T4-ADN-807

DATE DUE

DISCARDED

Demco, Inc. 38-293

AUG 1 2 2009

Figurations of Exile in Hitchcock and Nabokov

For my parents Elisabeth and Benno

Figurations of Exile in Hitchcock and Nabokov

Barbara Straumann

Edinburgh University Press

© Barbara Straumann, 2008

Edinburgh University Press Ltd
22 George Square, Edinburgh

Typeset in Sabon and Futura
by Servis Filmsetting Ltd, Stockport, Cheshire, and
printed and bound in Great Britain by
the MPG Books Group

A CIP record for this book is available from the British Library

ISBN 978 0 7486 3646 4 (hardback)

The right of Barbara Straumann
to be identified as author of this work
has been asserted in accordance with
the Copyright, Designs and Patents Act 1988.

This thesis was accepted as a doctoral dissertation by the Faculty of Arts of
the University of Zürich in the winter semester 2004/05 on the recommendation
of Prof. Dr. Elisabeth Bronfen.

Contents

Preface	vi
Abbreviations	vii
1 Introduction	1
Cross-mapping Hitchcock and Nabokov	1
Questions of Exile and Dislocation	11
Home and Exile in Hitchcock and Nabokov	22
Part I Nabokov's Dislocations	
2 Refiguring Loss and Exile in *Speak, Memory*	33
Chronophobia	38
Family Romance	51
Poetics of Memory	66
3 'Aesthetic Bliss' and Its Allegorical Displacements in *Lolita*	86
Childhood Romance	91
Textual Relocations	100
Language to Infinity	113
Part II Hitchcock's Wanderings	
4 Inhabiting Feminine *Suspicion*	127
Traumatic Fantasy	132
Family Murder	144
Aesthetics of Overproximity	153
5 Wandering and Assimilation in *North by Northwest*	165
Mad Traveller	170
Oedipal Voyage	178
Language of Exile and Assimilation	188
6 Epilogue: Psychoanalytic Dislocation	201
Bibliography	220
Index	237

Preface

Thanks are owed first and foremost to Elisabeth Bronfen, who kept insisting that I continue my work on the doctoral thesis which this book is based on. Not just a dissertation advisor, she has been a very important intellectual friend and definitely the best teacher I have ever had. In the process of research and writing, several other people also helped with critical advice and suggestions. Joan Copjec's seminars and ideas were extremely stimulating and proved most fruitful. Hanjo Berressem encouraged me with his astute comments to both expand and sharpen the argument as well as to show more verbal wit in the way I put things. For their generous and informed responses to preliminary papers, I also wish to thank Cathy Caruth, Aleida Assmann, Gabi Rippl and Renate Hof. For critical comments and readings that helped shape my manuscript, my thanks go to Martin Heusser, Christina Ljungberg, Benno Straumann, Tobias Weber, Daniela Janser and Anna-Katharina Straumann. Moreover, I am grateful for invaluable backing and encouragement from a number of other colleagues, friends, relatives and family members. To my partner Balz Bruder, I give my thanks for his ironic humour and his untiring support in all the stages of this project. Much of the work on my dissertation was done during a seven-month period spent as a visiting scholar at SUNY Buffalo and funded by the Swiss National Science Foundation; I would like to extend my thanks to the Foundation for awarding me a generous research grant. Finally I wish to express my deep gratitude to Jackie Jones at Edinburgh University Press, who immediately understood the critical project of this book and who ultimately made it happen.

Barbara Straumann

Abbreviations

The following abbreviations all refer to works by Vladimir Nabokov. Full references appear in the Bibliography.

A	*Ada or Ardor*
BS	*Bend Sinister*
D	*Despair*
IB	*Invitation to a Beheading*
KQK	*King, Queen, Knave*
LD	*The Luzhin Defense*
LL	*Lectures on Literature*
LO	*The Annotated Lolita*
LS	*Lolita: A Screenplay*
NWL	*Dear Bunny, Dear Volodya: The Nabokov-Wilson Letters, 1940–1971*
P	*Pnin*
SL	*Selected Letters 1940–77*
SM	*Speak, Memory*
SK	*The Real Life of Sebastian Knight*
TT	*Transparent Things*

Chapter 1

Introduction

Cross-mapping Hitchcock and Nabokov

In late 1964, Alfred Hitchcock and Vladimir Nabokov cross paths for a short period of time. Hitchcock, the filmmaker, approaches Nabokov, the writer, for a joint project. After a telephone conversation, the two exchange several plot ideas revolving around spectacular scenarios of dislocation: the story of a homeless girl whose widowed father manages a large international hotel with the rest of the family members posing as concierge, cashier, chef, housekeeper as well as a bedridden matriarch, while, in fact, they form a shady 'backstage' gang of crooks; a starlet whose astronaut lover appears to be curiously changed after his return from outer space to earth; a senator's daughter engaged to an Americanised secret agent who may potentially defect during his visit to his Russian homeland; and, finally, a defector from behind the Iron Curtain who is betrayed by a seemingly benevolent American couple on their western ranch to Soviet agents intent on either his death or abduction. In their letters both the director and author express interest in some of the material. Hitchcock writes that 'my needs are immediate and urgent' and Nabokov suggests that they meet in Europe the following year.[1]

What a film by Hitchcock and Nabokov might have looked like had they pursued their plans, we can only speculate. At the same time, the anecdote of their near-collaboration intrigues me because it evokes a host of correspondences between their oeuvres. In addition to the iconic status and stature that they had both attained by the early 1960s as at once distinctive and detached *auteur* figures, Nabokov himself may have thought of further affinities when, in his account of the gala premiere of Stanley Kubrick's *Lolita* on 13 June 1962, he described himself as the virtual double of Hitchcock rather than of Kubrick's male lead, James Mason.

Crowds were awaiting the limousines that drew up one by one, and there I, too, rode, as eager and innocent as the fans who peered into my car hoping to glimpse James Mason but finding only the placid profile of a stand-in for Hitchcock. (LS: xii)

As implied by Nabokov's impersonation of Hitchcock, there was indeed a remarkable resemblance between the two figures and their body gestures once they reached a certain age. Yet doesn't their doubling also extend to aesthetic attitudes and concerns? Isn't there a striking correspondence in their exchange of plot ideas, in which authorship cannot easily be attributed – unless we return to the letters, where we read that the hotel story and the relationship between the senator's daughter and the seemingly Americanised agent were suggested by Hitchcock, the starlet, her astronaut lover and the Russian deserter by Nabokov? Doesn't our speculation about the potential treatment of these scenarios refer us to compelling convergences in Hitchcock's and Nabokov's thematic and aesthetic interests? Are we not inevitably reminded of other plots of cultural and psychic dislocation in their oeuvres as well as their highly self-reflexive *mise-en-scène*?

Thus one can, for example, well imagine how their plans for a joint project could have tied in with their shared fascination for spying. Issues of perception and perspective, of knowledge and power shape their work to a large extent. Inspired as they are by elements of Gothic, detective and espionage fiction, many of Hitchcock's and Nabokov's literary and cinematic texts turn on sight and its refraction as a trope for cultural, political and/or psychic alienation. They frequently feature protagonists who not only observe other figures, but who also spy on themselves or else are spied upon by doubles or secret agents of political systems, thus pointing to subjectivities that are estranged or otherwise precarious. At the same time, questions of sight and control are also self-reflexively played out on the extra-diegetic level of Hitchcock's and Nabokov's texts, where readers and spectators are time and again caught in their potentially deceptive perception.

The focus of my comparison is on mutual concerns and preoccupations rather than on notions of explicit intertextuality and influence. In reading Hitchcock's and Nabokov's texts alongside each other, I take my cue from Elisabeth Bronfen's usage of the concept 'cross-mapping' (2002, 2004b). Referring to Stanley Cavell (1981) and his reading of George Cukor's romantic Hollywood comedy *Philadelphia Story* (1940) together with Shakespeare's *A Midsummer Night's Dream,* Bronfen suggests that certain aesthetic texts can be fruitfully mapped onto one another even if they do not stand in a direct intertextual relation. The critical interest at stake in such a cross-mapping lies in a thinking in analogies, in exploring the similarities and differences between the tropes brought into circulation by the texts in question. In cross-mapping such diverse cultural texts as film noir and Wagner's operas, Bronfen's core question concerns the cultural survival of texts, images, codes and rhetorical gestures as they migrate through different historio-cultural periods and media. How do they develop their compelling force to move us beyond the aesthetic medium and the historical moment from which they emerge? She suggests – similarly to Stephen Greenblatt (1988) – that it is through the cultural negotiation and exchange accompanying their historical transmission, transcription and transference that objects, practices and modes of expression gain their 'social energy'. Likewise it is their perpetual refiguration in different media which renders certain tropes particularly resilient for their audiences.

Picking up on Bronfen and Greenblatt, I would definitely make a claim for the cultural survival of Hitchcock's and Nabokov's aesthetic energies. The ongoing fascination of their texts may well be nourished by their specific refigurations of already existing cultural tropes as well as their subsequent absorption by our cultural imaginary. The *Phoenix Tapes* (1999) by the video artists Christoph Girardet and Matthias Müller enact a particularly compelling comment on this negotiation and exchange. By splicing together recurrent themes and images from Hitchcock films – incriminating pieces of evidence, railway tracks, over-present mother figures or the violent embrace of couples – they not only invoke specific movie memories, but their use of found footage actually appears to tap a collective cultural unconscious that these cinematic memory traces have helped shape in and through their compelling refigurations.[2]

Rather than focusing on the unorthodox trajectories in cultural history that can be rendered visible by virtue of a cross-mapping of texts from different cultural periods as Bronfen suggests, the dialogue I propose between Hitchcock and Nabokov foregrounds the way in which, while working in the same period but different media, they develop similar thematic and aesthetic concerns. What I am primarily concerned with is how their narratives and their highly aestheticised languages refigure a particular historicity, namely their concrete experience of cultural displacement. More specifically, by taking the seemingly relentless playfulness of Hitchcock and Nabokov as its point of departure, this book sets out to trace the figurations of exile negotiated by their texts as well as the specific ways in which they triangulate an exilic imaginary, aesthetic language and concrete cultural displacement.

As we begin comparing Hitchcock's and Nabokov's cinematic and literary texts, we quickly notice the self-reflexivity with which they foreground their mediality and their status as aesthetic representations.[3] Our attention is arrested first and foremost by the prolific puns and brilliant wordplay, by the various types of irony the filmmaker and writer invoke as well as the myriad games they play with their readers and spectators.[4] What Alfred Appel writes about Nabokov, namely that 'the process of reading and rereading his novels is a game of perception' in which the 'author and the reader are the "players"' (1991: xx–xxi), can equally be said about Hitchcock.[5] In a way similar to Nabokov, who ironically points to the unreliability of his narrators, even as their language keeps seducing us, Hitchcock's camera often aligns itself with charismatic criminals or deluded characters, thus rendering us partly complicitous in their crime and/or delusion.[6] Time and again, we are also derailed by the patterns and genres of detection invoked by their literary and cinematic texts. Nabokov's playful writing asks us to follow elaborate allusions and references which provide us with clues to complex aesthetic arrangements and/or turn out to be ironically refracted false leads. Even though Hitchcock's thrillers and espionage films may follow structures of detection in a more literal fashion, they often provide the spectator with empty decoys which trigger the movement and action of the figures, but prove to be tangential to the film's concerns or, to use Slavoj Žižek's words, 'purely auto-reflexive' in the overall structure of the film (1992: 6).

At stake, therefore, is not a hermeneutic solution but a deft game of power which the authors play with their audiences – as well as a reassuring sense of control in the way their oeuvres function as strikingly coherent systems. Much attention has been paid in both Hitchcock and Nabokov studies to the signature systems as well as the remarkably consistent and closed textual universes developed by the respective oeuvres.[7] Thematic elements traversing and thus connecting texts include figures and focalisers who impose their often deluded imagination on the surrounding world, masks, self-inventions and fictional biographies in Nabokov's writing; wrongly suspected protagonists, the fallibility of fathers and other representatives of the symbolic law, or the 'blockage' of sexual relationships in Hitchcock's cinema; and one could add the omnipresence, in both oeuvres, of psychic alienation, haunting obsessions as well as numerous double constellations.[8]

The self-referential economy created by these self-citational loops is both enhanced and epitomised by authorial masks and impersonations. Most prominent in this respect are the famous cameo-appearances of the director Hitchcock, who positions and promotes his prominent public persona as a distinct brand and popular trademark, not unlike the way in which Andy Warhol comments on himself and other celebrities as cultural signs.[9] Whether failing to board a bus in *North by Northwest* or getting on a train while carrying a double-bass which duplicates the rotund shape of his body in *Strangers on a Train*, the director inscribes himself in his films to pose as a riddle and to signal his authorial presence to the spectators who are in on the game he is playing with them. In Nabokov's writing, these authorial inscriptions find a correspondence not only in anagrammatic signatures such as 'Vivian Darkbloom' or 'Vivian Bloodmark' that riddle his texts,[10] but also in a cinematic cameo-performance written into his screenplay of *Lolita*, though omitted in Kubrick's film.[11] As Hitchcock fashions his deadpan persona, Nabokov uses his carefully scripted interviews, collected in *Strong Opinions* (1973), in order to construct an aloof mask of the author. Nabokov's prefaces and his postscript to *Lolita* come from 'an impersonation of Vladimir Nabokov talking about his own book' (LO: 311). Hitchcock, in turn, addresses his audience in directorial lead-ins featured in the trailers for *Psycho* and *Marnie* as well as the TV series *Alfred Hitchcock Presents*.

Is it perhaps indicative of their authorial role that Hitchcock and Nabokov had themselves repeatedly photographed with pointed index fingers or related hand gestures as in the two portraits on the cover of this book? While the indexical function manifested by these hand-signals remains, of course, pure speculation, we can safely say that the signature systems of their texts keep pointing to the author figure as at once the origin and centre of their worlds of artifice. Hitchcock and Nabokov are both inside and outside the games they play in their films and texts. They position themselves as detached observers of the plots and worlds whose rules they simultaneously create and manipulate. The impotence facing many Hitchcock protagonists stands in sharp contrast to the artistic control signalled by the director, while Nabokov often intervenes in his fiction to point to the fallibility of his ambitious narrators and his own superior power as author.

Nabokov, in one of his prefaces, refers to the authorial figure who frequently intrudes in his novels as 'an anthropomorphic deity impersonated by me' (BS: 11). Yet he could equally be describing how Hitchcock foregrounds the presence of his camera and thus wittily highlights the godlike position he occupies as director. In the introduction to his screenplay of *Lolita*, Nabokov evokes the complete control he would have exercised had he worked primarily for the theatrical stage or the cinematic screen. Again, the passage comes close to a characterisation of Hitchcock and his ambition to shape every aspect in the marking of his films and thus to imprint his authorial signature despite the highly collaborative system of cinema. 'If I had given as much of myself to the stage or the screen as I have to the kind of writing which serves a triumphant life sentence between the covers of a book', Nabokov writes,

> I would have advocated and applied a system of total tyranny, directing the play or the picture myself, choosing settings and costumes, terrorizing the actors, mingling with them in the bit part of guest, or ghost, prompting them, and, in a word, pervading the entire show with the will and art of one individual . . . (LS: ix–x)

In interview statements, Hitchcock and Nabokov both stress their artistic omnipotence and the power they have over actors and figures. Like Hitchcock's well-known description of actors as 'cattle' (in Gottlieb 1997: 301), Nabokov argues 'my characters are galley slaves' (SO: 95). Suggesting another image for the author's mastery, Alfred Appel characterises Nabokov's aesthetics as 'Nabokov's Puppet Show' (1991: xvii), and equivalent to the puppeteer who pulls the strings of his self-reflexive performances, Hitchcock often casts himself as the deft master not only of his cinematic suspense, but also of his spectators' affects and emotions. 'My suspense work', Hitchcock says, while commenting on the power he has over the audience of his thrillers, 'comes out of creating nightmares for the audience. And I *play* with an audience. I make them gasp and surprise them and shock them' (Hitchcock in Gottlieb 1997: 313).[12] Time and again, Hitchcock's and Nabokov's self-reflexive games can also be seen to ironically expose the strings of the puppeteer so as to refer to the mediated status of their texts.

Indeed, another close affinity can be observed in the ways in which the master game-players continually remind us that their films and novels constitute textual worlds and that what we witness is the virtuoso creation and manipulation of self-reflexive artifice. Their authorial interventions undermine rather than anchor any mimetic illusion, whether in the insistent foregrounding of narration, the subversion of narrative conventions, or the prominent practice of self-citation. As a result, the emphasis of their literary and cinematic languages lies on the signifier and non-mimetic representation, on a multiplicity of signs and the always refracted and mediated character of any 'reality'. This aesthetics plays itself out in the medial self-reflexivity already mentioned above and in the *mise-en-abîme* structures shaping many of the texts: the allusions to playacting and the star image of Cary Grant in *North by Northwest*, or to cinematic voyeurism in the protagonist played by James Stewart in *Rear Window*, the many Nabokov figures who constitute themselves as the narrators or even the writers of the texts we actually read. Yet their self-reflexive textuality is also nourished by a plurality of signs and images derived from both 'high' art and popular culture, psychoanalysis and a vast array of literary and cinematic traditions – as well as by the irony and parody with which these references, and the expectations they raise in spectators and readers, are undermined. In fact, if in their self-referential systems Hitchcock and Nabokov often allude to their own texts or authorial personae in self-ironical ways, they emerge as debunking arch-parodists when it comes to the play of and with cultural references, whether, for instance, in Nabokov's rejection of psychoanalysis or Hitchcock's hyperbolic invocations of its tropes and symbols.

Not surprisingly Nabokov once located his affinity with the filmmaker in their shared humorous stance. 'Actually, I've seen very little Hitchcock', he conceded, 'but I admire his craftsmanship. I fondly recall at least one film of his, about someone called Harry . . . his *humour noir* is akin to *my humour noir*, if that's what it should be called' (Nabokov in Appel 1974: 129). Ultimately it is here that the writer and the director may have left one of their strongest marks and imprints on the cultural imagination: in the penchant that they both reveal, in *The Trouble with Harry* and almost everywhere else, for the dark and the bleak, for abysses that appear to be at once deepened and distanced by their parody and irony.

While these resemblances between Hitchcock and Nabokov could be supplemented with many others, the question is how one can describe the implications and consequences of their convergence and comparison. Thus a structural analysis could explore further similarities between Hitchcock's and Nabokov's thematic and aesthetic overlaps, their manipulation of narrative conventions, or the traces of literary traditions in Hitchcock's filmmaking and the impact of cinematic techniques on Nabokov's writing.[13] A poststructuralist approach, in turn, may show how their privileging of cultural signs and references prefigures a postmodern aesthetics. For me, however, the significance of Hitchcock's and Nabokov's cross-mapping lies somewhere different – in their emphatic embrace of a highly aestheticised language and the question of how this gesture can be brought together with the particular historicity and the concrete experience of cultural displacement from which their texts emerge. In their public statements, the filmmaker and writer celebrate a similar aesthetic investment. 'I put first and foremost cinematic style before content', Hitchcock says. 'Content is quite secondary to me' (Hitchcock in Gottlieb 1997: 292). Similarly, in his postscript to *Lolita,* Nabokov declares that 'for me a work of fiction exists only insofar as it affords me what I shall bluntly call aesthetic bliss' (LO: 314). What, I ask myself, are the functions and gestures underlying Hitchcock's and Nabokov's pronounced embraces of aesthetic language? Rather than following their declarations and focusing on the self-reflexivity of their languages alone, I propose an analysis of their logic and condition which places them in the context of cultural exile and displacement.

Not only were Hitchcock and Nabokov born in the same year, 1899, but both of them also faced concrete cultural dislocation as a crucial juncture in their biographies.[14] In spring 1939, after Hitchcock had established himself as the leading British director of the time, he chose to emigrate with his wife and assistant Alma Reville and their daughter Patricia to the United States. Hollywood appears to have been the cultural site where he actually wanted to be since in retrospect he emphasises that long before his transatlantic move, he had already been closely associated with American cinema and its aesthetic language.[15] Similar to the American-trained director, Nabokov, too, was fluent in several cultural languages. His aristocratic St Petersburg family cultivated its cosmopolitan cultural orientation not only in regular travels to Western Europe but also in the early multilingual education of its children. In contrast to Hitchcock, who transplanted himself voluntarily and under no duress, Nabokov's politically liberal family was forced into exile by the Russian Revolution. Two decades into his Western European exile, during which he studied at Cambridge and established himself as a Russian émigré writer, he was again violently displaced. Together with his Jewish wife Véra, born Slonim, and their son Dmitri, he managed to escape Nazi totalitarianism in 1940 and to find refuge in the United States, where he began a second career as an author writing in English.

My wager, in invoking these biographic trajectories, is that Hitchcock's and Nabokov's languages stand in a close connection with their exilic dislocation and self-fashioning. Their textuality and self-referentiality, and also their desire for mastery and control, can be read as part of an aesthetics of exile. In order to re-introduce referentiality – and thus the question how aesthetic texts hook into the world – both into their oeuvres and their discussion, I propose that we reread their texts against the backdrop of exile as a momentous experience of twentieth-century history and culture, including the cataclysmic displacements and deaths in the Holocaust as well as a certain cultural dynamics surrounding exile from the 1920s to the 1950s. Whenever we refer to exile, we need to consider an irresolvable tension between two facets, namely an irreversible, potentially traumatic experience of loss, on the one hand, and a condition that may be enabling because it grants access to another cultural language, on the other hand. In the past century, displacement meant violent dispossession and death for many, notably for over six million European Jews who were systematically murdered in the concentration camps of Nazi Germany. For others, who managed to escape as political refugees or who emigrated for professional and/or economic reasons, exile could mean either cultural estrangement or an enriching exchange with the cultural codes of the respective host country.

Nabokov's autobiographical text *Speak, Memory* hinges on precisely this dynamics of exile and its ambivalence. According to his narrative, it is his Western European exile, described as a liminal existence largely devoid of, and hence alienated from, any cultural contact, which promotes his development as an author. Largely secluded during his years in England, he cultivates his mother tongue to become a Russian writer. Similarly, it is the phantom world of the Russian émigré circles in Berlin that is rewritten in his early fiction before American everyday culture comes to play a very different, more concrete role for his far more grounded 'American' novels *Lolita*, *Pnin* and *Pale Fire*. On the one hand, then, Nabokov fashions himself as an isolated figure who inhabits a purely textual world. On the other hand, he could not write his text unless he had lost an entire cultural world and several family members – unless 'the things and beings that I had most loved in the security of my childhood had been turned to ashes or shot through the heart' (SM: 92). Like so many others, his exilic trajectory is thus embedded in the very real exilic movements and cultural displacements of the time.

France, where Nabokov and his family moved before their emigration to the United States, was a site particularly rich in exilic resonances. The major destination of the mass exodus of Russians from Germany in the early 1920s and then again in the 1930s, Paris had from early on attracted American expatriates, who could have returned home any time but chose to live and work abroad. The rise of Nazism in Germany in the 1930s meant that as for Nabokov and his family, Paris became a temporary refuge for many exiles before they moved to England, as did for instance Sigmund Freud (who stopped over in Paris as he fled to London), or to further destinations especially in the United States.

The transatlantic route had, of course, long been established. Notably Hollywood had, from the very beginning, been influenced by the migration and immigration of European directors, including Josef von Sternberg, Ernst Lubitsch and Friedrich Wilhelm Murnau, as well as (a smaller number of) European stars, most famously perhaps Marlene Dietrich and Greta Garbo. In the 1930s, many European directors, including Fritz Lang, Billy Wilder, Douglas Sirk, Robert Siodmak, Otto Preminger, Max Ophüls, Jean Renoir and others, either chose emigration or were forced into exile (Baxter 1976). The 'hard core of political refugees' (Elsaesser 1999: 105), however, were intellectuals, writers and composers, among them Hannah Arendt, Max Horkheimer, Theodor

W. Adorno, Siegfried Kracauer, Bertolt Brecht and Hanns Eisler, several of whom moved to Los Angeles, the heart of American mass culture. This cultural environment inspired different responses ranging from Horkheimer and Adorno's cultural pessimism in their critique of the culture industry and its supposedly standardised production in *The Dialectics of Enlightenment* (1944) to the participation in and, in some cases, active contribution to its very economies. Especially filmmakers, by working in the American art *par excellence*, helped shape America's culture, which gained such influence in the twentieth century as to develop into a hegemonic paradigm travelling across the Atlantic and almost everywhere else.

In the years following the war, some exiles returned to Europe. Others stayed in postwar America, where the cultural and social climate was far from homogeneous. The investigations of the House Committee on Un-American Activities on Communism in Hollywood in 1947 resulted in the studio blacklist and in increased caution in its cultural production, while McCarthy's accusations, threats and witch-hunts formed a similar attempt, nourished by a paranoia over the ideologically other and alien, to install a Cold War hegemony. Media representations advertised an upbeat optimism together with commodity and consumer culture centred on the affluent middle-class family, its suburban home and domestic values. Yet as David Sterritt (1998) convincingly shows, conformity and conservatism simultaneously produced cultural dissidence and dissatisfaction. Sterrit chooses as his core example the Beat Generation and its interrogation of consensual norms and values in its disruption and transgression of narrative rules. Yet he also refers to mainstream culture, notably to film noir – a genre in which the influence of European directors was especially strong and which articulated a cultural malaise by depicting a particularly bleak vision of an urban America of violence and corruption – and to filmmakers such as Sirk and Hitchcock, who 'treated Hollywood conventions to audacious revisions and ironic interrogations' (Sterrit 1993: 64).[16]

Indeed, Hitchcock's work occupies an alternative position within the cultural hegemony as it points to dislocations by using its very codes. Unlike other European directors, Hitchcock was not forced into exile, but chose to move to Hollywood to gain access to the language of the predominant film system. Hollywood not simply allowed him to work with larger budgets and major stars. It represented an international language that addressed a global audience, while also offering his preoccupation with violence the imaginative potential of another cultural setting, namely 'the freer, larger, more dangerous, more socially mobile American society' (French 1985: 117). Initially, he appropriated Hollywood norms and conventions as a stranger to the studio system, which was more rigid than British filmmaking, and later in his career cultivated an imperturbable public persona that was stereotypically English. However, his work did enter American mainstream culture, in which he wished to participate. When he pokes fun at cinematic codes and points to contradictions in symbolic systems, he always does so from within the cultural language he incorporated into his own idiom.

Questions of Exile and Dislocation

While exile can produce powerful forms of cultural exchange, it also inevitably refers us to a murky interface. Exile as a trope of aesthetic creativity cannot be neatly separated from geopolitical displacement and its concomitant, potentially traumatic loss of an entire cultural world, nor can it be clearly distinguished from the fundamental dislocation of subjectivity as it is described by psychoanalysis. In *Speak, Memory*, this ambivalence is partly covered up when Nabokov celebrates exile as an invigorating impulse by claiming that 'the break in my destiny affords me in retrospect a syncopal kick that I would not have missed for worlds' (SM: 193). The text's assertion that exile forms a compelling source of inspiration is one of the core trajectories that I shall examine, that is, the question whether and how exile may be appropriated and refigured in an aesthetic framework as a both powerful and empowering trope. As we will see, Hitchcock's and Nabokov's oeuvres rework both cultural and psychic forms of dislocation into pivotal narrative themes and aesthetic textual structures. In *Speak, Memory*, for example, it is the topographical separation from the home and homeland which inspires a resilient nostalgic imagination as well as a seemingly freefloating self-fashioning of the author figure. Following a reversed but no less distinctive gesture, Hitchcock's early Hollywood film *Suspicion* invokes a fantasy scenario which stages the subject's violent separation from home.

Even as it forms an intriguing trope of textual production, exile inevitably refers to a rupture which is traumatic and hence real in a Lacanian sense. As a moment of the literal, its caesura resists symbolisation, which means that it cannot fully be recuperated by aesthetic language. In fact, exile and its aesthetic figurations can be seen in analogy to Fredric Jameson's argument according to which history inflects texts as an 'absent cause'. As a belated effect, Jameson points out, history 'is inaccessible to us except in textual form . . . our approach to it and the Real itself necessarily passes through its prior textualization, its narrativization' (1981: 35). At issue, therefore, is not a mimetic representation of exilic experience nor a notion of history as 'context' but the question of how exile inscribes itself in aesthetic texts as a vanishing point and how, in so doing, it articulates itself as the driving force of their language.

Likewise, to stress the notion of caesura means to situate exile somewhere different from issues highlighted by postcolonial and multicultural theory. Interested in the renegotiation and transformation of dominant and subaltern discourses and positions, postcolonialism focuses on hybridity, the cultural mixture and fusion of incommensurable signs, languages, codes and traditions that emerge in the perpetual migrancy of subjects, in the global circulation of commodities and signs. Exile, by contrast, refers us to an irreversible displacement from the homeland to a host country. Certainly the exile's liminality between two cultures can be fruitfully discussed in reference to postcolonial concepts of cultural hybridity or a 'third space' (Bhabha 1994). Yet the classic narrative trajectory that exilic rupture typically generates simultaneously has recourse to a prior chronotope of the home. As I shall suggest, the home is necessarily a belated construction and/or marked by internal difference from the very start. Nevertheless exile narratives posit the home as the site of origin and belonging as well as a significant pivot of the exilic imaginary. In so doing, they either highlight or displace the impact of exile.

My critical interest in exilic rupture concerns above all the void with which it confronts representation. How do narratives of exile refigure this lacuna? And in what ways may aesthetic language be seen to respond to the aporia of a non-representational referentiality? My critical desire to re-introduce referentiality into texts that are so evidently self-referential is also the reason why my analyses will not follow a classic poststructuralist or postmodernist stance. These approaches, I suspect, would be such perfect fits as to duplicate the economy of the primary texts themselves. By focusing on a freeplay of signifiers, such readings are likely to overlook the non-representational void of exilic rupture that forms the ground and vanishing point of the seemingly relentless playfulness, the irony and parody of the texts.

Nabokov's language especially is not as free-floating as it may seem at first sight. The creation of a world in and of signs is not only typical of postmodern aesthetics, but may also be seen as an existential appropriation of art in the reconstruction of a cultural world and its language after their actual loss. Similarly, the practice of self-citation may be understood together with a process of cultural self-translation, namely with the fact that in the United States Nabokov systematically translates his Russian novels into English and, as a result, keeps revisiting similar elements in his writing, while in Hollywood Hitchcock remakes some of his British films.[17] Finally, it is also along the lines of this exilic perspective that I wish to situate the paradoxical re-emergence of the author. At the same time as Nabokov's and Hitchcock's authorial impersonations posit the author as an effect of signs and discourses, there is also a biographical dimension at stake. Not only their investment in playful language and irony, but also their insistence on authorial control and self-reference may be closely connected to the cultural exile in which their textual production unfolds.

It goes without saying that the circumstances and conditions of Hitchcock's self-chosen emigration and Nabokov's enforced displacement are fundamentally different. Nevertheless I want to suggest that we read them together with Hitchcock's and Nabokov's respective aesthetics. More precisely, it is by mapping their self-reflexive languages onto questions of exile and displacement that we can isolate their specific rhetorical gestures. Self-reflexivity and irony can articulate as well as deny 'knowledge'. In reinserting the facticity of exile, I am, therefore, interested in seeing how their exilic texts mediate between referentiality and figurative language. I wonder, in other words, how their aesthetic texts gesture towards a vanishing point of the real. Do they self-consciously reflect on an 'exilic' knowledge or are they haunted by its inassimilable traces? To what extent does their language register the impact of dislocation and/or provide a site of imaginary belonging?

Given my critical interest, it appears particularly apt and pertinent to turn not only to biography and exile studies, but above all to psychoanalysis as the most paradigmatic critical discourse of twentieth-century culture to address questions of identity and belonging as well as a fundamental dislocation subtending all subjectivity. Freud's theoretical framework partly emerges in response to his concrete experience of cultural dislocation as a Jew living and working in the anti-Semitic culture of Austria and later literally displaced by Nazi totalitarianism. At the same time, psychoanalysis also develops its critical concepts in close contact and exchange with aesthetic texts. Aware of the fact that the choice of my analytical framework entails a certain critical loop, my argument is conceived as a model case of cultural analysis, where more often than not the tropes we use as critics are prefigured by the phenomena we seek to analyse and describe. As a possible way out of this dilemma, I suggest a critical cross-mapping which, by applying the theoretical discourse to the aesthetic texts as analytical key, brings the two into dialogue. The aesthetic texts of Hitchcock and Nabokov and the theory of Freud, I want to suggest, form part of the same cultural imaginary. My cross-mapping of the texts and Freud's concepts will, therefore, emphasise the difference but also the murky interface that can be observed between the circulation of cultural tropes and the irreducible experience of exile, between the universal claim of the subject's fundamental dislocation made by psychoanalysis and the particular figurations of exile created by individual texts.

In what follows, I will further specify and elucidate the stakes and consequences of my cross-mapping as well as develop the most important theoretical notions and questions that will resurface in the course of my readings of individual texts. At the same time, my preliminary discussion provides a wider critical context and framework by means of which the paradoxical redoubling of exile and its textual figurations can be decribed.

Edward Said points to one of the core contradictions of exile when he reminds us that 'exile is strangely compelling to think about but terrible to experience'. 'If true exile is a condition of terminal loss', he goes on to ask, 'why has it been transformed so easily into a potent, even enriching motif of modern culture?' (1984: 159). Following this aporia of exile as both a resilient trope and a potentially traumatising experience, we can say that, on the one hand, any instance of exile is irreducible in its historical contingency and individual condition and, on a certain level, eludes the imaginary as well as symbolic language. On the other hand, exile cannot be separated from a large repertoire of cultural metaphors and narratives. In fact, exilism appears to be one of the privileged tropes migrating through the Western cultural imaginary, whether we think of such different exilic figurations as the expulsion from Biblical Paradise, the homelessness cultivated by Romantic poets or the long-delayed homecoming of Odysseus. While these narratives imply different points of departure – that is, forced displacement in contrast to exile as a metaphor of aesthetic inspiration and creation as well as a wandering which may actually seek to avoid the home – the vast archive of exilic figurations suggests that our imagination centrally turns around conditions of exile and that it may be their perpetual refiguration that endows them with their social energy, the reason why they continue to fascinate and 'move' us.

As the literary critic Michael Seidel points out, exile is 'a symptomatic metaphor of the state of narrative imagination' (1986: 8). In the most general sense, imaginative narration allows us to explore foreign territory as well as to return to familiar topoi; and of course all narratives about exile inevitably thematise issues of the familiar and the foreign, of emplacement and alienation. In so doing, they vicariously address fundamental categories of subjectivity, which may be another decisive reason for their compelling social energy. Indeed, I want to suggest that exilic narratives highlight our need for fantasies of home and belonging. As it always exceeds a concrete material place of habitation, the home condenses a wealth of semantic meanings. As a site promising plenitude and protection, it can refer to one's family, homeland, culture and/or language, to a site of origin as well as refuge. Irrespective of its particular figuration, the imagination of a home is necessary for us in order to live in a certain psychic stability and identity. In a pivotal way, all narratives of exile thus play through various home fantasies just as narratives about the home often revolve around issues of dislocation, whether they pertain to actual or potential loss, or the question whether and how we can inhabit a home as a site of belonging.

It is important, however, to note that concrete exile raises questions of home and displacement, of belonging and dislocation with a particularly poignant urgency. Not causing material loss alone, exile marks a threatening situation. By displacing a familiar frame of reference, it triggers a heightened and necessary turn to the imaginary. Or put differently, exilic rupture confronts the subject with a radically alienating moment which provokes a need to rebuild the world and reinvent oneself. As Said argues, 'much of the exile's life is taken up with compensating for disorienting loss by creating a new world to rule' (1984: 167). In attempting to transform disempowering contingency into a narrative of meaningful necessity and coherence, the exilic subject, significantly enough, cannot but turn to the existing tropes of the cultural imaginary. 'The exile's new world', Said points out, 'logically enough . . . resembles fiction' (1984: 167), thus referring to the notion that the excessively real experience of exile comes to be paradoxically enmeshed with both the imaginary and figurative.

In contrast to the Latin adjective *exsul*, which means 'banished, living abroad, homeless', another probable etymology, *ex salire*, suggests that the word 'exile' refers not only to expulsion, but that 'it also expresses a sense of "leaping out" toward something or somewhere, implying a matter of will' (Israel 2000: 1). Regardless of whether exile is voluntary or enforced, the exilic 'leap' thus connotes a move toward fantasy and imagination. Ultimately the exile's imaginary can align itself with a cultural relocation and assimilation in a host country or another symbolic frame of reference, or it can sustain and fetishise the state of dislocation. Inextricably linked to loss, narratives of exile are fundamentally predicated on the imagination of the past and its absence. They form an attempt to re-present and thus render present again what was lost and/or what strictly speaking cannot be represented, namely the moment of exilic rupture.

In their emphasis on re-presentation, exilic narratives inspire an empowering gesture, which can be compared to Freud's account of the game played by his grandson Ernst in *Beyond the Pleasure Principle* (1955b: 14–17). If we want to go along with Freud's interpretation, the boy's attempt to re-enact the absence and return of his mother with a toy reel in a game of '*fort-da*' forms a symbolic activity over which he can exert mastery and control. Similar to the self-invented game of the child and its inspiration by the absent figure of the mother, the exilic return encodes the absent home not only as the site of one's origin but also as the site of one's imagination. Moreover, as in the case of Freud's narrative, which turns around the temporary absence of the mother and then her irrevocable loss through death, it is crucially the absence of the home which gives rise to symbolic representation and imagination alike. It is thus paradoxically only once the home has vanished that our imaginary can actually take possession of this site.

Owing to its representational metaphoricity, the exile narrative marks a paradigmatic aesthetic moment. As they highlight issues of representation and imagination, Elisabeth Bronfen suggests, exile narratives perform a self-reflexive or meta-textual gesture. Exilic representations, in other words, do not merely re-present the absent but, in a fundamental way, constitute the reality of what they represent (Bronfen 1993: 168). We can, therefore, say that because they centrally deal with issues of imagination and representation, exilic narratives actually figure as tropes of aesthetic production per se. Similarly, the exilic displacement of the writer is often refigured as a gain of a poetic language in analogy to the psychoanalytical narrative, where the separation of the mother-child dyad is synonymous with access to a symbolic system. Salman Rushdie points to the significance of a retrospective re-creation of the past when he suggests that 'writers in my position, exiles or emigrants or expatriates, are haunted by some sense of loss, some urge to reclaim, to look back . . .' (1991: 10). At the same time, he underlines the quintessentially literary character of this gesture. The re-creation of the past 'almost inevitably means that we will not be capable of reclaiming precisely the thing that was lost; that we will, in short, create fictions, not actual cities or villages, but invisible ones, imaginary homelands . . .' (1991: 10). Most importantly, however, Rushdie's notion of the 'imaginary homeland' implies that it is precisely in the move towards poetic imagination and language that the displaced writer may gain a site of habitation.

All the more resilient by virtue of its mobility, the 'imaginary homeland' of language confers a certain independence from any concrete home and its inevitable vulnerability. Yet, at the same time, the exile's valorisation of language may also mark a precarious state of dislocation. The writer and involuntary exile Joseph Brodsky, who was officially expatriated from the Soviet Union, offers a powerful image capturing the desperate counterpoint of linguistic exile. 'To be an exiled writer', he writes, 'is like being a dog or a man hurtled into outer space in a capsule (more like a dog, of course, than a man, because they will never bother to retrieve you). And your capsule is your language' (1994: 10). Imagination and language, Brodsky's image implies, not only form the immaterial possessions of an 'imaginary homeland' which, unlike real places of habitation, cannot be removed by exile. But it is precisely in the withdrawal to language and imagination that dislocation and alienation may register in a particularly acute and poignant way. 'To finish the metaphor off', Brodsky suggests, 'it must be added that before long the passenger discovers that the capsule gravitates not earthward but outward in space' (1994: 10). His argument that 'the condition we call exile is, first of all, a linguistic event' (1994: 10) thus highlights an ambivalence, namely an inseparability as well as a disjunction between exiled subjects and (their) language.

Of course, language always entails an 'exilic' element. As poststructuralist theory points out, signs and their reference stand in an opaque relation so that speaking subjects are never quite identical with themselves. Yet this structural dislocation becomes particularly virulent in exile, which redoubles the sense that there is no stable point of reference from which to speak. Indeed, exile denotes a state of radical liminality which can be located neither here nor there since it oscillates between an estranged past and a dislocated present. Aesthetically, this ambivalence may be renegotiated as a hybrid cultural affiliation or multilingual fluency developed, for example, by Rushdie and, to some extent, by Hitchcock and Nabokov. However, given their fundamental liminality, exilic languages are characterised by a particular instability in their reference to notions of home and belonging.

Any home narrative revolves around a paradoxical place of departure since the home is redoubled or refracted by either the fact or knowledge of dislocation. Although it may stand in for concepts of wholeness and safety, the home is inevitably troubled by an internal difference, by which any binary opposition between dislocation and the home is, from the beginning, deconstructed. In his essay 'The "Uncanny"' (1955a), Freud refers to scenarios in which the homely becomes frightening. While one might think that the familiar would inspire a feeling of comfort and well-being, the return of previously familiar psychic material that has been repressed produces an experience of the uncanny. As argued by Freud, this reversal of the homely into the alien and unknown hinges on the double meaning of the German word *heimlich*, which implies a fundamental ambivalence. While connoting the homely and intimate, *heimlich* simultaneously refers to the hidden, secret and repressed: 'the *unheimlich* is what was once *heimisch*, familiar; the prefix *"un"* ("un-") is the token of repression' (1955a: 245). Freud's analysis thus emphasises how the protective familiar is based on repression, the intimate secret of which returns, for example, in the double as a paradigmatic figure of the uncanny. While Freud suggests that the familiar is by definition always inscribed by an 'unfamiliar' knowledge, the psychic ambivalence of the uncanny is particularly pertinent to a discussion of exile. In exile, both the home and the self are split and reduplicated by their exilic doubles. In their ambivalent oscillation between past and present, the familiar and the unfamiliar can no longer be located. Yet even more importantly, exile in its continual, uncannily redoubled return 'home' highlights that the home may have been unfamiliar from the very beginning. We can, therefore, say that in analogy to the experience of the uncanny and its resurfacing of an alien knowledge about the most intimately familiar, exilic displacement re-articulates a secret contradiction by which one's site of belonging has been inhabited all along.[17]

Given its uncanny resonance, the exilic imaginary raises the question whether and how the subject can attain a psychic ability to be at home. In a psychic sense, the home becomes an indispensable category once it is either lost or perceived as threatened or troubled. In other words, it is paradoxically the loss of one's home which enhances or even constitutes the need for it. As the Austrian writer and Holocaust survivor Jean Améry points out, it is only if one is at home that the home is not needed.[18] Or put the other way round, we would not need a fantasy of the home if we were fully at home. In this sense, imagination and exile represent mutual tropes: any fantasy of the home signals that, literally or figuratively, something is out of place.

As argued by Freud, the subject's imaginary activity circles around a gap or lack, a psychic sense of dislocation which it wishes to correct (1959a: 146). In a manner particularly resonant with narratives of exile, Freud further suggests that daydreaming fantasies hover between three temporal moments. They revolve around a 'current impression' provoking one of the subject's great wishes, which it relates to a memory of an earlier satisfaction so as to create a future scenario of wish fulfilment (1959a: 147). Semantically, daydreams may follow various trajectories. Yet Freud's example focuses on the fantasy of an orphan which restores what the subject possessed in 'his happy childhood': 'the protecting house, the loving parents and the first objects of his affectionate feelings'

(1959a: 148). Fantasy may hence seem to return the subject 'home'. However, as a symptom or compromise formation, any fantasy scenario keeps pointing to the lack or loss which it seeks to cover up.

Imagination is, therefore, marked by a double articulation. In following a wish fulfilment, it simultaneously refers to the subject's psychic dislocation. A similar double movement also marks texts about exile. The turn to the imaginary which stages a return home is, in fact, refracted by the home's literal absence. Or we can go as far as to say that dislocation figures as the precondition of the aesthetic text. This exilic knowledge can, however, be negotiated in different ways. The question is thus always whether and to what extent exilic dislocation is played out in its psychic and rhetorical ambivalences, or whether it has to be encrypted as a textual secret. In other words, can uncanny ambivalence be articulated by the textual imaginary, or does it have to be negated and may hence return to haunt the text on another level? In what respects are textual scenarios structured around an imaginary of protection? And what may be gained by aesthetically re-enacting a knowledge of dislocation?

As my readings of Hitchcock and Nabokov will show, figurations of exile can be traced on both thematic and aesthetic structural levels. In showing what thematic tropes and narratives individual texts valorise, my core interest lies in their rhetorical gestures. How do texts map an imaginary of home against and with the condition of exile and dislocation? And what are the implications of the various narrative possibilities? Similarly we have to ask whether the 'language' of their imaginary comes to serve as a site of belonging and/or to what extent it continues to gesture towards the impact of displacement.

Humanistic narratives of exile, in the most classic form, presuppose a home or homeland as a distinct site of departure. In retrospect the home may be mythically transformed into a paradisiacal state, from which the exiled person has been banished. Yet, while this narrative trajectory commemorates an irrevocable separation from one's home and origin, it simultaneously holds on to the notion that there would in fact be a home if displacement could be undone. Exilic dislocation thus comes to be counteracted by the imagination of a stable origin and home. A similar imaginary is also at stake in the home narrative of nostalgia. Here the home is typically located in the irretrievable past so that the yearning for the home is staged as a desire for desire. Belonging is, so to speak, refigured as a longing for a vanished home. In its repossession of the past, nostalgia aligns itself overtly with imagination so that, paradoxically enough, the home has to remain absent in order not to disturb the distant familiarity of the re-created past.

In both nostalgic and humanistic narratives, exile figures as 'an enabling fiction' (Seidel 1986: xii) allowing them to maintain that there is a home one can inhabit in one's imaginary. Although these scenarios inevitably point to the separation they are based on, they provide an antidote to dislocation. Or we could also say that they function as 'protective fictions'. Elaborating on an early concept of Freud, Elisabeth Bronfen defines protective fictions (*Schutzdichtungen, Schutzbauten*) as fantasies and symptoms which screen the psychic gap demarcating the impact of traumatic knowledge (1998: 37–9).[20] Indeed, by relocating the home to a protective imaginary, nostalgia and the classic exile narrative may implicitly occlude that loss has occurred. Moreover, they may ward off the disturbing notion that one never has been – and never will be – entirely at home. In other words, exilic displacement allows one to posit a belated fantasy of wholeness and protection, which displaces the knowledge not only that one never actually inhabited such an ideal state, but also that one's home may have been troubled prior to exile. As powerful fantasies of the home, nostalgic and humanistic narratives may thus either mitigate a traumatic loss or they may also cover up the notion that the subject can never fully feel at home.

While these nostalgic and humanistic narratives affirm an imaginary protection of the home, the scenario of 'home paranoia' maps a very different relation between the home and the subject's fantasy work. Rather than recuperating an idealised home, its imaginary delineates a line of flight from a home plagued by psychic malaise. Imagination is, in other words, literally set in motion by a discontent with the home's real living conditions. On the one hand, the subject's wandering, whether mental or also geographical, figures as a liberating escape from a suffocating overpresence. Its mobile vagrancy celebrates a seemingly boundless imaginary which avoids any curtailment. On the other hand, the 'exilic' wandering of the mind also articulates that things are literally not in place, that the home one flees from is marked by inconsistencies and fissures. These fantasies then materialise Freud's notion how any site of belonging and of identity is haunted by uncanny secrets, whether we speak of the family home or the subject's psychic apparatus. By foregrounding a psychic homelessness, scenarios of 'home paranoia' do not affirm the integrity of the home but, on the contrary, underline that the subject is dislocated precisely in its fantasy work, which together with other psychic processes, points to the inaccessible 'other scene' of the subject's unconscious. Instead of supporting a fantasy of omnipotence, narratives of 'home paranoia' underscore the disturbing notion that the subject is 'not even master in its own house' (Freud 1963: 285). The fundamental dislocation of subjectivity and the fissures implicit in any notion of the home are thus mutually implicated.

The tropes of home paranoia and nostalgia are also at the core of the family narratives told by psychoanalysis. This renders them compelling models for the analysis of exile narratives. As Freud argues, the 'liberation . . . from the authority of the parents is one of the most necessary though painful results' in the development of the individual (1959b: 237). In emphasising the centrality of the family as well as the importance of separation for the mature subject, he provides us with two core narratives, which may bring the trajectories I have already introduced into sharper focus. Harking back to nostalgic narratives of exile, the typical fantasy of the so-called 'family romance' elevates the childhood home to a site of comfort. Staging a discontent with current family relations, subjects replace the parents they need to separate themselves from with the fantasy of a nobler origin. However, rather than abandoning the parents, the family romance actually exalts them together with the memory of childhood.

> The whole effort at replacing the real father by a superior one is only an expression of the child's longing for the happy, vanished days when his father seemed to him the noblest and strongest of men and his mother the dearest and loveliest of women. (1959b: 140–1)

Maintaining that childhood was in fact happy, the family romance thus recaptures a fantasy of wholeness and protection.

By contrast, the resolution of the Oedipal trajectory requires the individual's separation from its primary attachments. In its Lacanian reformulation, the Oedipus complex turns into the crucial passage from imaginary plenitude to the mediation of subjectivity by the symbolic law as a register of lack, difference and curtailment.[21] On the one hand, the Oedipal journey is 'exilic' because it implies a loss of imaginary omnipotence. In contrast to the nostalgic fantasy of the family romance, its emphasis is on 'the opposition between successive generations' (1959b: 237), which characterises the subject's context as one of contingency as well as mortality. On the other hand, the subject's access to a symbolic position resonates with the notion how in exile one may arrive in another cultural language.

The family serves as a core trope of the home, whether it is configured as a site of happiness or discontent. In the context of exilic loss and displacement, family and home narratives are so resilient because they may displace as well as stand in for other (related) issues. Thus they provide a narrative language to refigure questions of lack and loss, the disturbing knowledge of which they may either highlight or occlude in the form of screen memories or protective fictions. In so doing, they simultaneously negotiate the ability of a subject or a text to re-establish a home and thus to reside in its narratives and languages. If mapped onto the situation of cultural displacement, Freud's family romance, for example, may be read together with nostalgic retrospection and its imaginary privileging of family bonds over the rupture of exile. The separation from the family, on the other hand, may highlight a sustained movement of dislocation. The resolution of the Oedipal *rite de passage*, in turn, provides a model for the assimilation of a new set of cultural codes. Family narratives may, therefore, stand in for different forms of psychic and cultural departure and arrival. By referring to these different narrative figurations, exilic texts both draw on and establish a compelling interface between family narratives and cultural as well as psychic notions of dislocation and belonging.

In their different figurations of fantasy and its (dis)location, thematic tropes and narratives cannot be separated from the aesthetic structures and gestures which they develop in particular texts. At stake, therefore, is what one may want to call a 'poetics of exile'. In tracing how narratives and tropes are inspired by exile, I am simultaneously interested in whether they rhetorically ward off a traumatic knowledge of displacement or articulate that dislocation is inevitable, both in cases in which exile occurs as an actual event or cases in which it registers as a psychic condition. How, in other words, is the double movement of displacement and belonging refigured aesthetically? Is the uncanny psychic ambivalence of exile reflected by the aesthetic structure and argument of the individual text? Or is its 'exilic' knowledge denied so that a text may come to be haunted by the blind spots of a secret double articulation?

Home and Exile in Hitchcock and Nabokov

This double perspective on aesthetics and exile is particularly pertinent to a reading of Hitchcock and Nabokov. From the very beginning, their homes are highly fictional, both in their cultural affiliations and the imaginary of their textual representations. In reading Hitchcock's and Nabokov's textual homes together with the question of exile and cultural displacement, I wish to follow the exilic traces permeating their languages. Bearing in mind the various narratives and tropes of exile I have introduced above, my readings in the subsequent chapters will focus on the question how literary and cinematic texts engage in an exilic imaginary and aesthetics as well as how their specific implications are played out. Or asked differently, what is brought to the fore by their particular thematic tropes and rhetorical gestures? And what are the auspices under which aesthetic language forms an 'imaginary homeland'?

While this book posits similarities and analogies between Hitchcock's and Nabokov's aesthetic concerns, it also forms an attempt to determine the distinctive ways in which their texts triangulate exilic rupture, narrative imagination and textual aesthetics. My cross-mapping of texts is thus to highlight rhetorical shifts and displacements that occur both within and between the two oeuvres. Hitchcock and Nabokov meet in their transatlantic move and their interest in aesthetic language, but they differ vastly in their exilic departures and cultural arrivals. More specifically, I will argue that Hitchcock emphasises scenarios of wilful self-dislocation, whereas Nabokov's texts can be read as a commemoration of traumatic rupture. In addition to the different exilic departures that refract their poetics, I shall also trace the consequences that these different points of departure and trajectories have for the ways in which their texts arrive in American culture. What does it mean for their work to migrate to another cultural context and what are the preconditions and implications of their respective arrivals?

Throughout much of my analysis, I will treat literary and cinematic texts in an analogous fashion, namely as narratives raising thematic and aesthetic questions. In fact, the close correspondences between Hitchcock's and Nabokov's oeuvres are not least of all a result of their medial hybridity, of the ways in which the director's films evoke the literary and the writer's texts the cinematic. Not only do Hitchcock movies, like most films, adapt literary sources, but the focus of his psychothrillers on the subject, its fantasies, fears and anxieties, clearly picks up on the ways in which the individual psyche has been explored in literary texts over the past two centuries, especially in traditions and authors that are also particularly important to Nabokov, including Romanticism, Gothic, detective and espionage fiction as well as writers such as Poe and Stevenson. Strongly resonant of the literary is also the way in which the director positions himself as a distinct author figure. Despite – or perhaps precisely because of – the highly collaborative media system of film, in which work is divided and distributed among many different departments, Hitchcock creates a visual language and a narrative style that unmistakeably carry the mark of his authorial signature, a feature traditionally associated with literary discourses of creativity. Rather than producing the type of mimetic illusion and spatial continuity so typical of classical Hollywood film, Hitchcock's camera, for instance, foregrounds itself as a conspicuous presence – through tilted angles, unusual frames or movements, which suggest that the camera has a 'will of its own'.[22] Hitchcock thus positions his camera as a narrative instance reminiscent again of literary narration.

Although Nabokov's texts reveal an ambivalence towards film as a popular medium potentially complicitous with clichés and commonplaces, they are yet deeply immersed in cinematic culture. Nabokov not only lived in Berlin, the interwar film mecca second only to Hollywood, where Hitchcock had gathered some of his early experience and where he himself worked as an extra, auditioned as an actor and entertained hopes to turn his novels into film and/or to find work in Hollywood (Appel 1974: 270–4, Boyd 1993a: 232, Zimmer 2001: 64–5, 126, Grayson 2001: 61–3). His novels also make extensive reference to film. The protagonist Ganin in *Mary*, for instance, works as an extra, while several female figures – Margot in *Laughter in the Dark* as well as Dolores and Charlotte Haze in *Lolita* – appear to be the products of the movies they have watched (Appel 1974: 109).

Most importantly, however, 'Nabokov is an intensely visual writer – "I see in images, not words," he says – and his work abounds in images and scenes that are cinematic by design' (Appel 1974: 195). As he begins to dissociate himself from his body in order to be in two places at once, Hermann Karlovich in *Despair* (1932/1965), for instance, watches his bodily alter ego making love to his wife in a quasi-cinematic set-up, 'with the harps of rain aphrodisiacally burbling in the orchestra as I was sitting at my maximum distance of fifteen rows of seats' (D: 33). After his supposedly artistic murder of a figure he mistakes for his double, he is uncomfortably cornered by the French police and several hundred onlookers. In this situation, Hermann Karlovich fantasises how he could exit from his rented room by announcing the rehearsal of a famous film actor playing the escape of a criminal – a scenario which anticipates the brilliant final scene of Billy Wilder's *Sunset Boulevard* (1950), in which the former silent film star Norma Desmond (Gloria Swanson), having murdered her young lover and screenplay writer, eventually lets herself be persuaded to leave her room as she is duped into believing that the cameras, rather than belonging to Paramount News, have returned to film her in her comeback role as Salome. Similar to the dissolution of Desmond's close-up into pure light as the element of the cinematic medium *par excellence*, Hermann Karlovich narrative ends with the cinematic exit scenario scripted by his narrative imagination, which the text has been foregrounding all along. Together with other filmic modes and moments in his texts, this example suggests that Nabokov incorporates cinematic elements in order to refer either to the deluded imagination of his protagonists or to the aesthetic artificiality and medial self-reflexivity of his writing.[22]

In spite of Hitchcock's and Nabokov's medial cross-overs, differences in the media systems as well as in the narratives and tropes they develop do gain urgency as we turn to issues of exile and dislocation. In *Lolita*, I shall argue in the second chapter, the dislocation of the European emigrant Humbert Humbert is signalled by the fact that he eclipses the world beyond his image repertoire and imposes his solipsistic imagination on Dolores Haze. The violent power and predominance of Humbert Humbert's idiosyncratic focalisation and unreliable narration can be convincingly conveyed in literature. In film, however, any control of the 'verbal track' by a narratorial voice-over will inevitably be undermined by the co-existence of audio-visual channels as well as the undeniable physical presence, the positions and voices of other characters (Stam 2005a: 38). In fact, it is precisely in the multiplicity and juxtaposition of channels, codes and images that I will locate a cinematic aesthetics of dislocation.

At the same time, differences between the literary and cinematic media system also come into play when we consider how, after their exilic move, Hitchcock and Nabokov relocate their work in relation to American cinema and literature. Hinging on a visual grammar which is to some degree global, film lends itself more easily to cultural translation than literature. For a writer, literary language may provide an 'imaginary homeland' in exile. Yet loss can register all the more acutely when language becomes the one and only possession shored up against the ruins of loss. As suggested by Brodsky's metaphor mentioned above, the isolated possession may turn into an isolating impulse as writers, dislocated from the cultural context of their literary language, resemble individuals encapsulated in their language and launched on a one-way journey into outer space.

Questions of exile and/or psychic dislocation are prominently foregrounded by a great majority of Hitchcock's and Nabokov's texts. However, so as to highlight issues of exilic transfer, my readings focus on their American texts (or, in the case of Nabokov, on texts he wrote in English). Furthermore, I have selected my textual examples in view of their particularly emblematic condensation of exilic and aesthetic concerns. Thus Nabokov's autobiography *Speak, Memory* (1951/1967) retraces the exile's home in the past, whereas *Lolita* (1955/1958) represents 'the record of my love affair' with the English language (LO: 316). In *Suspicion* (1941) Hitchcock returns to the British associations of his first Hollywood film *Rebecca* (1940). *North by Northwest* (1959), in turn, not only represents a paradigmatic Hitchcock thriller, but also marks the director's position in the system of classic Hollywood cinema. The examples, in other words, are chosen as counterpoints reflecting the liminal displacement of exile, on the one hand, and the question of cultural assimilation, on the other.

I begin with a reading of *Speak, Memory* (1951/1967), which serves as a foil for the analysis of the other texts. Nabokov's autobiography follows a classic trajectory of exilic nostalgia. Its nostalgic re-creation of an extraordinarily blissful childhood not only serves as a powerful source of aesthetic inspiration. Its family romance simultaneously represents a screen memory which occludes and yet also preserves traumatic reminiscences of loss through dislocation and death, which trouble the seemingly happy family home. In the second chapter, I suggest that similar to the 'imaginary homeland' which *Speak, Memory* restores in poetic language, *Lolita* creates a home in literary texts and imagination. In so doing, the novel produces an aestheticisation of the world which is apotropaic and violent at the same time. On the one hand, *Lolita* (1955/1958) points to the violence with which Humbert Humbert elides the disturbing knowledge represented by the separateness of the other, the world beyond his image repertoire. On the other hand, the narratorial and the authorial levels, that is the textual voices of the first-person narrator Humbert Humbert and the implied author Nabokov, uncannily converge in their investment in poetic language. As a result, I claim, the novel's aesthetic project comes to be haunted by a blind spot, by an exilic knowledge that cannot be addressed by its textuality but instead must be occluded. The displacement played through on the thematic level, that is the migration of the cultural exile Humbert Humbert across the United States, is thus supplemented by a dislocation on the aesthetic level.

Both in analogy and counterpoint, the second part of the book is devoted to Hitchcock's cinematic texts. While Nabokov's 'imaginary homelands' invoke an ambivalent protection, it is precisely imagination which brings about dislocation in Hitchcock's nightmare scenarios. Using the family home and the subject's psychic apparatus as interchangeable tropes, his narratives of home paranoia underscore a fundamental dislocation of subjectivity. The heroine of the female paranoia film *Suspicion* (1941) engages in a wandering of the mind which liberates her from her parental home. At the same time, the murder fantasy that accompanies her Oedipal move towards sexual and cultural difference culminates in a traumatic enactment. *North by Northwest* (1959) equally turns around a scenario of troubling home paranoia. Yet more distinctly than the earlier film, the protagonist's traversal of the Oedipal voyage works towards a symbolic curtailment of the imaginary. The mutual re-establishment of the couple and the national law reflects the film's recuperation of a symbolic frame of reference. At the same time, the ironical alignment of the film's language with Hollywood codes signals on a meta-texual level that symbolic re-integration always remains ambivalent. As a result, *North by Northwest* and *Suspicion* both point to an irresolvable antagonism which haunts the subject in its imaginary as well as symbolic relations.

Moving through these different configurations, my critical narrative is to trace how exile, whether a biographical and/or psychic reality, is refigured. In so doing, I want to examine the ways in which notions of home and dislocation inform the rhetorical gestures of the different narratives and their imaginary. In their respective ways, both Nabokov's textual abundance and Hitchcock's predilection for scenarios of home paranoia serve as signals that something is 'out of place'. The question, however, is whether and how this dislocation comes to be self-consciously reflected by their aesthetic languages. Nabokov's writing, I shall suggest, encrypts a void of trauma, which commemorates but cannot articulate the violent rupture of geopolitical loss and displacement. Given his voluntary self-dislocation and assimilation in the Hollywood system, Hitchcock occupies far safer ground to explore an exilic knowledge. In fact, it is by traversing tenebrous territory that he can ironise its disturbing impact on our imaginary and symbolic resolutions. By contrast, it appears as though Nabokov's textual irony were to create a distance that actually remains out of reach. His aesthetics not only engages in an exilic self-fashioning but is simultaneously propelled by a real rupture.

Hitchcock's and Nabokov's figurations of exile, I finally argue, are also inflected by the distinct ways in which they allude to psychoanalysis. Significantly enough, psychoanalysis not only theorises dislocation in its psychic forms but is itself strongly inflected by concrete cultural displacement. This is tangibly documented by *Moses and Monotheism* (1939), a text which Freud wrote before and after his exilic displacement from Vienna to London. By way of a summary, my epilogue will look at psychoanalysis as a highly allegorical language. Returning to the murky interface between concrete exile and its transformation into a critical and aesthetic trope, I will discuss psychoanalysis as the theoretical framework used in this book as well as one of the most recurrent discourses quoted by Hitchcock and Nabokov. My cross-mapping concludes with Nabokov's first English novel *The Real Life of Sebastian Knight* (1941) and Hitchcock's first all-American film *Shadow of a Doubt* (1943). The two family and *doppelgänger* narratives illustrate not only the divergent attitudes of Hitchcock and Nabokov towards psychoanalysis as the cultural discourse of dislocation *par excellence*. The ways in which they either invoke or reject Freud's figures of thought provide yet another perspective from which we can evaluate the differences of their exile and aesthetics. While scenarios of psychic dislocation serve as the primary motor of Hitchcock's cinematic language, Nabokov's writing is doubly exilic as it remains haunted by what can never be translated into any language.

Notes

1. See the two letters included in Nabokov's *Selected Letters* (SL: 361–4) as well as two additional letters in the Berg Collection of the New York Public Library (Alfred Hitchcock to Vladimir Nabokov, Universal City, California, 3 December 1964; Véra Nabokov to Alfred Hitchcock, Montreux, Switzerland, 10 December 1964). The abbreviations of Nabokov's texts are listed at the beginning of the book.
2. For a selection of film still sequences from the *Phoenix Tapes*, see the catalogue *Notorious: Alfred Hitchcock and Contemporary Art*, edited by Kerry Brougher et al., accompanying the exhibition of artwork recycling Hitchcock's visual language at the Museum of Modern Art, Oxford, 1999.
3. Hitchcock time and again plays on what films do, notably on the idea that cinema centrally deals with questions of proper and improper viewing. At the beginning of *Psycho* (1960), the camera 'hops' onto a window sill just like a bird in order to then pry into the illicit intimate scene inside the room. In a similar vein, *Rear Window* (1954) presents a protagonist who reflects back on the spectator and the viewing of film in general. Lying immobilised at his window during a heat wave, Jeff (James Stewart) awakens from his sleep to observe his neighbours as if they were figures moving on a screen of projection. In so doing, the film offers one of Hitchcock's many comments on the voyeurism, fantasy work and other psychic processes built into the cinematic medium. *The Real Life of Sebastian Knight* (1941) and *Lolita* (1955/1958) are, in turn, two examples of Nabokov texts which appear not only to be written by their protagonists as we are reading them, but which, moreover, thematise issues of literary imagination by mixing elements of biography, memoir and fiction.
4. Surprisingly, the two oeuvres have rarely been read together. To my knowledge, the only sustained comparison of Hitchcock and Nabokov to date is James Davidson's article 'Hitchcock/Nabokov: Some Thoughts on Alfred Hitchcock and Vladimir Nabokov' (1997). Alfred Appel, in *Nabokov's Dark Cinema*, makes a few brief references to the joint project of the author and the director, their humour and the games in which they involve their readers and spectators (1974: 129, 132–3, 252). Discussing Hitchcock's black humour in the context of 1950s culture, James Naremore invokes Nabokov's *Lolita* (2004: 30), while Fredric Jameson refers to the irony and the presentation of American everyday life by the two European exiles (1992a: 104–5, 116). Beverly Gray Bienstock mentions the tight control characterising the work of both Hitchcock and Nabokov as well as the authorial appearances they frequently make in their literary and cinematic

texts (1982: 128–9). Barbara Wyllie (2003), finally, repeatedly touches on Hitchcock in her study exploring the relevance of film to Nabokov's writing.
5. On the game structures in Hitchcock's films, see Thomas M. Leitch (1991).
6. For a full-length study on the unreliability of Nabokov's narrators, see Renate Hof (1984).
7. Not only was Hitchcock a prominent example for the *auteur* theory developed by the *Cahiers du Cinéma* group in the 1950s, but his aesthetic signatures also form the focus of later analyses, notably by William Rothman (1982), Slavoj Žižek (1992) and Tom Cohen (1994, 2005a, 2005b). A classic equivalent in Nabokov studies is Appel's *Annotated Lolita* (1991). A similar approach can also be found in Leona Toker's study on literary structures in Nabokov's texts (1989).
8. The doubles in the two oeuvres range, for example, from Hermann Karlovich and his dissimilar murder victim in *Despair* to Humbert Humbert and Clare Quilty in *Lolita*, from Bruno Anthony and Guy Haines and their criss-cross of murders in *Strangers on a Train* to Roger O. Thornhill and his non-existent alter ego George Kaplan in *North by Northwest*.
9. There is a strong resemblance between Hitchcock's usage of his iconic profile in his self-advertisement, on the one hand, and Warhol's serial silkscreen portraits of stars and celebrities, on the other hand. In both cases, individuals are reduced to and reproduced through a few recognisable features. It is hardly a coincidence that in 1974, Andy Warhol chose to interview Alfred Hitchcock for his celebrity magazine *Interview*. The conversation is reprinted in the volume *Alfred Hitchcock: Interviews* edited by Sidney Gottlieb (2003: 186–212).
10. There are a great number of anagrams in Nabokov's oeuvre with which he marks and signs his authorial presence and control, including, for example, 'Adam von Librikov' (TT: 78, SO: 196), 'Vivian Badlook' (SO: 110), 'Vivian Bloodmark, a philosophical friend of mine' (SM: 169), 'Vivian Darkbloom (a shy violet in Cambridge)' (SO: 192) as well as 'Vivian Darkbloom', the name of Clare Quilty's mistress and the anagram of Nabokov in *Lolita* (LO: 4, 31, 221).
11. As they are lost in a canyon on their cross-continental journey, the screenplay figure of Lolita suggests that Humbert Humbert ask 'that nut with the net over there' (SL: 127–8) – the butterfly hunter Nabokov, who puts a killed specimen on the palm of his hand just before Humbert Humbert asks him for directions.
12. See Hitchcock's distinction between terror and suspense, his comments on the experience of 'thrills', the genre of the thriller and the director's power over the audience (Hitchcock in Gottlieb 1997: 109–12, 118–21, 256–7, 272).
13. James Davidson's article explores structural analogies between the two oeuvres (1997). For the relevance of film for Nabokov's writing, see Alfred Appel's book *Nabokov's Dark Cinema* (1974) and Barbara Wyllie's *Nabokov at the Movies* (2003).
14. For biographical details, see Brian Boyd (1993a, 1993b) and Jane Grayson (2001) on Nabokov, Donald Spoto (1983), John Russell Taylor (1996), Patrick McGilligan (2003) and Charlotte Chandler (2005) on Hitchcock.

15. In his long conversation with François Truffaut, Hitchcock affirms that from a young age, 'I certainly was deeply entrenched in American cinema . . . It never occurred to me to go and offer my services to a British company'. When he started out in the film business as a title card designer in 1921, he did so in an American studio which 'happened to be located in London' and which provided him with an 'American training' so that he 'never set foot in a British studio until 1927' (Hitchcock in Truffaut 1985: 124–5). While, as he points out, the years in Britain were instrumental to his technical formation – 'as a matter of fact, the techniques and camera precepts that I learned then have continued to serve me ever since' – it was only in Hollywood that he could fully realise his cinematic ideas, thereby making productive a so far latent intuition. 'For want of a better term, we might label the initial phase the period of the sensation of cinema, and the second phase, the period when the ideas were fertilized' (Hitchcock in Truffaut 1985: 123).
16. For related examples in the fine arts, see Barbara Haskell's exhibition catalogue *The American Century*, especially the chapter 'Postwar Anxiety and Subjectivity' (1999: 353–61).
17. Note in particular the British and the American version of *The Man Who Knew Too Much* (1934/1956), *The 39 Steps* (1935) and its American remake *North by Northwest* (1959).
18. In her book *Strangers to Ourselves* (1991), Julia Kristeva works with an allegorical analogy between the exilic foreigner and the 'foreign body' constituted by the unconscious in the subject's psychic apparatus.
19. 'Man muss Heimat haben, um sie nicht nötig zu haben' (Améry 1966: 79).
20. See Freud's correspondence with Wilhelm Fliess (1986: 177–8, 253).
21. On Lacan's conception of the Oedipus complex, see Dylan Evans (1996: 127–30).
21. Note, for instance, how at the beginning of *Rebecca* the camera appears to literally follow the narrative movements of the spectral voice-over, how at the beginning of *Psycho* it 'hops' on a window sill to pry into an illicit scene inside the room, or how the camera marks a panoptic and omniscient position by looking down on the fire following the fuel explosion in the famous shot in *The Birds*.
22. Surprisingly perhaps Nabokov's screenplay of *Lolita* is one of his least cinematic texts. Consisting mainly of dialogue, the text lacks not only a coherent development of visual tropes, but also a plurality of narrative levels and 'channels' so pivotal for the production of irony in both Nabokov's and Hitchcock's texts.

Part I

Nabokov's Dislocations

Chapter 2

Refiguring Loss and Exile in *Speak, Memory*

Nabokov's autobiography *Speak, Memory* (1967), which first appeared as *Conclusive Evidence* (1951), is marked by multiple revisitations. The memoir returns to powerful scenes of an autobiographical past not only to re-create and repossess a lost geocultural world together with a childhood family home of extraordinary bliss, but also to pretend that, on some level, displacement, death and loss have not occurred. As I shall argue in this chapter, it is precisely in its attempt to undo a cataclysmic past that the survior text comes to be haunted and revisited by the burden of a disturbing knowledge.

As we consider Nabokov's biography, we quickly notice that his re-creation of the family home occurs against the backdrop of several dislocations, notably his geocultural displacement and the death of several family members. As a result, the home, which forms both the point of departure and the object of reconstruction, is troubled by loss – a fact that appears to ineluctably haunt the author and his text. Yet in spite of, or precisely because of, these radical dislocations, first through the Russian Revolution and then the Second World War, Nabokov still has recourse to home narratives. More specifically, his autobiography invokes a classic humanistic narrative of exile, a type of text that presupposes the chronotope of a home or homeland which, in retrospect, comes to be mythically refigured as a paradisiacal site or state from which the exiled person has been expelled.

It is thanks to this former, supposedly secure emplacement that the exile can remain connected to the home. His nostalgic longing implies that there is actually a home one could inhabit, if only exilic separation had not occurred. In the same gesture, the scenario of nostalgia allows the exile to repossess the home in the imaginary, notably in narratives inspired by its absence and shaped by its consequent phantasmatic idealisation. As already emphasised in the introductory chapter, this valorisation of the imaginary and imagination is, of course, a quintessentially poetic gesture. Yet it is also emblematic of the situation of exile, in which recourse to a mythopoetic home, its narratives and fantasies becomes all the more precious – and necessary. The family and home narratives Nabokov presents in his autobiography coincide with Salman Rushdie's notion of the 'imaginary homeland' (1991). In the absence of an actual home, the exile re-creates an imaginary home as a result of his or her desire to reclaim imaginatively what is no longer there. Although it is necessarily belated and displaced in relation to the 'real' home, which has been lost, the imaginary homeland forms a powerful pivot. As a protective fiction, it covers up the lacuna of loss and displacement and simultaneously offers a new form of habitation.

My reading of *Speak, Memory* claims that Nabokov's imaginary homeland is not formed by family and home narratives alone but equally resides in a strong investment in aesthetic language. Not simply conveyed by linguistic means, Nabokov's imaginary home 'dwells' in poetic language so that the text can be said to create a home both in and through its writing. In an interview he gave for the fashion magazine *Vogue*, Nabokov emphasises his valorisation of the aesthetic by subordinating biographical events to the primacy of poetic language. 'The best part of a writer's biography', he argues, 'is not the record of his adventures but the story of his style' (SO: 154–5). Apart from a few scenes dealing with the writer's early poetic experiments, his autobiography does not offer an account of his style in a strict sense. Yet the text is steeped in a highly aestheticised language, which, indeed, attests to his interest in technique and 'style'. With its textual patterns, *Speak, Memory* revels precisely in the language games for which Nabokov became known and celebrated. Yet in contrast to his call to shift focus from a writer's 'adventures' in life to the 'story of his style', I argue that in the case of Nabokov, the two are closely interlinked.

Even as it seeks to turn away from biographical facticity, Nabokov's aesthetics cannot be separated from the real rupture of exile and bereavement. On the contrary, it is against the backdrop of these experiences that his wordplay unfolds. The reason why my rereading reintroduces referentiality is not because my interest is primarily biographical, but because I want to trace the stakes of Nabokov's aesthetic investment. What, in other words, is the relation between the facticity of loss and exile, on the one hand, and an emphasis on textual patterns, on the other hand? What are the rhetorical gestures of Nabokov's poetic language? Nabokov's writing, I claim, cannot be subsumed under a postmodern textuality, nor can it be reduced to the aesthetic self-reflexivity emphasised so often in his public statements. On the contrary, I attribute pivotal importance to what tends to be overlooked or simplified if we read Nabokov as a postmodern author, namely the political and historical implications of the nostalgia and mourning underpinning his writing.

The seemingly relentless playfulness conjured up by Nabokov's autobiography serves as an antidote to the referential moments that ruptured his vita. That is, by continuously turning back upon itself, his aesthetics seeks to stave off those moments in his biography which point to loss and displacement.[1] Rather than forming a self-sufficient means, his poetic language is inscribed by a gesture that can be called apotropaic. This is to say that Nabokov valorises aesthetic technique so as to avert, and protect himself against, the facticity of loss and bereavement. The protective rhetoric of Nabokov's writing is all the more significant in view of the claim I want to make that *Speak, Memory* can be read as a survivor text. The memoir, which was entitled *Conclusive Evidence* in an earlier version, is not only to give evidence of the author's life, but also to provide a testimony of his survival. As a survivor narrative, Nabokov's autobiography is haunted by contingencies that he survived but others close to him did not.

Nabokov's contingent survival may well be the reason why his text seeks to deflect the painful impact of history. In *The Political Unconscious*, Fredric Jameson defines history as that which 'hurts' because it sets limits to individuals, their desire, imagination and control (1981: 102). Not only does history happen in a random and contingent fashion. As Jameson points out, history resembles the Lacanian real as it resists symbolisation and can be approached only indirectly through textual and narrative refigurations (1981: 35). Picking up on Jameson's notion of history as 'an absent cause' and belated effect, one might say that Nabokov creates the surfeit of his textual patterns not only against the backdrop of something that eludes representation. His extremely controlled language games are simultaneously written against history as that which poses a limit to human stability and power. By embracing a highly aesthetic language, Nabokov thus challenges history as that which insists beyond individual language and imagination and, at the same time, forms the ineluctable ground and vanishing point of his survivor narrative.

As Brian Boyd emphasises in his biography, Vladimir Nabokov could hardly ignore the catastrophic events of twentieth-century history which ruptured his life so dramatically and traumatically (1993a: 3). In Russia, Nabokov's family belonged to the aristocratic ruling class, and his parents stood for liberal political positions and intellectual affiliations. They spoke several cultural languages with equal fluency. Their double orientation towards both Slavic and Western European cultures was, for instance, reflected by their extensive travelling in Western Europe and their fond return to the Russian homeland, the children's education first by English and French-speaking governesses and later by Russian tutors, the English novels and bedtime stories that the Anglophile parents would read to them, or the effortless switching between Russian, French, German and English in everyday conversations.[2] Nabokov's paternal grandfather, Dmitri Nabokov, had opposed anti-Semitism in his capacity as minister of justice, and his father, Vladimir Dmitrievich Nabokov, a trained criminologist, defended individual rights and minority groups, especially Jews and homosexuals. He was also an editor of the liberal daily newspaper *Rech'* (*Speech*), a prominent member of the Constitutional Democratic Party and a chancellor of the first Provisional Government in 1917. When the Bolshevik Revolution forced the family into exile in 1919, it not only dislodged them from their aristocratic houses, possessions and privileges – just three years earlier, Nabokov himself had inherited a fortune and an estate from his uncle. The Revolution also destroyed the cosmopolitan culture that had been so important for the family's self-definition.

Most important of all, Nabokov lost several family members under tragic circumstances. His cousin Yuri Rausch von Traubenberg, to whom he had been closely attached, was killed fighting the Red Army. While the games of the two boys narrated in *Speak, Memory* come close to playful rehearsals of Yuri's death, it is almost only in passing that the text makes mention of his disfigured corpse, which Nabokov saw on the Crimea shortly before his escape to Western Europe (SM: 155–6). The most traumatic experience, however, must have been the violent death of Nabokov's father, which is again only obliquely rendered in the autobiography. In 1922, a few years into the family's exile in Berlin, where Vladimir Dmitrievich Nabokov was one of the editors of the émigré newspaper *Rul'* (*Rudder*), he was fatally shot by two Russian extreme rightists at a public lecture as he shielded the speaker, his friend Pavel Milyukov, the intended victim of the assassination. After her husband's death, Nabokov's mother moved to Prague. Nabokov's economically difficult circumstances meant that he 'was unable to visit her frequently' (SM: 40). Although some of her children and a former family governess joined her, she died in 1939, isolated and destitute, in Prague, which by then had been occupied by the Nazis. During the war, Sergey, one of Nabokov's brothers, was deported to the concentration camp Neuengamme near Hamburg, where he died four months before the capitulation of Nazi Germany.

Nabokov himself, his Jewish wife Véra, born Slonim, and their son Dmitri made a narrow escape from Fascist violence and terror. Not having followed the mass exoduses of Russians from Germany to Paris in the early 1920s and then again in the 1930s, they only left Berlin after Véra was no longer allowed to work because of her Jewish identity and after one of the two murderers of Nabokov's father had been designated under-secretary in Hitler's Department of Émigré Affairs (Grayson 2001: 69). In France Nabokov was refused a work permit; he could have been drafted into the French army at any moment, thus having had to leave behind Véra and Dmitri, who would have been at great risk as Jews in a country vulnerable to a Nazi invasion (Boyd 1993a: 521). Given their poverty and the dangerous geopolitical situation in Europe, Nabokov and his family 'would hardly have survived and would certainly not have been able to flee Hitler for the United States' had it not been for the generous support of relief organisations and admirers (Boyd 1993a: 3). A ship, the *Champlain*, had been chartered for a refugee crossing by a Jewish New York rescue organisation, which

> was directed by Yakov Frumkin, an old friend of Nabokov's father, who like many other Russian Jews was glad to be able to repay the dead man for his bold stands against the Kishinyov pogroms and the Beilis trial by now offering his son a cabin for half fare. (Boyd 1993a: 521)

A part of the still considerable sum for the remaining half-fare was raised at a benefit reading, and several Jewish families paid the amount outstanding. The German invasion of France advanced so rapidly that the ship could not depart from Le Havre as initially scheduled but had to leave from St Nazaire further south–west. On its very next crossing to the United States, the *Champlain* was sunk by a German U-boat (Boyd 1993b: 11).

These referential moments are important to consider because they suggest that Nabokov's biographical trajectory both provides and confronts him with an excess rather than a lack of memories. Indeed, the crucial characteristic of *Speak, Memory* appears to be an overabundance of reminiscences, some of which resist integration into the family home narrative, return to haunt the text and – by irrupting with a painful force – confront the survivor with a troubling knowledge. Contrary to the culturally powerful discourses that in recent years have evolved around notions of memory and trauma, Nabokov's text is haunted not by a memory shortage but by the need on the part of the survivor to forget. So far several studies on Nabokov have focused on memory. Yet while they tend to highlight the images, metaphors and 'intertextual reminiscences' of Nabokov's 'art of memory',[3] I am primarily interested in the surplus of Nabokov's memory text.[4] As I shall argue, it is a surfeit of reminiscences that constitutes the vanishing point of Nabokov's aesthetic project; or put differently, it is from a troubling referentiality that the game of his aesthetic patterns seeks to turn away. Designed to undo painful referentiality, the crux of Nabokov's aesthetic investment entails a significant aporia. While the rhetorical empowerment of his language and narrative is pitted against disturbing memories, the text implicitly has to return to the knowledge it seeks to stave off.

In what follows, I will trace the ambivalences of the imaginary home which Nabokov creates in and through his aesthetic language. Asking how the past inscribes itself into his text, my reading will focus on three areas, namely aesthetic language, the text's family romance and, finally, the poetics of memory that underpins the re-construction of this imaginary home. Paradoxically, it is in these three textual domains, which are designed as safeguards, that ruptures return and articulate themselves most prominently. In seeking to restore the disrupted network of family bonds in his memory text, Nabokov's family romance cannot but refer to irrevocable loss, which forms the paradoxical and precarious ground of his writing. My reading thus examines the double gestures in which the imaginary home narratives both highlight and deflect the losses that keep revisiting the survivor text. Likewise the re-insertion of referentiality into Nabokov's 'story of style' will allow us to explore the connection between aesthetic language and troubling facticity so as to move both beyond a purely aesthetic as well as a merely semantic reading of Nabokov's writing.

Chronophobia

Nabokov's autobiographical text begins with a striking home movie scenario. In contrast to the private screening of the home movies in Hitchcock's *Rebecca*, where happy honeymoon scenes are juxtaposed with the precarious relation of the newly-wed couple watching themselves on film, the discomfort of Nabokov's scenario derives from the home movie itself. While the young person is viewing the home movies of his family for the first time, he is presented with a disturbing vision of his own absence prior to his birth. In an uncanny reversal of chronology, the subject's prenatal absence is taken to prefigure its irrevocable absence in death:

> I know . . . of a young chronophobiac who experienced something like panic when looking for the first time at homemade movies that had been taken a few weeks before his birth. He saw a world that was practically unchanged – the same house, the same people – and then realized that he did not exist there at all and that nobody mourned his absence. He caught a glimpse of his

mother waving from an upstairs window, and that unfamiliar gesture disturbed him, as if it were some mysterious farewell. But what particularly frightened him was the sight of a brand-new baby carriage standing there on the porch, with the snug, encroaching air of a coffin; even that was empty, as if, in the reverse course of events, his very bones had disintegrated. (SM: 17)

The anticipation of mortality even before life has begun is remarkable. Having been introduced in the foreword as 'conclusive evidence of my having existed' (SM: 8), the autobiography opens not with a reassuring point of origin but with a troubling scenario, in which 'a young chronophobiac' – whom I take to stand in for Nabokov himself – is confronted by the possibility of his non-existence.

The scene's reversal of life and death discloses a disturbing knowledge pertaining to the contingency of our existence. What the movies bring home to the young chronophobiac is our contingency, the idea that the world could exist – and be complete – without us. As the chronophobic child notices distressedly, his absence in the world of the home movie is not even as much as registered, let alone mourned. With the 'brand-new baby carriage' uncannily presenting itself as a coffin in which his body seems to have disintegrated in either a curious reversal of time or some enormous quick-motion effect, the scene also suggests that we are faced with the inevitable contingency of death from the very beginning of our lives. Death emerges as the only event in life that we are certain to experience, while it is also the most contingent since we cannot know when and how it will occur.[5]

While the scenario in this passage poses the disturbingly open question of the origin and end of human life, it is also distinctly marked by death. As Sabine Baumann notes, the mother's waving is clearly not intended as a signal to the (as yet unborn) child (1999: 254). Rather, the 'mysterious farewell' addresses the father, who must be standing behind the camera, so that the scene comes to form an uncanny prolepsis of his utterly contingent and violent death some twenty years later. From the survivor's belated perspective, which may be implied by the ambiguous expression 'a world that was practically unchanged' – it not only looks 'unchanged' to the child, but it also seems untainted by losses experienced later – the mother's 'unfamiliar gesture' poignantly anticipates this particularly painful separation together with other instances of dislocation, notably the loss of the family home and the geocultural homeland.

In *Camera Lucida*, Roland Barthes argues that the photographic medium is characterised by an intrinsic fatality. By arresting and capturing a particular moment in time, it documents what undeniably 'has been' and will, therefore, die or already be dead by the time the picture is looked at (1993: 77, 96). This lethal effect also marks the photographs included in *Speak, Memory*. As a family album, they may seem to preserve a blissful plenitude. Yet many of the portrayed family members are, in fact, dead by the time of the text's first publication. Although Barthes writes about the medium of photography and not film, his argument is also pertinent to the opening of the autobiography. To the surviving family member, the 'homemade movies' present the family *sujet* in the light of a double loss. Not only do they represent what 'was' and is no longer, but while the survivor is absent from the world documented by the home movies, they are inhabited by those whom he has survived by the time of writing. This paradoxical constellation points to the inexplicable contingency of his own survival and further underlines the irrevocable loss of his dead family members. The film representation – just as the home narratives of the text – may temporarily inspire the dead with spectral life. But in the same gesture their phantomatic resurrection also emphasises their separateness from the surviving family member. As the opening of a survivor narrative, the home movie scenario is particularly resonant because the scene encodes the home as a site which has been vulnerable from the very start, even before the subject was born into it and long before it came to be marked by fatality.

The 'origin' posited by the home movie scene haunts the text both on a semantic and a representational level. The opening passage underscores that an unambiguous return home is impossible. The knowledge of the family's fragility and destruction is inevitable from the perspective of the one who has survived separation and loss. Moreover, the mortal mark on the home narrative can be thought together with Freud's notion of the 'navel of the dream', that is his critical metaphor for a moment which resists integration into any symbolic or imaginary narrative and which he, therefore, describes as 'unplumbable – a navel, as it were', that is in 'contact with the unknown' (1958: 111). Mortality marks a radically 'unfamiliar' moment in Nabokov's family narrative because it is connected to experiences of painful parturition and is hence particularly difficult for the survivor to confront. In fact, death evokes a structure that may be called traumatic. As a critical moment of which we cannot have any direct knowledge, death is situated beyond the representational register. As has been argued by trauma theory since Freud, trauma posits a void for which, similar to the 'navel' of the dream, there can be no adequate representation.[6] Since the subject is not actually 'there' at the moment of traumatic impact, it will always remain cut off from the actual trauma together with any representations that come to refigure the psychic gap which separates the 'traumatic wound' from consciousness. Trauma continues to call for symbolic refigurations, but these belated representations will never fully fill the lacuna trauma has opened. As a result, the traumatic void keeps insisting by triggering an infinite loop of refigurations.

The gaps and surplus structures that characterise Nabokov's text are two sides of one and the same coin. His language creates a realm which is so self-referential that aesthetic technique becomes a way of at once turning away from and pointing to the traumatic effects of history. Because it cannot ever be addressed and 'filled' by representation and language, the traumatic void of loss reproduces itself infinitely. It triggers a surfeit in the form of language games as well as fantasies and narratives about the home. The autobiography, its ellipses, its narrative and aesthetic excesses are by no means reducible to collective history. Yet its fictional surplus and verbal artifice, which can seem compulsive at times, are written both towards and against a very particular individual pain connected to a cataclysmic history. Or put differently, aesthetic language and narrative are literally shored up against the ruins of loss.

I have started with my close reading of the home-movie scenario to suggest that the ambivalent way in which it presents death as its unfathomable 'navel' is paradigmatic for Nabokov's autobiography and perhaps his writing at large. The contingency of life and death literally forms the text's point of departure. As suggested by the beginning of the memoir, it is against the backdrop of death and loss that Nabokov's writing unfolds even as it also seeks to undo these excessively real moments. This ambivalent gesture is palpable in the double articulation in which the beginning, on the one hand, makes explicit reference to a fatal facticity and, on the other hand, seeks to ironically distance itself from the unsettling issue by deflecting panic onto the 'young chronophobiac'. While bringing a moment of high anxiety so strikingly to the fore, the rhetoric of the text simultaneously turns to a protective distance.

As suggested by the chronophobic moment that frames the textual beginning, Nabokov's interest and investment in aesthetic language can be described as a desire to avert and undo the fatality of the past which has disrupted the family home in the form of traumatic history. His text challenges the notion that death forms a realm of radical alterity which is inaccessible to the subject and, therefore, poses a limit to imagination and thought alike. 'I rebel against this state of affairs', Nabokov writes in the face of this and argues instead for a transcendence of 'the impersonal darkness on both sides of my life . . . caused merely by the walls of time separating me and my bruised fists from the free world of timelessness . . .' (SM: 17–18). Already the text's very first sentence designates non-existence and its inaccessibility to human subjects as received ideas and rejects them in line with Nabokov's trenchant critique of commonplaces: 'The cradle rocks above an abyss, and common sense tells us that our existence is but a brief crack of light between two eternities of darkness' (SM: 17). Vladimir Alexandrov (1991: 24) also refers to this passage, albeit to make a rather different point. Instead of reading death as a troubling moment the text writes itself against, he regards the reference to 'common sense' as an ironical signal, undercutting the entire passage on chronophobia tongue-in-cheek. He then goes on to argue that *Speak, Memory* gestures towards a realm of transcendence. In contrast, I would propose that this transcendental gesture might be read as a way to 'rebel' against the irrevocable limit of death. Following Alexandrov's study, the notion of a transcendental otherworld has gained prominence and wide currency in Nabokov criticism. While studies in this area focus on a metaphysical notion of 'a timeless otherworldly realm that hosts idealized memories and provides personal immortality' as well as 'the intuition that souls of the deceased inhabit a parallel world, communicate with the living, and participate in their lives' (Shrayer 1999: 75), I am interested in moments in which death and the deceased pose a radical alterity and, in so doing, bar the possibility of 'communication'. Perhaps one could argue that death as a radical limit forms the backdrop against which Nabokov constructs the notion of the 'otherworld', where death is 'understood as the birth of the eternal self, as an awakening from sleep . . .' (Bronfen 1988: 595). But ultimately the attempt to establish a line of communication between the dead and the survivor remains bounded by death. 'Death remains an irrevocable limit', the transgression of which is beyond our 'image repertoire and beyond the symbolic process of signification' (Bronfen 1988: 595).[7]

As if to counteract the fatal temporality haunting the home movie scenario, the very next passage offers another, more assuring scene of 'origin' as well as a more benign notion of time. The scene revolves around a walk in the family's estate, Vyra – 'the occasion may have been my mother's birthday' (SM: 18). Walking between father and mother, the child recognises for the first time his own and his parents' identity by developing a sense of time: 'The inner knowledge that I was I and that my parents were my parents seems to have been established . . . when it was directly associated with my discovering their age in relation to mine' (SM: 18). Echoing the chronophobiac's panic, the child in this scene is also given a shock of recognition; yet in this instance the effect is 'tremendously invigorating' (SM: 18). Time is now described as a 'radiant and mobile medium' (SM: 19) in which the child's self-discovery in relation to his parent's identity and hence to his family ties occurs in a moment of plenitude.[8] The recollection may be cherished all the more because, retrospectively, it represents an experience of time which is not yet tainted by later events. By contrast, time is almost negated by the exiled Nabokov and his position, which he describes as 'my present ridge of remote, isolated, almost uninhabited time' (SM: 19). While this isolated situation and its transcendence of time may be embraced by the text, they are also marked by a poignant sadness. It is as if to render himself immune against the ruins and losses of history that the survivor leaves time 'almost uninhabited'. The concept '"uninhabited" makes direct sense here', Nabokov notes in an interview, 'since most of my former companions are gone' (SO: 144).

In the park passage, the discovery of time not only coincides with the emergence of identity, it is also equated with 'the awakening of consciousness' (SM: 18). It appears as though the unplumbable navel haunting the home movie scenario had to be juxtaposed with 'my first gleam of complete consciousness' (SM: 19). A later passage underscores this textual move by asserting that it is 'when one is wide awake, at moments of robust joy and achievement, on the highest terrace of consciousness' that

> mortality has a chance to peer beyond its own limits, from the mast, from the past and its castle tower. And although nothing much can be seen through the mist, there is somehow the blissful feeling that one is looking in the right direction. (SM: 41)

However, the park passage not only juxtaposes the home movie scenario with 'my first gleam of complete consciousness'; it also signals a shift towards space, which is pivotal to Nabokov's aesthetics. The memory of the child's emerging consciousness is described as fragmentary, but it is given 'a slippery hold' by 'a series of *spaced* flashes' which gradually condense into 'bright blocks of perception' (SM: 18; my emphasis). Just like the 'awakening of consciousness' in the child, the autobiography, too, operates with what one might call 'spaced flashes'. It invokes, arranges and connects autobiographical details so as to cover more and more territory and thus create a text that can itself be described as 'spaced'.

One of the ways in which *Speak, Memory* dispels chronophobia is by revisiting a myriad of other parks and gardens. In so doing, the text evokes both a geographical topography and the space of an aesthetic pattern or textual network. Particularly significant is the square that forms the setting of another family walk at the very end of the text. Here, in an equally joyous family scene, Nabokov is walking together with his wife Véra and their child Dmitri across a green square in St Nazaire on 'our way to the docks, where, behind the buildings facing us, the liner *Champlain* was waiting to take us to New York' (SM: 237).

On their walk, Nabokov and Véra anticipate 'the blissful shock, the enchantment and glee' Dmitri is about to experience as he will catch sight of the gigantic ships looming behind the row of harbour-front houses (SM: 237). Nabokov's rendition of the scene describes 'a splendid ship's funnel' which is visible as a fragment behind a clothes-line not as an object having to do with the family's escape, but as part of a picture puzzle: 'as something in a scrambled picture – Find What the Sailor Has Hidden – that the finder cannot unsee once it has been seen' (SM: 237). Yet the text ends before Dmitri can make his discovery. As a result, time appears arrested by the happy recollection of this 'one last little garden . . . laid out on the last limit of the past and on the verge of the present' (SM: 237).

Although Nabokov writes his text for the most part in 'the present' of his American exile, he neither describes his transatlantic journey nor his life in the United States. Instead his writing sustains the temporal and geographical liminality of the final scene at the harbour, which points towards but then elides the family's embarkation. In the same gesture, his description occludes the very real danger of the geopolitical circumstances in which, prior to escaping to the United States, the family found itself, as well as the precarious happiness of this very moment – one of only a very few oblique references to the family's narrow escape from Nazi terror. Instead Nabokov emphasises the 'clever thematic connexion with transatlantic gardens and parks' (SM: 237) so as to integrate the scene into a pattern which interconnects all the parks and gardens revisited in the text and which thus comes to serve as a trope of memory: 'Roots, roots of remembered greenery, roots of memory and pungent plants, roots, in a word, are enabled to traverse long distances by surmounting some obstacles, penetrating others and insinuating themselves into narrow cracks' (SM: 235). In an earlier passage, the '"English" park' at Vyra, always on the brink of 'reverting to the wild state', is taken to stand in for the continuation of another 'disintegrating process': 'When, nowadays, I attempt to follow in memory the winding paths from one point to another, I notice with alarm that here are many gaps, due to oblivion and ignorance . . .' (SM: 107). Nevertheless Nabokov's park pattern resembles the act of memory performed elsewhere to evoke another English park. In the narratorial frame of Hitchcock's *Rebecca*, the voice-over of the exiled heroine follows the overgrown winding drive towards Manderley as she returns to the once magnificent country estate in her wishful dream. Nabokov's *Speak, Memory* also reaches for an empowering form of recollection. It is by connecting the various parks and gardens through the mapping and patterning of his text that Nabokov seeks to take possession of the past.

Although the author was twice uprooted by exile, the two park scenes in Vyra and St Nazaire remain firmly connected by memory through some robust and ineradicable network of 'roots'. Serving as a frame and thus literally holding the text together, the two scenes maintain an 'organic' connection between distant moments and places despite their separation through ruin and rupture. In the last two chapters, continuity is further reinforced by Nabokov's invocation and direct address of Véra, the person who survives together with him and Dmitri. In the final paragraph, the walk of the two parents across the square, with their son between them, refers back to the blissful family triad evoked at the beginning of the text and, in so doing, underscores the stability of the family lineage despite the fact that Nabokov's father and mother are by now dead. In fact, the two scenes taken together suggest that the same constellation could be re-enacted in a 'transatlantic' park or garden and perhaps in a future generation, which would still remain connected – through the text's 'patterns of greenery' (SM: 18) – to that memorable walk along 'an alley of ornamental oaklings in the park of our country estate, Vyra, in the former Province of St Petersburg, Russia' (SM: 19). The park scenes are thus blended into the space of a textual pattern which recuperates the plenitude and coherence that have been ruptured by historical temporality.

The notion that the spacing of aesthetic language can retrieve the past and hence trick, if not completely transcend, time is characteristic of Nabokov's writing. It also underpins the image of the 'magic carpet' which he presents as if to offer a poetological trope for the way in which his spaced writing seeks to challenge and counteract the passage of time:

> I confess I do not believe in time. I like to fold my magic carpet, after use, in such a way as to superimpose one part of the pattern upon another. Let visitors trip. And the highest enjoyment of timelessness – in a landscape selected at random – is when I stand among rare butterflies and their food plants. This is ecstasy, and behind the ecstasy is something else, which is hard to explain. It is like a momentary vacuum into which rushes all that I love. (SM: 109–10)

As a miniature of the entire text, the poetological image promotes a 'magic' that promises to move beyond the facticity of time as if there were indeed scope for disbelief. After its flight through different times and places, the 'magic carpet' – and, by implication, the times and places traversed by its traveller – are literally folded into a 'pattern' which condenses into a state of timelessness.

By analogy, the autobiography repeatedly propels itself into 'a momentary vacuum' by having myriad moments and details mirror each other in the complex layers of recurrent patterns. One of the most prominent examples is Nabokov's imaginary butterfly hunt which introduces his comment on the 'magic carpet'. It begins with the lepidopterist exploring 'the vast marshland beyond the Oredezh' on a July day in 1910. Coming to the end of the Russian bog, he catches sight of an American mountain scenery to be visited several decades later: 'In the distance, fleeting cloud shadows dappled the dull green slopes above timber line, and the gray and white of Longs Peak' (SM: 108–9). At the beginning of the same chapter, a similar connection is established between 'a summer morning, in the legendary Russia of my childhood' and the rediscovery of the same contrast of 'the dark velvet of fir trees against a blue of extraordinary intensity' later in Colorado (SM: 94). The pattern continues as a butterfly, having escaped from the boy's wardrobe, is 'finally overtaken and captured, after a forty-year race, on an immigrant dandelion under an endemic aspen near Boulder' (SM: 95). While the text's weaving of an elaborate tissue of self-reflexive patterns may temporarily disorientate its readers ('Let visitors trip'), it ensures that 'a landscape selected at random' will reverberate with other privileged scenes of the exile's life. The losses and separations that occurred between distant moments come thus to be negated and undone by the simultaneity of the aesthetically self-reflexive text(ure).

Could one go as far as to say that the textual aesthetics of Nabokov's memory text resembles a butterfly collection? They both trace aesthetic patterns and, in order to do so, depend on 'killing agents' (SM: 95). The text 'kills' time by arresting certain moments so as to assemble them in recurring themes and thematic patterns. In *Speak, Memory*, Nabokov describes how a particular 'killing agent', ether, would always bring back one particular moment:

> Soon after the wardrobe affair I found a spectacular moth, marooned in a corner of a vestibule window, and my mother dispatched it with ether. In later years, I used many killing agents, but the least contact with the initial stuff would always cause the porch of the past to light up and attract that blundering beauty. (SM: 95)

As Nabokov flippantly adds, the memory of the moth also returns when during an operation as an adult, he is himself 'under ether' (SM: 95). Picking up on this memory under anaesthesia, one might say that by remembering the past as a pattern, Nabokov's aesthetic language, too, works like a pain-relieving substance.

At the same time, the spatial mapping of *Speak, Memory* resonates with the notion of the writerly text and the act of rereading introduced by Roland Barthes in *S/Z*. In contrast to the readerly text, which the reader consumes in a linear fashion and as a finished product, the writerly text emerges as a proliferation of meaning, a textual plurality and infinity of language. This 'stereographic space of writing', as

Barthes calls it (1990: 15), goes hand in hand with a continual rereading of various textual codes, a process which not only turns readers into the producers of a text whose plurality of links and networks develops into many different directions but, even more important for my discussion, allows them to approach the text through a multiplicity of different entry points. It is precisely the 'reversibility' of the writerly text highlighted by Barthes (1990: 13, 19) that is also at stake in *Speak, Memory*. Nabokov creates patterns and connections between seemingly disparate details because this allows his mnemonic writing not only to come back and return to particular moments at will, but also to reread and rewrite the past and, in so doing, reverse what is irreversible.

Despite the close resemblance, there is a crucial difference between Barthes's postructuralist notion of textuality and Nabokov's almost compulsive creation of patterns. The two of them meet in privileging an attention to detail. Yet while Barthes cuts the text up into arbitrary segments so as to emphasise that 'the fragment, the shards, the broken and obliterated network' are not to be subsumed under any formal unity (1990: 20), Nabokov's text seeks to restore what has been ruined and ruptured to a coherent form. In one passage in particular, Nabokov offers a compelling image for the coherence he wishes to create. He refers to the 'small bits of pottery' found by Dmitri among glass pieces, pebbles and shells on a beach in Mentone and goes on to suggest that the fragments and shards collected by several generations are not only united by the same pattern but, taken together, would make up the complete object:

> I do not doubt that among those slightly convex chips of majolica ware found by our child there was one whose border of scroll-work fitted exactly, and continued, the pattern of a fragment I had found in 1903 on the same shore, and that the two tallied with a third my mother had found at that Mentone beach in 1882, and with a fourth piece of the same pottery that had been found by *her* mother a hundred years ago – and so on until this assortment of parts, if all had been preserved, might have been put together to make the complete, the absolutely complete, bowl, broken by some Italian child, God knows where and when, and now mended by *these* rivets of bronze. (SM: 236)

Like this wishful fantasy of re-collection ('if all had been preserved'), his textual patterns also form part of an attempt to find and create coherence where there can be none since so many have died. In recent years, the reading of Nabokov's aesthetic networks as exuberantly playful and self-reflexive has been supplemented by an approach that regards them as imprint or 'patterns' of transcendence and hence as clues to a metaphysical, otherworldly dimension.[9] Yet whether they reach out to a self-reflexive playfulness or to an otherworld of an equally timeless transcendence, is it not their rhetorical function in so doing that matters most?

Nabokov's memory text, I have been arguing, seeks to posit the past as a scene in which everything can be revisited in and as a simultaneous presence. By evoking a space of aesthetic self-reference, his patterns literally 'dis-place' time and, in so doing, seek to reverse the losses brought about by history. At stake for me is thus Nabokov's attempt to aesthetically undo referentiality. The novelist John Lanchester makes a similar point when he writes in reference to Michael Wood's Nabokov monograph *The Magician's Doubts* (1994):

> It is, I think, possible to read this emphasis on pattern as a way of resisting loss – even, perhaps, of denying the idea of loss . . . Nabokov's emphasis on pattern, on structures in which everything seems to be simultaneously present, can seem like a magic charm against loss and against history. (Lanchester 1995: 179–80)[10]

Viewed in this way, the playful language of Nabokov's writing refers us to an existential dimension. Not only do his language games stage an aesthetics that, in line with his flight on a magic carpet, seems entirely disconnected from the geopolitical situations that actually forced him to take flight, but his writing, which can sound rarefied and over-written at times, is marked by a desperate attempt to restore broken connections.

This means that Nabokov's writing differs from Barthes's notion of the writerly text in a decisive way. Rather than presenting itself to readers and their rereading as a plural and infinite network of fragments, its connections appear to be carefully crafted by an author who is in urgent need of their re-assertion. This emphasis on aesthetic coherence is particularly pronounced in *Speak, Memory*. However, the desire for coherence characterises not only this text but Nabokov's overall project. His textual universe is interwoven with details which all seem to intertwine and interlink with each other. Some of the most prominent thematic lines and patterns include the posy of violets in *The Real Life of Sebastian Knight*, the oblong puddle in *Bend Sinister*, the squirrel in *Pnin* and the sunglasses in *Lolita*. As we shall see in the next chapter, *Lolita* also teems with (inter)textual allusions and cross-references. The fact that some of them appear to elude the protagonist narrator Humbert Humbert goes to underline the control of their creator, the implied author Nabokov.

Nabokov's language games and patterns are not as free-floating and detached as they may seem at first sight. Rather, they appear to be inspired by a wish for coherence – and by the need of the exile to re-create a world in and through language after an entire geocultural home and homeland have been lost and ruined. As an authorial signature, Nabokov's textual patterns form part of the attempt to inscribe his mastery as author, but perhaps also to prove his existence as a suvivor. Whichever way one reads the gesture, it is deeply desperate and far from self-assured.

Several of Nabokov's patterns illustrate how he writes against historical referentiality. Fully in keeping with the seemingly timeless design of his text, they deflect precarious geopolitical moments and their contingent survival. Nabokov's references to chess, for instance, are literally pitted against his flight during the Russian Revolution and his narrow escape from Europe during the Second World War. The eventual success in obtaining a *'visa de sortie'*, needed to flee from France to the United States, coincides with the conception of a particular chess problem: 'All of a sudden, I felt that with the completion of my chess problem a whole period of my life had come to a satisfactory close' (SM: 224). About twenty years earlier, the young refugee Nabokov seems equally absorbed by chess. Already here it appears as if he were trying shield himself from the historical upheaval taking place in his immediate surroundings:

> Over the glassy sea in the bay of Sebastopol, under wild machine-gun fire from the shore (the Bolshevik troops had just taken the port), my family and I set out for Constantinople and Piraeus on a small and shoddy Greek ship *Nadezhda* (Hope) carrying a cargo of dried fruit. I remember trying to concentrate, as we were zigzagging out of the bay, on a game of chess with my father – one of the knights had lost its head, and a poker chip replaced a missing rook . . . (SM: 194)

As a self-contained system of rules, the game of chess can be read as another trope for Nabokov's writing and the way in which its textual games turn away from referentiality as well as the strategy of resistance they thus perform. What Nabokov writes about the composition of chess problems – 'these highly specialized, fanciful, stylish riddles' – also holds for the patterning of his text: 'It might be a new way of blending an unusual strategic device with an unusual line of defense . . .' (SM: 221–2).

Nabokov explicitly argues that 'the following of . . . thematic designs through one's life should be, I think, the true purpose of autobiography' (SM: 23). To illustrate his claim, he refers to the so-called 'match theme'. In association with the Russo-Japanese war, he remembers meeting General Kuropatkin. The friend of the family entertains the boy by first spreading out a horizontal line of matches, 'the sea in calm weather', and then turning 'the straight line into a zigzag – and that was "a stormy sea"'. Before the General can show what the child hopes will be 'a better trick', they are interrupted – by the war, it appears, since on that very day the General 'had been ordered to assume supreme command of the Russian army in the Far East' (SM: 23). The match theme is, however, resumed fifteen years later. On his flight from St Petersburg, controlled by the Bolsheviks, to Southern Russia, Nabokov's father is approached by an old man in 'rustic disguise'. 'He asked my father for a light. The next moment each recognized the other' (SM: 23). Nabokov expresses the hope that Kuropatkin's flight was successful but adds 'that is not the point. What pleases me is the evolution of the match theme' (SM: 23). The question, in other words, is not whether Kuropatkin managed to escape and survive. Rather, the appeal of the theme lies in its 'matching' of details. Thus although, or precisely because, so much has been lost and ruined – 'everything had fallen through' (SM: 23) – Nabokov emphasises the coherence of his textual patterns.[11]

Nabokov's myriad language games suggest that by turning away from the *hors*-textual, history and the real could be magically avoided. The seemingly relentless playfulness of his aesthetics serves as a strategy of avoidance, which resists or even denies the notion of loss. Yet what he says about the discovery Dmitri is about to make at the text's close also holds for his language and its readers; there is something 'that the finder cannot unsee once it has been seen' (SM: 237). Nabokov may conceive of his patterns as hide-and-seek games he plays with his readers. After all they draw on the very principles which characterise his obsession for chess and lepidopterology and which he himself uses to describe his writing, namely the magic of deception, defence and deceit that is displayed by the mimicry of the butterfly and practised in the composition of chess problems (SM: 98, 222). Yet once we have realised that Nabokov's patterns enact a structure of surplus and repetition refiguring the void of loss and catastrophe, it is difficult to 'unsee' their pointed sadness.

Speak, Memory performs both the necessity and limitation of an escape into aesthetic language. When Nabokov describes 'the following of thematic designs' as 'the true purpose of autobiography', this may be to express the wish that the material of one's past may be shaped and mastered 'exactly as if it were a work of art' (Lanchester 1995: 180). Similarly, in tracing continuity and coherence in spite of irreversible rupture, Nabokov's language seeks to retrieve a sense of control fundamentally undermined by history as that which 'hurts'. Yet, in evoking a surplus structure, his patterns point towards a momentous void. As the ground and vanishing point of his aesthetic project, loss triggers an abundance of language games which, forever cut off from the death of the others, nevertheless remains connected to this gap. Rather than eliding and eluding the impact which cataclysmic history had on the family home, Nabokov's aesthetics of chronophobia forms an ambivalent act of commemoration.

Family Romance

Similar to his aesthetic language, Nabokov's family narrative also forms an attempt to undo the passage of time and the impact of history. It suggests a mythical reversal of loss by resurrecting the chronotope of a childhood home that seems untainted by later geopolitical turmoil and upheavals. Like many of his fictional texts – including *The Real Life of Sebastian Knight*, *Lolita* or *Ada* – *Speak, Memory* revisits a childhood past as an imaginary paradise. By continually affirming 'the harmonious world of a perfect childhood' (SM: 21), the narrative recasts itself not only as a classic 'family romance', but it also elevates the childhood home through scenes which reassert its extraordinary bliss and happiness in the face of historical catastrophe. In other words, Nabokov revisits the past first and foremost through the family because his turn to 'family values' such as plenitude and protection makes it possible to refigure geopolitical displacement as a mythical expulsion from a quasi-paradisiacal state. Yet under what auspices does Nabokov re-create 'the legendary Russia of my boyhood' (SM: 94)? What scenes and figurations allow him to imagine the family home as an idealised site of plenitude and protection? What, finally, are the implications that emerge in his refiguration of the childhood home as a mythical locus? As I shall argue in the following, it is precisely in its transformation into the privileged pivot of both nostalgic longing and poetic imagination that the family home becomes ambivalent.

Clearly, the text's return to an idealised past resonates with Freud's well-known concept of the 'family romance'. The deeply nostalgic scenario gives voice to the regret that the 'happy days' of childhood are 'gone'. Typically subjects express their 'longing for the happy, vanished days' by ennobling the home of their early childhood. Often they will develop the fantasy that they have been adopted by foster-parents who have come to replace their actual parents of far nobler origin. According to Freud, this recurring scenario harks back to the 'over-valuation' of the parents during the earliest years when the child perceives them as figures of utmost perfection (Freud 1959b: 240–1). In holding onto the idealised parents of early childhood, the family romance functions as a protective fiction. It answers a discontent with current family relations by converting the home into a site to which one wishes to belong and return in one's fantasy work. Although the satisfaction and safety of early childhood are a fantasy we come to cherish in retrospect, the scenario of the family romance allows us to postulate, and also nostalgically yearn for, the existence of such an Edenic state.

The nostalgia for a 'perfect childhood' also underpins the refiguration of exile as a loss of childhood in *Speak, Memory* (and, as later chapters will show, in *The Real Life of Sebastian Knight* and *Lolita*). Following the scenario of the classic family romance, Nabokov's homage to the family home represents a quest for a sense of wholeness afforded by a happy childhood, which is formulated first and foremost as an affectionate declaration of love to his parents. At the same time, Nabokov's script of a happy childhood radicalises Freud's scenario and its desire for protection in a significant way. His particular romance cannot be divorced from the family's violent separation. Unfolding on this backdrop, its nostalgic desire for a lost childhood comes to deflect the loss of the family in an apotropaic manner. The classic scenario invokes a romanticised childhood so as to formulate an implicit critique of one's imperfect family home – a critique which is, in fact, necessary for the subject's emancipation from the parents in a line of generational succession. By contrast, Nabokov's nostalgic return to the happiness of his childhood home suggests a recuperation of violently severed ties in the form of an imaginary family reunion. His narrative follows the desire to re-create an 'imaginary homeland' in the literal absence of an actual home, in the face of the family's violent separation. Going beyond the classic family romance and its protection against domestic discontent, Nabokov's narrative of a happy childhood serves as a screen memory, which covers up the concrete loss of his family.

Not merely resurrecting the past but restoring it in such a way as to affirm the family's integrity and wholeness, *Speak, Memory* displaces the multiple bereavements that have come to mark the family. Yet, even as Nabokov's family romance may present itself as a powerful protective fiction, it remains haunted and revisited by the 'family secret' of loss and death. In fact, it is precisely in reclaiming the family's happiness within the framework of the family romance that its violent loss is felt most poignantly, that plenitude comes to be juxtaposed with pain. In what follows, I shall trace this uncanny ambivalence in some of the most resilient strands of Nabokov's family narrative so as to highlight that, in spite of its empowering gesture, the imaginary restoration of symbolic family bonds is repeatedly ruptured by the register of the real, the facticity of irrevocable loss.

Nabokov's reconfiguration of the past as a family romance is inspired first and foremost by his mother. Following mythopoetic traditions of the maternal, Elena Ivanovna Nabokov stands in for the imaginary, for the inheritance and transmission of the mother tongue. In fact, Nabokov's text goes as far as to invoke her as the muse of his text. This is underscored by the oversized present – 'a giant polygonal Faber pencil, four feet long and correspondingly thick' (SM: 32) – which the mother gives to her son as if to inspire him with his poetic gift, as well as by Nabokov's description how he recites and addresses his first poem excusively to her (SM: 174–6).[12] As his muse of memory, nostalgia and poetic language, Elena Nabokov both inspires and corresponds to the text's poetics. As we shall see in the following, the mother is not merely remembered as a parent. She is simultaneously cast as an allegorical figure of and about memory, who plays out the ambivalence of the text's family romance.

It is under the auspices of the mother that the home is invested with a nostalgic sensibility and imagination. By allegorising her as the figure who commemorates the family home and the homeland of geocultural belonging, the text harks back to the notion of the Russian *rodina*, the homeland which in Russian carries maternal connotations encoding the homeland as 'motherland' (SM: 76). Elena Nabokov is closely associated with the home and its topography. Returning from St Petersburg to Vyra, the family's country estate, and already the summer home of her own childhood, she is said to always kneel down and kiss the ground (SM: 193). As if to mark it as a realm of retrospective imagination, she adorns the home with 'special tags and imprints' (SM: 33). Likewise she offers a perspective already refracted by nostalgia as she invites her son to rejoice in moments of intense happiness experienced at their home:

> '*Vot zapomni* (now remember),' she would say in conspiratorial tones as she drew my attention to this or that loved thing in Vyra – a lark ascending the curds-and-whey sky of a dull spring day, heat lightning taking pictures of a distant line of trees in the night, the palette of maple leaves on brown sand, a small bird's cuneate footprints on new snow. (SM: 33)

Framed by the mother's call to remember, these shared moments appear to be proleptically translated into future recollections in the very instant they are occurring – a scenario that attests as much to a desire for nostalgia as it articulates a love for the evanescent manifestation of these moments in time. Rather than haunted by chronophobia, the passage appears to be inspired by 'chronophilia', a heightened awareness of and love for the fleetingly fugitive and volatile presence of these privileged instants, which are commemorated in their transience.[13] While this chronophiliac desire can be read as a powerful act of mnemonic preservation and possession, it also reverberates with an acute sense of finitude and fragility.

Given its inherent nostalgia, which is after all a longing for what is no longer present, the home's imaginary investment is inhabited by a precarious premonition. When, in cultivating 'an extraordinary consciousness of the various time marks distributed throughout our country place', Elena Nabokov stores her memories in the home's topography, she does so 'as if feeling that in a few years the tangible part of her world would perish' (SM: 33). Thus while the mother is presented by the text as a figure of powerful memory, if not total recall, her commemoration of the home also acts as an uncanny anticipation of its later loss. This means that from the exile's belated perspective, the family home can neither be separated nor protected from the precariousness implied by its proleptic commemoration.

Although their nostalgic memory of the home paradoxically entails an uncanny prefiguration of, or even desire for, its absence, the text nevertheless presents mother and son as always having been at home in nostalgic longing. Absorbing the legacy of his mother, Nabokov can be seen to celebrate premature remembrance and nostalgia, which conceive of the home as intrinsically absent long before the family's actual displacement. As a result of his 'cosmopolitan childhood' (SM: 182), the five-year-old Nabokov is already widely travelled when, during a protracted holiday, he maps a detailed topography of the far-away summer residence of Vyra so as to nostalgically evoke the home in its absence.[14]

> In a villa which in the summer in 1904 we rented . . . aged five, mooning in my cot after lunch, I used to turn over on my stomach and, carefully, lovingly, hopelessly, in an artistically detailed fashion difficult to reconcile with the ridiculously small number of seasons that had gone to form the inexplicably nostalgic image of 'home' (that I had not seen since September 1903), I would draw with my forefinger on my pillow the carriage road sweeping up to our Vyra house, the stone steps on the right, the carved back of a bench on the left, the alley of oaklings beginning beyond the bushes of honeysuckle, and a newly shed horseshoe, a collector's item (much bigger and brighter than the rusty ones I used to find on the seashore), shining in the reddish dust on the drive. (SM: 61)

To the child, Vyra represents 'home' although he has spent only a few summers in the countryside and although – or perhaps precisely because – he has not seen it for almost an entire year.[15] In fact, it is precisely absence which emphatically renders the summer estate the quintessential home. Similarly, it is after an entire year's absence that Russia is for the first time experienced as the home country:

> An exciting sense of *rodina*, 'motherland,' was for the first time organically mingled with the comfortably creaking snow, the deep footprints across it, the red gloss of the engine stack, the birch logs piled high, under their private layer of transportable snow, on the red tender. I was not quite six,

but that year abroad, a year of difficult decisions and liberal hopes, had exposed a small Russian boy to grown-up conversations. He could not help being affected in some way of his own by a mother's nostalgia and a father's patriotism. In result, that particular return to Russia, my first *conscious* return, seems to me now, sixty years later, a rehearsal – not of the grand homecoming that will never take place, but of its constant dream in my long years of exile. (SM: 76)

Both scenarios, the child's nostalgic longing and his 'first conscious return' to Russia, suggest that the home and the imaginary are inextricably linked. Furthermore, their nostalgic experience is not only constitutive of how Nabokov conceives of the home. It also quite literally anticipates the exile's recurring recollection of the absent home both in his 'constant dream', in which he keeps returning home, and his writing, which turns the home's absence into an scenario of poetic inspiration.[16]

The idea that the home has always been nostalgically inflected gains particular significance with the concrete loss of the actual family home. 'She cherished her own past with the same retrospective fervor', Nabokov writes about his mother, 'that I now do her image and my past. Thus, in a way, I inherited an exquisite simulacrum – the beauty of intangible property, unreal estate . . .' (SM: 33).[17] The immaterial legacy of remembering allows him to deflect loss both analeptically and proleptically. After the home's irreversible loss, absence and nostalgia – the immaterial qualities on which the maternal home has always rested – turn into a crucial inspirational source of the writer's 'imaginary homeland'. Similarly, if one's home is nostalgically invested and thus, to some degree, absent from the very start, if, in other words, one's home emerges only against the backdrop of absence, what is there to lose in the first place?

The 'unreal estate' of nostalgic imagination is conceived as an insurance against potential disposession and, in retrospect, comes to be re-encoded as 'a splendid training for the endurance of later losses' (SM: 33). As a site of nostalgic longing and as an imaginary topography in which memories could be stored securely, the home remains safe since, unlike material possessions, it cannot be taken away. On the contrary, it is precisely the imaginary and mnemonic force invested in their *rodina* that – over and beyond any material support – allows mother and son to ceaselessly stage the home's return despite its actual loss. In her 'pitiable lodgings' in Prague, Elena Nabokov is said to be surrounded by material rem(a)inders of her past such as 'the dim little photographs in crumbling frames she liked to have near her couch', a cast of her husband's hand together with a picture of his grave and albums of her favourite Russian poems (SM: 40). However, as the only remnant of their Russian heritage, the 'intangible property' of powerful nostalgic recollection allows Nabokov to assert that 'she didn't really need them, for *nothing had been lost*' (SM: 40; my emphasis). About himself he says that 'all the Russia I need is always with me: literature, language and my own Russian childhood' (SO: 9–10). As if to visually underline that he has indeed absorbed the immaterial legacy transmitted by his mother, *Speak, Memory* includes a picture showing the exiled writer working at a hotel room table. The small tabletop evokes the soapbox used by the mother to display her 'dim little photographs in crumbling frames'. What is more, the writing appears to occur in direct response to and inspiration from the family photos, which, significantly enough, are propped by Dahl's four-volume Russian dictionary, the repository of the mother tongue in exile.

The nostalgic inheritance passed on from mother to son is, however, far from unequivocal. The 'exquisite simulacrum' of maternal memory also forms a disturbing void. The claim that nothing is lost to Elena Nabokov because 'she had with her all that her soul had stored' is ambivalent (SM: 41). Not referring to her powerful recollection of her *rodina* alone, it also suggests that Nabokov's muse of memory has incorporated the lost home so as not to have to 'swallow' its loss. The rhetoric that in spite of material dispossession and multiple bereavement 'nothing had been lost' is reminiscent of Abraham and Torok's concept of the crypt (1994). As a melancholic formation, the crypt stores the lost object and keeps it alive so as to deflect or even deny its loss. Yet, while sheltering the object from which the subject has been severed, this intrapsychic tomb hosts, on some level, nothing but a void. Not only does the lost object occupy an unreal, phantasmatic and ghostlike status, but similar to the impact of trauma, the encrypted loss forms a secret knowledge from which the cryptophoric subject necessarily remains separated.[18] As a result, one might say that the void of loss is not directly available to Elena Nabokov, but instead permeates her memory as an encrypted secret.

Given their shared memory work, one could speculate that, following a line of transgenerational haunting, the encrypted loss also reverberates in Nabokov's text. This would mean that their imaginary return home not only attests to a powerful memory but is equally possessed by a secret knowledge. Thus along with 'this almost pathological keenness of retrospective faculty', conceived of as a 'hereditary trait' (SM: 60), Nabokov inherits loss, absence, nothing in short – not so much because the family fortune and possessions could not be preserved through the Russian Revolution, but rather because, together with the 'nothing' of nostalgic absence, he and his mother share an unspeakable secret. While the text cannot directly address this phantomatically transmitted knowledge, we may yet surmise that given their shared preoccupation with the home, the encrypted legacy may well be related to its precariousness, to a secret knowledge which – inhabiting their nostalgia all along – anticipates losses connected to the home and confronting them later in an very real manner.

The cryptophoric ambivalence of nostalgic inheritance is perhaps most compellingly materialised by the only object that is left to the exiled Nabokov from both his mother and motherland. Characteristically enough, the sole material remainder is a travel bag. Evoking a 'cosmopolitan childhood' (SM: 182), the bag is, on the one hand, reminiscent of the voluminous luggage the family used to take when they travelled for their summer vacations accompanied by an extensive entourage of tutors and servants. On the other hand, having undergone remarkable changes as a result of its possessor's exile and dispossession, the remnant piece can be read as a perfectly materialised metaphor of the cryptophore's burden of survival.

> I still treasure an elegant, elegantly scuffed piece of luggage once owned by my mother. Its travels through space are finished, but it still hums gently through time for I use it to keep old family letters and such curious documents as my birth certificate. I am a couple of years younger than this antique valise, fifty centimeters long by thirty-six broad and sixteen high, technically a heavyish *nécessaire de voyage* of pigskin, with 'H.N.' elaborately interwoven in thick silver under a similar coronet. It had been bought in 1897 for my mother's wedding trip to Florence. In 1917 it transported from St. Petersburg to the Crimea and then to London a handful of jewels. Around 1930, it lost to a pawnbroker its expensive receptacles of crystal and silver leaving empty the cunningly contrived leathern holders on the inside of the lid. But that loss has been amply recouped during the thirty years it then traveled with me – from Prague to Paris, from St. Nazaire to New York and through the mirrors of more than two hundred motel rooms and rented houses, in forty-six states. The fact that of our Russian heritage the hardiest survivor proved to be a traveling bag is both logical and emblematic. (SO: 204; a slightly altered version of SM: 112)

If we follow the idea of a secret family legacy in the form of an intangible void, it is significant that, as the only residue of 'our Russian heritage', the bag should be stripped of its valuable contents so that an empty shell is all that remains. Acting as a trope of the exile's family romance, the travel bag literally transports the notion of dislocation. As a benign souvenir, it metonymically evokes happy scenes of a lost childhood, which as a result of its cosmopolitan travels and seaside holidays always entailed (temporary) displacement. Its deprived state, on the other hand, insists on the family's irrevocable uprooting. The rhetoric of this resilient metaphor thus works along the lines of a fetishistic double articulation; the travel bag encrypts the family home so as to deflect its loss and, at the same time, commemorates the painful parturition from both the mother and motherland.

In the same way as a *'nécessaire de voyage'* can potentially be filled by any contents depending on one's needs and desires, the 'nothing' stored in the crypt can be replenished with fantasies about the lost object, which turn its absence into an imaginary presence. By analogy, while its rich decorations and the transported jewels were sold to support the family in the harsh reality of exile, its later textual contents ('old family letters and such curious documents as my birth certificate') are of a far more symbolic and imaginary quality in line with the 'intangible property' privileged by mother and son. As textual supplements of troubling losses, the bag's contents could be said to implicitly refer to the autobiographical text, which, as a refiguration of these losses, also has its place in the bag, at least metaphorically. After all, the text stands in relation to 'such curious documents as my birth certificate' because, in re-creating a family romance, it also functions as 'conclusive evidence' (SM: 8) of the writer's existence as well as his filial and geocultural origin.

The textual material potentially stored in the bag functions as a refiguration of the losses survived. This is suggested by Nabokov's claim that the material loss of the jewels and the bag's 'valuable receptacles . . . has been amply recouped during the thirty years it . . . traveled with me'. Standing in for far more dramatic, and traumatic, losses in the family, the material objects are replaced by textual supplements. The bag appears to have accumulated its imaginary value both as a witness of its possessor's survival and as a shell hosting textual material, which objectifies a traumatic gap. The 'old family letters' in the survivor's luggage address the dead, however obliquely. As a textual corpus, they evoke the imaginary presence of the dead family members and simultaneously point to their actual absence as well as their irrevocable separateness from the surviving family member. As comforting as it may be, 'the hardiest survivor' keeps insisting that in turning loss into a family romance, the exile's and survivor's work of imagination is forced to constantly return to its origin, namely to the momentous 'nothing' and the stubborn reference of displacement and bereavement, also metaphorically stored by the bag. Always travelling and thus staying with the survivor, the bag's shell also transports a cryptophoric burden which is 'all in the family' in a double sense – on the one hand, because it is bound up with the facticity of the family's losses and, on the other hand, because this knowledge remains a 'family secret'.

If Nabokov's family romance is thus haunted by the void of real loss, this becomes most palpable in the portrayal of his brother Sergey as well as the representations of his father. In the memoir, the latter's violent death forms a rupture that is so disastrous that it can be neither integrated into the meaningful coherence of the family romance nor explicitly named. Its unspeakable status is enacted by an early passage in the text. Indicating the precise date and time, it describes how mother and son spend the evening of the assassination up to the ringing of the phone, but then cuts short its account so as to avoid the sad news and instead goes on to describe the mother's exile in Prague, where she would move after her husband's death:

> On the night of 28 March 1922, around ten o'clock, in the living room where as usual my mother was reclining on the red-plush corner couch, I happened to be reading to her Blok's verse on Italy – had just got to the end of the little poem about Florence, which Blok compares to the delicate, smoky bloom of an iris, and she was saying over her knitting, 'Yes, yes, Florence does look like a *dïmnïy iris*, how true! I remember –' when the telephone rang. (SM: 40)

After surfacing in an indirect reference – the paternal grandfather died 'peacefully' on 28 March 1904, 'exactly eighteen years, day for day, before my father' – the death of the father is postponed to 'a short biography of my father' in a later chapter. Here the fatal accident, though explicitly related, is distanced by the formal, impersonal style of its rendition: 'Vladimir Dmitrievich Nabokov, jurist, publicist, statesman . . . was born on 20 July 1870 at Tsarskoe Selo near St Petersburg, and was killed by an assassin's bullet on 28 March 1922 in Berlin' (SM: 48, 135). The same detached, matter-of-fact tone also subtends the reference to 'his assassination in 1922 by a sinister ruffian' a few pages later (SM: 138).

The ellipsis of the father's assassination suggests that certain reminiscences at the very heart of the home cannot be assimilated. In this respect, the impact of the father's death resembles the memory of Sergey. After a straightforward sketch of the life of Kirill, the youngest brother, the passage on Sergey begins with Nabokov stating that 'for various reasons I find it inordinately hard to speak about my other brother'. In contrast to Nabokov's otherwise vivid and extremely dense memories, Sergey is described as 'a mere shadow in the background of my richest and most detailed recollections' (SM: 198). Hinting at some of the 'various reasons' for his reserve in speaking about Sergey, Nabokov describes their divergent interests as well as the 'miserable memory' of how 'rowdy, adventurous and something of a bully', he would disturb the younger but more mature and older-looking brother, 'who had a bad stammer that hampered discussions of doubtful points', while he was playing the piano (SM: 198). In contrast to the elective affinities between Nabokov and his youngest brother Kirill, who not only spoke several languages but was interested in literature and wrote his own poetry, Sergey did not share Nabokov's interests. 'We seldom played together, he was indifferent to most of the things I was fond of – toy trains, toy pistols, Red Indians, Red Admirables' (SM: 198). Instead, Sergey, like their father, developed a passionate interest in music (SM: 198), an art form which, as Nabokov emphasises repeatedly, is completely alien to himself (SM: 30, SO: 35). He also hints at his difficulty in accepting his brother's homosexual identity, recalling in particular how he passed on a page of Sergey's diary to his tutor, which 'abruptly provided a retroactive clarification of certain oddities of behavior on his part' (SM: 198). Their father, in one of his essays, argued for 'a very liberal and "modern" approach to various abnormal [sic] practices, incidentally coining a convenient Russian word for "homosexual": *ravnopolïy*' (SM: 139). Yet, as Brian Boyd writes, 'Sergey's homosexuality had always made Vladimir awkward . . .' (1993a: 396).

Nabokov's 'bleakest recollections' appear to be closely connected to his own survival in contrast to the disturbing facticity of Sergey's death. Although he writes that they were 'on quite amiable terms' at the time, Nabokov, critically enough, did not let his brother in on his escape plans so that 'he learned of our departure to America only after we had left . . . I am sorry he had to stutter his astonishment to an indifferent concierge' (SM: 199). During a visit to Berlin in 1943, Sergey was arrested because of his homosexuality. After a cousin managed to effect his release five months later, he found a job in a half-Russian office in Prague, where he expressed his contempt for Hitler's Germany. Immediately informed upon by his colleagues, he was arrested as a British spy and deported to the concentration camp Neuengamme near Hamburg, where he died of malnutrition on 10 January 1945 (Boyd 1993b: 88). One night several months later, Nabokov dreamed of Sergey. 'Although in waking life he supposed Sergey to be safe in the Austrian castle of his lover Hermann, in the dream he saw him in agony on a bunk in a concentration camp' (Boyd 1993b: 88). The very next day he heard about his death from Kirill, who worked as a translator with the American forces in Germany and traced Nabokov through a story he had published in the *New Yorker*. As Brian Boyd notes, Nabokov had 'spoken rather harshly of his brother in recent years' – their relationship appears to have been further complicated by the fact Sergey's lover was not only male but also a native speaker of German (Boyd 1993b: 89). Learning about Sergey's death, he must have realised that it was now definitely too late to make up for previous failures of recognition. The portrait of his brother concludes on precisely this note: 'It is one of those lives that hopelessly claim a belated something – compassion, understanding, no matter what – which the mere recognition of such a want can neither replace nor redeem' (SM: 199). The text thus points to a poignant gap, an abandonment which can never be recuperated, and silence ('I find it inordinately hard to speak about my brother'), which is caused by the horror of the brother's death and perhaps also by a sense of guilt about having survived.[19]

One of Nabokov's earliest letters to his sister Elena after the end of the Second World War underlines that his imaginary family reunion is disrupted by the brother's death. After describing the daily routine of his American life, Nabokov expresses his relief at Elena's well-being and survival: 'What a joy that you are well, alive, in good spirits' (26 November 1945; SL: 60). However, before going on to reflect on a possible regrouping of the surviving family members in the United States and the circumstances of his own transatlantic emigration but not his abandonment of Sergey, Nabokov's letter suddenly turns, in an abrupt shift of addressee, to an exclamation followed by an ellipsis: 'Poor, poor Seryozha . . .!' (SL: 60).[20] Not only do words fail Nabokov in connection with the sibling who did not survive, it also appears as though his own survival as well as his sister's were haunted by the question highlighted by Roland Barthes, namely 'why is it that I am alive *here and now*?' (Barthes 1993: 84). While Barthes reflects on death and survival in reference to the medium of photography, his formulation can also be applied to the home movie introducing Nabokov's survivor text. As shown by his treatment of Sergey's death, the question remains unsettling since there is no answer to the luck of survival, which is as contingent as the other's perishing.

Ultimately there appears to be too much difference for the brother's life and death to be integrated into a recuperative recollection of the family home. Yet, at the same time, this difference cannot be overlooked so that it keeps haunting the survivor's memory text, where it remains encrypted and preserved as a foreign body. In fact, there is a troubling discrepancy in the fact that highlighting all along how unique his childhood and his love for his parents were, Nabokov's autobiography elides the brother – until he is gone. Fashioned simultaneously against and towards the void opened up by Sergey's starvation, Nabokov's 'imaginary homeland' fills and sediments on this gap not unlike the comforting flesh and fat that he repeatedly says in his letters to Elena build up in his body. His letter mentioned above, for example, concludes with a reference to the transformation of his body: 'Did I write you that I have gained a huge amount of weight . . .?' (SL: 61). Subsequent letters pick up on this topic:

> I am fairly fat, just as before (190 pounds), I have false teeth and a bald pate, but I am capable of walking up to 18 miles a day in mountainous terrain and usually do ten, and I play tennis better than I did in my youth. (Letter to Elena, 29 September 1953; SL: 139)

Rather than using the Russian weight measure, poods, Nabokov, significantly enough, refers to pounds, thus underlining the American context in which his bodily transformation takes place: 'I weigh 195 pounds – I don't know how much that is in poods' (letter to Elena, 24 February 1946; SL: 66). In a later interview, finally, Nabokov describes his increase in weight as an overt Americanisation of his body:

> I came to America in 1940 and decided to become an American citizen, and make America my home . . . I became as stout as Cortez – mainly because I quit smoking and started to munch molasses candy instead, with the result that my weight went up from my usual 140 to a monumental and cheerful 200. In consequence, I am one-third American – good American flesh keeping me warm and safe. (March 1963; SO: 26–7)

Since Nabokov conceives of his bodily bulk as 'good American flesh keeping me warm and safe', the accumulated corporeal weight could be regarded as a trope both for the 'imaginary homeland' he creates in exile and for his host country that is distinguished from Europe – where so many family members died – as a culture of survival, vitality and longevity: 'Over here our American oldsters live to be ninety-seven, and walk five miles a day with a pedometer' (letter to Elena, 14 September 1957; SL: 226).

While the disturbing traces of Sergey's memory cannot be restored to a reassuring family romance, the memory of Nabokov's father serves as an apotropaic charm. In so doing, it wards off contingency and mortality that are inevitably also part of his remembrance. If, in other words, the father is first and foremost associated with blissful scenes, this is to counteract his death, which subtends the text as its 'family secret' (Wood 1994: 87). Yet, even as they seek to deflect this cryptophoric knowledge, the protective memories nevertheless have to touch on death. A particularly resilient scene dealing with the memory of the father describes how, as a token of their gratitude for his liberal treatment, the villagers would repeatedly toss up and then securely catch their *barin* (master in the sense of 'feudal landlord'), thus creating a scenario in which the father is elevated both literally and metaphorically to the noble and perfect parent we know from the family romance.

> From my place at table I would suddenly see through one of the west windows a marvelous case of levitation. There, for an instant, the figure of my father in his wind-rippled white summer suit would be displayed, gloriously sprawling in midair, his limbs in a curiously casual attitude, his

handsome, imperturbable features turned to the sky. Thrice to the mighty heave-ho of his invisible tossers, he would fly up in this fashion, and the second time he would go higher than the first and then there he would be, on his last and loftiest flight, reclining, as if for good, against the cobalt blue of the summer noon, like one of those paradisiac personages who comfortably soar, with such a wealth of folds in their garments, on the vaulted ceiling of a church while below, one by one, the wax tapers in mortal hands light up to make a swarm of minute flames in the midst of incense, and the priest chants of eternal repose, and funeral lilies conceal the face of whoever lies there, among the swimming lights, in the open coffin. (SM: 26–7)

Arresting the flux of time, the passage captures the brief moment when in the father's lofty flight, the physical laws of gravity, to which all mortal life is subject, seem to be suspended. Propelled into the air and soaring in his relaxed pose, the father is strangely transfixed as if he were congealed into a celestial fresco on a church ceiling so that translated into the virtual space of painting, the elevated paternal figure is juxtaposed to the funeral scene below. Yet, simultaneously, the father's body, 'reclining, as if for good', also mirrors the corpse resting in 'eternal repose' and, as a consequence, comes to hover uncannily between life and death.

This ambivalence is doubled by the fresco. The aesthetic code invoked through the painting lets the father ascend from mortal life to the seemingly immortalising realm of art, thus transforming him into an aesthetic figure. As a *mise-en-abîme* of his own writing, the scenario allows the son to fashion himself as the artistic begetter of an enduring representation of the dead father, thus seemingly overcoming the transience of human existence in an empowering gesture of resuscitation. But even as a mythical figure, the father keeps oscillating between aesthetic immortality and real, 'down-to-earth' mortality. Not at all clear about who is lying in the coffin, the text is on the contrary deliberately mysterious about the corpse's identity – 'funeral lilies conceal the face of whoever lies there . . . in the open coffin.' Yet given the simultaneous juxtaposition and reflection of the two bodies, we have all reason to assume that the passage both evokes and deflects the father's funeral following his contingent death.[21] The scene's constellation is thus characterised by a double articulation. The passage exalts the father to a figure of immortality so as to reach out for the family romance and its promise of plenitude and protection, but it also at the same time points to his later death.

In a later but similar scene, another happy childhood memory is made to overlap with the catastrophic moment of the father's death so as to affirm and underscore a comforting sense of security. Here the child fears for his father after learning from a magazine, passed around at school, that his father has been offended together with his friend Milyukov by 'the most powerful of the Rightist newspapers' and has, as a result, challenged its editor to a classic duel (SM: 147). During his agonisingly slow journey home, the twelve-year-old reviews and reminisces over the happy memories, the veneration and harmony that inspires their affectionate relationship:

> And behind it all there was . . . a very special emotional abyss that I was desperately trying to skirt, lest I burst into a tempest of tears, and this was the tender friendship underlying all my respect for my father; the charm of our perfect accord . . . Our relationship was marked by . . . all those private jokes which are the secret code of happy families. (SM: 149)

Then, finally arriving at home, the anxious child is overjoyed to find out that the duel has been cancelled after an apology from the newspaper editor, meaning that the acute danger – his father's potential death – has been averted.

> With the opportuneness of dream arrangements, my uncle the Admiral was coming downstairs . . . my parents were still speaking to him, and as he came down the steps, he looked up with a laugh and slapped the balustrade with the gloves he had in his hands. I knew at once that there would be no duel, that the challenge had been met by an apology, that *all was right*. I brushed past my uncle and reached the landing. I saw my mother's serene everyday face, but I could not look at my father. And then it happened: my heart welled in me like that wave on which the *Buyniy* rose when her captain brought her alongside the burning *Suvorov*, and I had no handkerchief, and ten years were to pass before a certain night in 1922, at a public lecture in Berlin, when my father shielded the lecturer (his old friend Milyukov) from the bullets of two Russian Fascists and, while vigorously knocking down one of the assassins, was fatally shot by the other. *But no shadow was cast by that future event upon the bright stairs of our St Petersburg house; the large cool hand resting on my head did not quaver*, and several lines of a difficult chess combination were not blended yet on the board. (SM: 150–1; my emphasis)

The recollected scene does not simply focus on the retrieved comfort following upon intense anxiety but instead doubles the duel challenge defending the honour of the father as well as his friend Milyukov with the father's literal (and fatal) defence of Milyukov ten years later, thus condensing two distant moments of danger averted and danger realised respectively. Nabokov's suggestion that the happy outcome of the duel episode resembles 'the opportuneness of dream arrangements' is, I think, significant. It implies that like the previous scene of the father's levitation and the family romance in general, this passage, too, follows a logic of wish fulfilment. Explicitly marked as the realisation of a wish, the scenario is characteristic of Nabokov's project in suggesting that like the duel, the father's death and all other losses might equally be averted. The 'dream arrangement' foregrounds an undoing of contingent death in and through the imaginary – as if survival were possible the second time, too.[22]

By denying the 'shadow' of loss and bereavement, Nabokov evokes a scenario which, untainted by 'that future event', reinstalls the father as a safeguard of the family's happiness both at that particular moment and in his memory at large. As in the the previously quoted scene, the text elevates the father to a figure of plenitude and protection and, in so doing, turns to the comforting framework of mythical invulnerability as it is promised and maintained by the family romance. Yet, as Michael Wood points out in his analysis of the passage, 'the mere naming of the shadow, even in the form of a denial, ensures its persistence. Death, like time, like parting, can be averted but not forgotten; it haunts even the happiest occasions of its avoidance' (1994: 86). Like the father's marvellous levitation cited above, the scene is necessarily bound to gesture towards the father's ultimate demise. Paradoxically enough, it is only over his later death that he can be reinstated as a figure of safety and invulnerability – 'the large cool hand resting on my head did not quaver.'

The images of the father bespeak far more than a nostalgic longing for a past childhood. They underline the protective gesture of Nabokov's family narrative at large. Owing to the cataclysmic incidents at the heart of the family, Nabokov's text appears to depend all the more on childhood memories in which privileged moments of the past seem permanently arrested in a state of bliss:

> I see again my schoolroom in Vyra, the blue roses of the wallpaper, the open window. Its reflection fills the oval mirror above the leathern couch where my uncle sits, gloating over a tattered book. A sense of security, of well-being, of summer warmth pervades my memory. That robust reality makes a ghost of the present. The mirror brims with brightness; a bumblebee has entered the room and bumps against the ceiling. Everything is as it should be, nothing will ever change, nobody will ever die. (SM: 62)

The passage re-creates the past as a 'robust reality' through the childhood memory of the way in which the uncle revisits his own childhood with the help of the very books he once loved as a child. The crux, however, is again that Nabokov has to explicitly deny and, therefore, name what makes 'a ghost of the present', namely change and death – 'nothing will ever change, nobody will ever die.'

Nabokov's childhood romance invokes memories of the family so as to pit them against later losses. In one passage, he argues that his 'earliest impressions' provided him with a particularly rich reservoir of memories making up for the loss of an entire geocultural world:

> In regard to the power of hoarding up impressions, Russian children of my generation passed through a period of genius, as if destiny were loyally trying what it could do for them by giving them more than their share, in view of the cataclysm that was to remove completely the world they had known. (SM: 21)

When he describes his nostalgia as 'a hypertrophied sense of lost childhood' (SM: 59), Nabokov exalts the memory of his family so as not to give in to its loss – at least in the imaginary of his family romance text. However, as I have been arguing, both the blissful images of the father and the nostalgia of the mother are inhabited by a fundamental ambivalence. If the mother's nostalgia is to forestall potential loss, it also turns her into the cryptophoric bearer of precisely this secret. Similarly, if the father of the family romance restores the plenitude and protection of the earliest years, this is to turn away from the pain inflicted by his actual death. Yet aesthetically restored family ties are repeatedly ruptured by the real, referenced by traces that cannot be fully integrated into the family narrative. It is to screen this knowledge that Nabokov's romance reclaims the plenitude and protection of childhood.

Nabokov underlines that his particular childhood was distinguished by a singular happiness. His assertion is reminiscent of Freud, who also contends that the vanished days were intrinsically happy even though his own theory suggests that any sense of childhood plenitude is a belated, if necessary fantasy (Bronfen 1998: 144). It also reminds us of his (ironic) reformulation of the well-known beginning of *Anna Karenina* in his last novel *Ada*, according to which all unhappy families resemble each other, whereas 'all happy families are more or less dissimilar' (A: 9). Emphasising the difference and uniqueness of happy families, Nabokov takes the remembered 'secret code' of the elevated, singular happiness of his family to deflect its violent separation. Put differently, the assertion of the family's unique happiness serves as an attempt to elude history as Fredric Jameson defines it, namely as what hurts and sets painful limits to the individual and its imagination (1981: 102). It is for this reason that Nabokov pits the private against the political, the mythical against the historical – that he not only develops a family narrative but puts so much emphasis on its felicity.

Poetics of Memory

Individual autonomy is not only celebrated with respect to the family's singular happiness in spite of history's painful impact, it also forms the wager underpinning Nabokov's poetics of memory. Together with its textual patterns, which turn away from historical contingency, his memory text creates a supposedly free-floating realm. In so doing, it affirms what Jameson, though writing not about Nabokov but about the role of fiction and aesthetics, calls 'some autonomous force in which it could also be seen as negating that context' (1981: 38). Importantly enough, *Speak, Memory* not only recounts reminiscences, but memory turns out to be the pivot of Nabokov's poetic project and its attempt to claim command and control of the past despite all fissures and ruptures. Not surprisingly, Nabokov advocates a thoroughly controlled (and controlling) form of memory which has the power to aesthetically shape the past: 'I witness with pleasure the supreme achievement of memory, which is the masterly use it makes of innate harmonies when gathering to its fold the suspended and wandering tonalities of the past' (SM: 134). The emphasis on his own control over memory is even stronger in the introduction, where he describes his memoir as 'a systematically correlated assemblage of personal recollections' (SM: 7). In thus asserting mnemonic control, Nabokov appears to allow no other source of inspiration. Or, as Michael Wood puts it, 'Nabokov will have no truck with involuntary memory, or indeed with anything involuntary. Memory is an act of will . . .' (1995: 87). Indeed, Nabokov's authorial voice rejects all psychic modes beyond consciousness and control. As a chronic insomniac, he describes sleep as 'the nightly betrayal of reason, humanity, genius' and notes that 'the wrench of parting with consciousness is unspeakably repulsive to me' (SM: 85).[23] Instead what counts for him are states in which the individual is 'wide awake . . . on the highest terrace of consciousness' (SM: 41).

As I have been arguing, it is in and through poetic language that Nabokov constructs a new world governed by a self-contained set of aesthetic rules. It is here, in the realm of his writing, that the past can be re-created as an imaginary homeland, where coherence is restored, where the family becomes an act of memory. Nevertheless, as I will show in this final part of the chapter, the forces of memory are double-edged. Not only does memory allow the survivor to resurrect a pre-exilic past, but as a 'faculty of impassioned commemoration, of ceaseless return' (SM: 134), it also entails a perpetual revisitation. Rather than possessing the past, the survivor himself comes to be possessed by the relentless return of reminiscences, which render him a 'possessor and victim' of memory alike (SM: 10). While the text posits the past as an indestructible home – 'one is always at home in one's past' (SM: 91) – the memory of the past cannot be separated from the shadows cast by so many bereavements. As a result, the shield of consciously controlled recollection is supplemented by material which doubles (and troubles)

Nabokov's notion of memory as an act of will. Or put differently, his empowering poetic memory is haunted by real revisitations, and his extremely controlled writing is inscribed by a radically 'other scene'.

One of the most ambivalent aspects of *Speak, Memory* lies in its invocation of a 'thanatopoetics', that is a poetics which establishes a close relation between death and writing. By translating both life and death into text and art, the autobiography engages in a game of '*fort-da*' that has both empowering and disturbing effects. In the involuntary mode of sleep, the departed may return as the ghosts of a deadly silence and melancholy. As Nabokov writes: 'Whenever in my dreams I see the dead, they always appear silent, bothered, strangely depressed, quite unlike their dear, bright selves . . . They sit apart, frowning at the floor, as if death were a dark taint, a shameful family secret' (SM: 41). By underlining the mute separateness of the dead, the dream brings to the fore a cryptophoric knowledge and thus a dark flip side of memory. In contrast to the dream passage and its nightmarish effect, the aesthetic realm, however, re-animates the dead by writing them back to life. As if to negate that death forms a 'family secret', Nabokov stresses his act of re-presenting the dead and maintains that 'the bright mental image (as, for instance, the face of a beloved parent long dead) conjured up by a wing-stroke of the will . . . is one of the bravest movements a human spirit can make' (SM: 28). Not only does Nabokov aesthetically resurrect the dead father as suggested in the passage of his literal elevation cited above, but the poetic representation of his survivor text appears to be endowed with the power of inspiring an entire world of the past, now dead and destroyed, with new life. A favourite memory scenario he says he likes to revisit is the celebration of summer birthdays and name-days at Vyra. At the outdoor banquet table, which he always approaches like a stranger from the park rather than from the house, 'I distinguish the features of relatives and familiars, mute lips serenely moving in forgotten speech', when suddenly, thanks to memory's precision and omnipotence, 'some knob is touched and a torrent of sound comes to life: voices all speaking together, a walnut cracked, the nutcracker carelessly passed, thirty human hearts drowning mine with their regular beats' (SM: 134).

The notion that memory has re-animating powers is related to a larger issue having to do with a mutual implication of art and death in many of Nabokov's texts. Especially in *Lolita*, the logic of representation turns out to have fatal side effects. By invoking numerous literary allusions to immortalise his love and, above all, the power of his art, the protagonist narrator Humbert Humbert literally writes Dolores Haze out of her individual life. In *Despair*, Hermann Karlovich, another would-be artist, plans to create a masterpiece by literally executing a perfect murder (a scenario which, of course, resonates with several Hitchcock films revolving around the 'art of perfect murder', such as *Strangers on a Train*, *Rope* or *Dial M for Murder*). Although these texts signal a distinct difference and distance between their psychotic narrators, on the one hand, and the implied author Nabokov, on the other hand, there is nevertheless a sense that their thanatopoetic logic is part and parcel of Nabokov's own aesthetic project.

In *Speak, Memory*, too, aesthetic representation is inseparable from death and de-animation. Not only do scenes of death have to be touched upon in order to re-animate the past and, by implication, assert the power of consciously controlled memory to resurrect life once it is gone. But the very logic of representational re-animation has a de-animating effect in that persons, objects and memories of the past appear to fade as they are transformed into literature. 'I have often noticed', Nabokov writes, 'that after I had bestowed on the characters of my novels some treasured item of my past, it would pine away in the artificial world where I had so abruptly placed it' (SM: 75). This aesthetic depletion is at work in explicit appropriations – for example, in the modelling of the mother in *The Real Life of Sebastian Knight* on Nabokov's own mother Elena Nabokov (note that they both wear their husbands' wedding rings tied to their own). Yet it also underlies the larger project and its attempt to preserve the past by shaping it like a work of art. Paradoxically enough, it is by absorbing the world into the register of representation that Nabokov's writing de-animates what it seeks to return to life.

Nabokov's thanatopoetics can, however, also be read in a far bleaker way. It is not just that the register of representation implies a rhetorical de-animation, but *Speak, Memory* presupposes the actual death of those whom it resurrects. Nabokov could not write his memorial text had he not lost an entire geocultural world, had not his father, mother and brother died under tragic circumstances. On some level, he needs them to be dead for his art to come into existence: only after 'the things and beings that I had most loved in the security of my childhood had been turned to ashes or shot through the heart' can his writing resurrect them (SM: 92). His text is inspired by loss, and only because of loss can he inspire what is lost with new life. Nabokov's attempt to turn dislocation into an empowering narrative of exile and poetic inspiration – 'the break in my own destiny affords me in retrospect a syncopal kick that I would not have missed for worlds' (SM: 193) – may well be the most disturbing moment of the text. The 'break in my own destiny', which is equated with the 'syncopal kick' of poetic inspiration, refers not only to exile, but also quite literally to the dead family members. It is their death that allows him to fashion himself as an artist following the romantic notion that artistic creation is predicated on loss and pain. While he seeks to inspire them with life in and through his text, it is their death that serves as the ground and vanishing point of his writing. At stake is thus again the void of radical alterity posed by death, around which the text circles and which it also takes as its source of inspiration. As loss is always part of Nabokov's thanatopoetics, the textual and narrative refigurations remain inevitably connected to the radically 'other scene' of death, which they at once deflect and preserve.

The aesthetic refigurations of the text, its language and narratives, are inspired by loss, but loss cannot be adequately represented by any of the refigurations it calls forth. As Slavoj Žižek, picking up on Claude Lévi-Strauss's work on myth, convincingly argues, we tell stories in order to resolve real contradiction, thus translating contingency into coherence (Žižek 1997: 10–13). This notion is particularly resonant with respect to the real rupture of loss and exile. As implied by Žižek's compelling formula, any coherent and hence meaningful narrative of past events will cover up the antagonism at its origin. Indeed, revisited not by a lack but a troubling surplus of real memory traces, *Speak, Memory* is marked by a need to 'forget' the unbearable complexity of loss through death. It is accordingly to deflect or even deny the rem(a)inders of the real that Nabokov's text invokes forms of memory that are controlled in their poetic codification.

However, as Joan Copjec points out, the 'negation of the real by the symbolic presents a special problem'. Because the real has 'no adequate signifier', negation can take place only through implicit repetition: 'It is in this way – in the circumscription of the real – that its nonexistence or its negation is signified *within* the symbolic' (Copjec 1994: 121). The survivor's necessity to forget within a framework of controlled memory is thus heightened by a structural impossibility of getting rid of the real, which inscribes itself as a void into the symbolic refigurations or which, as Fredric Jameson would put it, articulates itself as 'absent cause' in and through textuality (1981: 35). As a result, Nabokov's writing opens itself to a performative dimension over and beyond his explicitly formulated conception of memory. By attempting to distance itself from disturbing reminiscences and revisitations, the text deconstructs itself through the internal difference of a textual movement or rhetorical displacement. It is precisely here that we can locate the crucial gesture of *Speak, Memory*.

In highlighting the question of how Nabokov's memory text refers to real-life exile, my reading has traced the ways in which history, understood as an 'absent cause', inscribes itself into his writing. This focus, I have been arguing, allows us to locate textual moments and movements which, rather than mastering loss, are haunted by its disturbing effects. The key figure in *Speak, Memory* has, in other words, turned out to be a rhetorical double gesture. The remaining part of this chapter shows that, while catastrophic loss is deflected or even negated by Nabokov's memory text, its cryptophoric secret nevertheless continues to act as the propelling force of his writing. How can we describe the aesthetics of dislocation thus enacted by the text? In what forms does 'exilism' play itself out?

The losses at the heart of the Nabokov family home are at once covered up and commemorated by a 'loss' of language and place. At the linguistic level, loss is at stake in the unspeakable void, which, as I have been arguing, punctuates and punctures the family narrative ('I find it inordinately hard to speak about my other brother') and which then also produces a fetishistic fixation on the signifier – a language that may at times seem playful and then again compulsive. At the same time, Nabokov's geopolitical dislocations are accompanied by the shift from Russian to English in his writing, which ultimately led to his extraordinary career as an American author. The most significant reversal of loss is, however, Nabokov's deliberate cultivation of exile, in which concrete displacement is transformed into a more or less chosen movement of continual dislocation and perpetual migration.

In *Speak, Memory*, Nabokov enacts a logic of exilism which leaves the translation of exile forever incomplete. Never actually arriving in the United States, the exiled writer and his aesthetics remain curiously suspended in a liminal state, where it is impossible to determine the location of the 'other shores' invoked by the title of Nabokov's Russian translation of the text, *Drugie berega*.[24] Nabokov does not remain exclusively connected to the Russian *rodina* nor does he adopt the host country as his privileged focus of identification. As a result, he chooses neither complete cultural assimilation nor potential ossification in nostalgia. Instead he can be seen to identify with exilic displacement and its lack of any concrete place or position. The Russian émigré circles, in which he spent his European exile, are described as a 'spectral world' (SM: 212). Later, too, he sustains a movement of dislocation. On the one hand, he maintains his retrospective rapport with the maternal *rodina*, the 'Russia of my legendary boyhood' re-created in *Speak, Memory* (SM: 94), while on the other hand, he develops a new identity as an American writer. As he notes in *Strong Opinions*:

> I am an American writer, born in Russia and educated in England where I studied French literature, before spending fifteen years in Germany. I came to America in 1940 and decided to become an American citizen, and make America my home. (SO: 26)[25]

Even as his American novels *Lolita*, *Pnin* and *Pale Fire* are far more grounded in the details and objects of American everyday culture than their European counterparts, Nabokov remains literally on the move – and thus enacts a trajectory which may, in fact, coincide with a particularly American way of life. In the course of their two American decades, which do not feature in *Speak, Memory*, he and his family never settle down but move nomadically between rented homes of fellow professors on sabbatical leave during winter and motels and cabins on their extensive travels in the summer months. While the Grandhotel Montreux Palace, where he and Véra reside after their final move to Switzerland, may remind him of the noble resorts and residences visited in his cosmopolitan childhood, he continues to live in a state of exile, however privileged. This is underscored by the fact that he is now longing for America, his new but absent home: 'I think I am trying to develop, in this rosy exile, the same fertile nostalgia in regard to America, my new country, as I evolved for Russia, my old one, in the first post-revolutionary years of West-European expatriation' (SO: 49). In fact, he goes as far as to play with a potential remigration: 'I feel very nostalgic about America and as soon as I muster the necessary energy I shall return there for good' (SO: 56).[26]

In thus fetishising dislocation, Nabokov implicitly returns to his childhood home, which by virtue of its absence, both imagined and real, has always served as a source of nostalgic imagination. In this way, concrete displacement comes to be recuperated as the origin and source of poetic inspiration. As the 'pangs of exile' are belatedly translated into a 'fertile emotion' (SM: 189), loss and displacement are paradoxically seen to produce their own means of mitigation, namely poetic language, memory and imagination. Yet the powerful triangulation of absence, nostalgic memory and imagination also revolves around a disturbing ambivalence. It allows – in fact, inspires – the exile to re-create the past as an 'imaginary homeland', while on the other hand it implies that the childhood home must remain an imaginary scene. The exiled Nabokov sometimes plays with the idea of revisiting his former home 'with a false passport, under an assumed name' – indeed, he claims that it 'could be done'. Yet the scenario significantly eludes his imagination: 'What it would be actually to see again my former surroundings, I can hardly imagine' (SM: 193).

In *Speak Memory*, Nabokov's childhood home represents first and foremost a scene of poetic memory. As a belated re-construction, his home is necessarily mythical. The 'imaginary homeland' may never have existed in quite this form, but at the same time it is the only 'home' that the exiled writer can inhabit in and through poetic imagination.[27] This is underlined not least of all by the visual representations included in the autobiography. While the sequence of photographs is introduced by the family's house in St Petersburg, Vyra is absent except for the foliage of the park, which appears in the blurred background of two pictures. Instead the site encoded as the 'actual' home features in the drawing printed at the very beginning of the memoir and sketching the topography of the family's three country estates, Vyra, Batovo and Rozhestveno. As if to signal its non-referential status, the map is adorned by two butterflies which are of supernatural size. As Nabokov explains in an interview, they belong to the *Parnassius mnemosyne* species, thus further embedding his text about the home in poetic memory (SO: 90; also see Baumann 1999: 236). Serving as a visual preface, the map underscores the imaginary character of the home that is to be reconstructed by the text.

Interviewed about whether he would ever consider visiting Russia, Nabokov responds emphatically that his *rodina* is preserved exclusively in literature, language and the memory of his childhood. Under no circumstances are his imaginary home and homeland to be 'contaminated' through an actual return. As he emphasises: 'I will never go back, for the simple reason that all the Russia I need is always with me: literature, language and my own childhood. I will never return. I will never surrender' (SO: 9–10).[28] The childhood home, it seems, must remain an imaginary site in order to support the protective fiction that there is in fact a home to which he could return if it had not been for his exile. Likewise when the exiled Nabokov wonders 'what would happen if I put in a long-distance call from my desk right now' to the family's St Petersburg ground-floor telephone, it appears again vital not to make the call. A failing connection ('No answer? No such number? No such country?') would confront him with the irrevocable loss of his home (SM: 181), while a response coming from the foreign territory of present-day Russia would call into question the powerful imagination of his homeland. As Michael Wood notes: 'What looked like a call to a vanished past becomes a call to an unknown and certainly mangled present' (1994: 88).[29] In order to preserve the 'imaginary homeland', absence and dislocation have to be crucially sustained. Similarly the exile cannot – in fact, must not – adopt a new home because 'nothing short of a replica of my childhood surroundings would have satisfied me. I would never manage to match my memories correctly – so why trouble with hopeless approximations?' (SO: 27). If the childhood home is thus re-created in purely poetic and mnemonic terms, this is because any concrete return would undermine the fantasy and fiction of 'home', the empowering support of the exile's imaginary homecoming and the source of his exilic self-fashioning.

Under the auspices of the imaginary homeland, exile thus turns into a trope of poetic creation regardless of the pain caused by the actual geopolitical displacement. As it transforms dislocation into a poetic vantage point, Nabokov's exilic self-fashioning implies the notion formulated by Rushdie that while we usually assume that 'something always gets lost in translation', 'something can also be gained' (1991: 17). Locating this gain in the very condition of exile and migration, Rushdie suggests that thanks to their double affiliations implicit in their liminal state, exiled or migrating writers 'are capable of writing from a kind of double perspective . . . This stereoscopic vision is perhaps what we can offer in place of "whole sight"' (1991: 19).[30] While reflecting on the loss of his beloved childhood home, the 'things that fate one day bundled up pell-mell and tossed into the sea, completely severing me from my boyhood', Nabokov asks himself 'whether there is really much to be said for more anesthetic destinies, for, let us say, a smooth, safe, small-town continuity of time, with its primitive absence of perspective . . .' (SM: 193). Like Rushdie, he thus implies that despite its painful implications, exilic displacement from one set of cultural codes to another affords him with a double vision that is both liberating and enabling.

Rather than providing unequivocal empowerment, the perspectival split between past and present opens up a liminal realm in Nabokov's writing, where the past keeps refracting the present in a spectral fashion. As a 'robust reality', the past 'makes a ghost of the present' (SM: 62). Owing to the sense that both the past and the otherworld of the dead are more 'real' than the present of his exile, Nabokov himself appears to become a ghost, too. It is from his 'present ridge of remote, isolated, almost uninhabited time' (SM: 19) that he revisits the past of his childhood – similar perhaps to the spectral disembodied voice-over that revisits the destroyed former home at the beginning of Hitchcock's *Rebecca*. Seeking to possess the past, the exiled Nabokov is, in turn, possessed by its continual return as well as by an intellectual uncertainty pertaining to the time and space of his (dis)location – and his existence at large.

A particularly compelling image for the liminal realm, the temporal and spatial doubling of the exiled subject and his writing is offered by Nabokov's imaginary reconstruction of the wintry arrival of the Swiss governess. Not only is this a scene which, significantly enough, he had not witnessed in person and which is thus fundamentally inflected by the imaginary, but the 'stereoscopic vision' of the scenario also resonates with a host of doubling and spying constellations in other texts by Nabokov and the ways in which these figurations work as tropes of psychic and geopolitical dislocation. While poetically evoking the governess's sleigh drive as well as the moon at this moment – 'for surely there must be a moon, the full, incredibly clear disc that goes so well with Russian lusty frosts' (SM: 78) – the writer enters the imagined scene as a displaced adult, as if to enact another instance of his imaginary homecoming, 'of its constant dream in my long years of exile' (SM: 76).

> Very lovely, very lonesome. But what am I doing in this stereoscopic dreamland? How did I get here? Somehow, the two sleighs have slipped away, leaving behind a passportless spy standing on the blue-white road in his New England snowboots and stormcoat. The vibration in my ears is no longer their receding bells, but only my old blood singing. All is still, spellbound, enthralled by the moon, fancy's rear-vision mirror. The snow is real, though, and as I bend to it and scoop up a handful, sixty years crumble to glittering frost-dust between my fingers. (SM: 78)

Initially, it may seem as though the past were haunted by the 'passportless spy'. Since he did not witness the scene at the time, the exiled Nabokov returns to visualise the scene 'by proxy'. Earlier on the station platform, his double welcomes the governess: 'My ghostly envoy offers her an arm that she cannot see' (SM: 77), and during the sleigh ride, objects are doubled by shadows, as if referring to an intrusion of the exile's 'stereoscopic' perspective. Yet, rather than the nocturnal winter scene of his *rodina*, it appears to be the exiled adult who is revisited and dislocated by the spectral return of the past. Displaced by the material snow, sixty years literally 'crumble' away. It remains uncertain whether in this process time is turned back to a solid past; whether it is the past that is crumbling away and comes to elude the exiled Nabokov; or if the crumbling is perhaps even to signal that the companions of the past have literally returned to 'dust'. Whichever reading we privilege, the past obviously has the power to transfer the transfixed exile into its enthralling hold. In fact, one might even see a convergence, whether coincidental or uncanny, between Nabokov's use of the word 'spellbound' and Hitchcock's film *Spellbound* (1945), which features another winter scene, in this instance clearly located in America but also refracted by the past of one of the figures, who is 'enthralled' by the traumatic memory not only of his guilt in his brother's fatal accident, but also of a skiing accident, which supposedly brought about the death of the 'double' he then came to embody.

Just like the crumbling snow and the two disappearing sleighs, the past eventually eludes Nabokov's grasp but, at the same time, continues to possess him. His imagination remains 'spellbound' by retrospective imagination ('fancy's rear-vision'), which propels him into the 'stereoscopic dreamland' and its disorienting topography: 'But what am I doing in this stereoscopic dreamland? How did I get here?' The scene thus uncannily dissolves the boundary between past and present without, however, bridging or closing their difference.[31] As if to indicate that his dislocation cannot be transcended, the 'passportless spy', though wearing New England winter gear, is significantly enough without a document of identification. Retrospective imagination may be the passage, the figurative 'passport' allowing him to spy on the 'stereoscopic dreamland', but it also implies that he is radically dislocated in the present situation of his exile. The absence of an actual passport, on the other hand, may be taken to suggest that he is a spy at the service of both past and present, but homeless in both.

Spies and doubles feature prominently in Nabokov's texts. In reality, he could not return to his homeland, where the world of his cultural milieu had been destroyed and where, as an author whose books were banned during his lifetime, he did not exist. The spying and doubling constellations of his oeuvre may not be as openly political as the spies and secret agents in Hitchcock's thrillers, which refer to the division between two political systems.[32] Nevertheless Nabokov's spy persona and the stereocopic situation of exile in which he finds himself resonate with scenarios of dislocation at stake in Hitchcock's espionage plots, especially in the case of unsuspecting protagonists who realise all of a sudden that, mistaken for the wrong man, they have become involved in the intrigues of two opposed groups of agents. Prominent of course is also the connection to other Nabokov texts featuring both a division and a mutual implication of two spaces, for example the preoccupation of the Russian émigré community with potential infiltration by communist agents in *The Eye*, the imprisonment of Cincinnatus in an absurd totalitarian world while he is exiled from the spiritual 'reality' of the otherworld, the soul and God in *Invitation to a Beheading*, or the *ideé fixe* Kinbote entertains in *Pale Fire* that an assassin has been dispatched by the totalitarian regime of his former kingdom Zembla to kill him in his American exile.

At the same time, the notion of a stereoscopic vision can also be read together with the ways in which many of Nabokov's characters double themselves through narration and self-observation. Both V in *The Real Life of Sebastian Knight* and Kinbote in *Pale Fire* write texts about other figures and their texts and, in so doing, come to be doubled both by those figures and their own textual production, which is propelled by these doubles. Humbert Humbert in *Lolita* and Hermann Karlovich in *Despair* fashion themselves as narrators and simultaneously observe and comment on themselves as figures. As suggested by Humbert's doubled name, they are structurally divided between experience and narration – and of course they also come to be doubled by their texts. The textual character of Nabokov's narrators and figures entails a shift towards a disembodiment in and through imagination. Hermann Karlovich wishes to be in two places at once and to disappear once he has created his artistic masterpiece by murdering his supposed double. Similarly, the protagonist of *The Eye* enacts a self-division so as to move into the immaterial realm of the imaginary. Obsessed from the very beginning with self-scrutiny and the fear of being spied upon (note the novel's Russian title *Soglyadatay*, meaning 'spy' or 'watcher'), the protagonist narrator allegedly shoots himself after a scene of painful humiliation. Not only does his disembodied imagination survive, but the protagonist actually splits himself into a narrated figure and the eye/I that controls both narration and perception. As a shade that is both insubstantial and invulnerable, he continues to watch the countless masks of a figure who eventually turns out to be himself as well as a world that is largely shaped by his own imagination.

The doubled spaces and figures in Nabokov's fictional texts are important to invoke here because they raise political, psychic and aesthetic questions which also pertain to the situation of exile and its intellectual uncertainty in *Speak, Memory*. As the epilogue will discuss in greater detail, Hitchcock uses the psychoanalytic conception of the double as an agent of the repressed and its return. By contrast, Nabokov's texts often feature doubles to thematise a potential split between the subject and the world. They ask such questions as what is my relation to the world? How do I know that I exist? What if I am a ghost, a shade, a spook? What is the status of my imagination? Texts such as *The Eye*, *Despair* and *Lolita* negotiate these and related questions by having the imagination of their narrator-protagonists turn into delusion and madness. At the same time, there is an overlap between the fictional texts and the valorisation of the imaginary in *Speak, Memory*. The aesthetic project of Nabokov's autobiography, I have been arguing throughout this chapter, bespeaks a belief in the power of representation and imagination as well as in the idea that individuals can invent and fashion themselves – even in exile, where identity becomes problematic. The novel *Invitation to a Beheading* (originally written in Russian) focuses on the imagination of its protagonist Cincinnatus, who finds himself in a prison world of absurd rules and characters. In contrast to all the other figures in his surroundings, who are without exception trivial and transparent, he is characterised by a uniquely individual imagination and perception. Whether we read the novel as an explicit commentary on totalitarian collectivity and surveillance (as well as the opacity of Cincinnatus to both), whether we see him as a captive to the fear of death, or as a soul imprisoned in a material world awaiting its awakening to a spiritual realm of transcendence, it is his imagination and the textual production it inspires that lead to his liberation in the end. At the same time, individual imagination often goes awry in Nabokov's novels. Not only do many of their narrators impose their delusions and obsessions on themselves and others, like Hermann Karlovich, whose mistaken assumption that Felix is his double results in murder. Imagination also often brings about isolation by shutting out the world as in the case of *Lolita*'s Humbert Humbert, who becomes a prisoner of his solipsism.

In Nabokov's autobiography, representation and imagination are ambivalent, too. While his fictional texts show the problems that may arise if there is too much fiction, Nabokov himself requires imagination to survive the onslaught of history. As a means of mitigating loss and pain, the realm of poetic language offers existential protection. Yet while representation may be liberating and empowering in its potential creation of poetic worlds, it can also evoke as well as resemble a phantom world of ghostly spectres and shades. The emphasis on representational and imaginary registers not only raises the question how autobiography hooks into the world of real experience. The autobiographic genre is also precarious because in contrast to his fictional narrators, who are indeed pure textual effects composed of signs, the exile and survivor Nabokov inscribes himself into his autobiographic writing in order to exist and to give proof of his existence. This project becomes all the more problematic if the pre-exilic past appears to be more 'real' than the spectral present; if writing about oneself and the world implies a certain effect of deanimation; if the world recedes from one's words. Nabokov's figures may be postmodern figurations but, given the existential reasons for his privileging of the imaginary and his extremely controlled writing, Nabokov is not a postmodern author. On the contrary, the coherence of his text, the consistent system of his patterns, is the one certainty Nabokov has in his exile and survival.

In conclusion, we can, therefore, say that Nabokov's project remains without any firm ground. As the very pivot of poetic creation and its protective gesture, imagination and representation are precarious. In a similar vein, the stereoscopic vision of exile may be empowering, but its liminality also reverts into an uncanny doubling. As suggested by the doubled time and space of the 'stereoscopic dreamland', the exiled Nabokov not only recollects but is also revisited by the past. His sustained dislocation then presents an ambivalent form of commemoration.[33] On the one hand, perpetual displacement may function as a line of flight, as an attempt to escape facticity. On the other hand, Nabokov's ongoing migrancy also effectively preserves the dislocating impact of his losses. Because they cannot be translated into the representational register, they are commemorated in a performative manner – in the literal migrancy he sustains in his exilic self-fashioning, but also in the poetics he creates in his memory text.

A proleptic reference to Hitchcock may further elucidate the movement at stake. In Hitchcock's aesthetics, the real repeatedly erupts in the form of a blot or stain, which threatens to engulf the visual field. By contrast, as carriers of both nostalgia and a family secret, Nabokov and his text encrypt their 'navel' as an absence rather than as an overpowering presence. That is, the impact of the real – or its belated traces (for here the actual impact occurs prior to any articulation) – are incorporated as a cryptophoric void. While the horror evoked by Hitchcock's thrillers is always too close, Nabokov's autobiography seeks to deflect the traces and effects of the real. Yet, even as the manner in which it is preserved creates a certain distance, the encrypted void continues to act on both Nabokov and his text. As a real rem(a)inder, it dislocates them and makes them move both literally and metaphorically, in a nomadic way of life and a poetics of exile.

Nabokov's writing is itself radically dislocated. Ceaselessly oscillating between past and present, between violent dislocation and recuperative recovery, it keeps wandering in a liminal zone. Spectrally revisited by the ambivalence of the past and its remembrance, Nabokov's 'stereoscopic' writing enacts a scene of doubled memory, which disrupts potential ossification in nostalgia. His memory text hovers between the restorative recollection invested in an inherently imaginary homeland, on the one hand, and the mourning of irrevocable losses, on the other hand. While it celebrates poetic imagination inspired by 'a hypertrophied sense of lost childhood' (SM: 60), it simultaneously commemorates the real impact of loss and exile. Even as it seeks to aesthetically displace history, it simultaneously opens itself up to, and hence comes to be dislocated by, its encrypted knowledge. The 'other scene' of disturbing memories is not sealed off but forms the limit against and towards which Nabokov writes his memory text in an unresolvable double gesture.

Notes

1. Incidentally, the semantic range of 'adventures', which Nabokov replaces by 'style' and which he would probably choose to translate as events both unexpected and exciting, also entails a more troubling meaning, namely the chance of danger or loss (note the entry on 'adventure' in *The Shorter Oxford English Dictionary*).
2. How common the switching of languages must have been in the family is suggested by Nabokov's rendition of his parents' reaction to the news of Tolstoy's death:

> My father ruffled the German newspaper he had just opened and replied in English (with the parody of a possible quotation – a manner of speech he often adopted in order to get going): 'That, my boy, is just another of nature's absurd combinations, like shame and blushes, or grief and red eyes.' '*Tolstoy vient de mourir,*' he suddenly added, in another, stunned voice, turning to my mother. '*Da chto ti* (something like "good gracious")!' she exclaimed in distress, clasping her hands, in her lap. '*Pora domoy* (Time to go home),' she concluded, as if Tolstoy's death had been the portent of apocalyptic disasters. (SM: 162)

3. See in particular John Burt Foster's book *Nabokov's Art of Memory and European Modernism* (1993). Sabine Baumann (1999) makes reference to the importance of family memory, mourning and trauma as well as the Holocaust, but does not discuss the ambivalences of Nabokov's aesthetic memory which, as I argue, are intricately linked to the disturbing aspects haunting Nabokov's memoir. Emphasising in her essay that 'death and loss were among the most moving experiences of Nabokov's life', Phyllis Roth outlines important links between a desire for aesthetic mastery, controlled memory and consciousness, on the one hand, and 'the underside of the idyllic life' (1982: 56, 51), notably the deaths of Nabokov's father, brother and cousin, on the other hand – trajectories which I should like to trace in more detail. While Roth's project appears to be the recovery of 'the man behind the mystification', my focus is on the aesthetic language and the rhetorical gestures of the text.

4. In my reading, I am particularly indebted to Michael Wood (1994) and John Lanchester (1995), both of whom read Nabokov's texts against the backdrop of exilic loss.

5. Note Slavoj Žižek's succinct formulation of this aporia: 'We live only in so far as a certain letter (the letter containing our death warrant) still wanders around, looking for us . . . the bullet is already on its way, sooner or later, it will hit its mark – such is the fate of all and each of us, the bullet with our name on it is already shot' (2001: 21).

6. On the concept of trauma, see Cathy Caruth (1996), Ruth Leys (2000), Dominick LaCapra (2001) as well as Jacques Lacan's notion of trauma as a 'missed encounter' with the real (1981: 55). Cathy Caruth describes trauma in a manner similar to Lacan, namely as a missed experience which the subject cannot claim as its own but which, for this reason, has to be confronted again and again; see in particular her chapter 'Traumatic Departures: Survival and History in Freud' (1996: 57–72).

7. In a similar vein, Phyllis Roth refers to 'Nabokov's awareness of death as that which finally cannot be transcended' (1982: 44).

8. A more detailed discussion of this passage would have to trace how Nabokov defines 'the pure element of time' in relation to 'the spatial world, which', as he claims, 'not only man but apes and butterflies can perceive' (SM: 19). Nabokov was an avid reader of Henri Bergson (SO: 43, Toker 1995: 367–73). As pointed out by Boyd, he 'heartily approved Bergson's cutting time off from space . . . and he accepted Bergson's stress on time as a richer mode of being than space . . .' (1993a: 294). Given my focus on the implications that historical time and rupture have for Nabokov's aesthetics, the question of Nabokov's re-encoding of time as an expanding and liberating dimension is cut short in my reading. Nabokov states that he is

not interested in the 'lapse' or 'passage of time' (SO: 185). Yet this appears to be precisely what his aesthetic patterns are erected against.
9. In *Nabokov's Otherworld*, Vladimir Alexandrov argues that 'Nabokov's textual patterns and intrusions into his fictional texts emerge as imitations of the otherworld's formative role with regard to man and nature: the metaliterary is camouflage for, and a model of, the metaphysical' (1991: 18).
10. Highlighting the impact of loss throughout his Nabokov monograph, Michael Wood makes a similar point and argues that Nabokov 'is saying, I think, and may himself half-believe it, that pattern is a redemption of loss . . .' (1994: 94).
11. Yet another version of the thematic pattern revolving around flight from political turmoil returns in Nabokov's remark that supposedly 'one of Kerenski's aides asked my father for a sturdy car the premier might use if forced to leave in a hurry . . .'. Again the memory is said to be notable because it connects to a much earlier, analogous event: 'if I treasure the recollection of that request (recently denied by my eminent friend, but certainly made by his aide-de-camp), it is only from a compositional viewpoint – because of the amusing thematic echo of Christina von Korff's part in the Varennes episode of 1791' (SM: 143). Earlier, in Nabokov's account of his family genealogy, we learn that von Korff, a great-grandaunt of Nabokov's grandmother, 'lent her passport and her brand-new custom-made traveling coach . . . to the royal family for their escape to Varennes' during the French Revolution (SM: 45–6).
12. In Nabokov's description, the mother figures not only as his privileged addressee, but also as the supportive figure in his poetic birth: 'As I carried it homeward . . . I did not doubt that my mother would greet my achievement with glad tears of pride . . . Never in my life had I craved more for her praise' (SM: 175). At the same time, Nabokov undercuts this scene in a self-ironical way. Not only does he characterise his first poem as 'a miserable concoction, containing many borrowings' (SM: 174), the description of the recital also resonates with retrospective self-criticism of the young poet's self-centredness, which leaves him completely oblivious of the mother's anxiety and concern for her husband in St Petersburg, who is 'being detained by the tension of approaching war' (SM: 175). At the scene's conclusion, the mother 'passed me a hand mirror so that I might see the smear of blood on my cheekbone where at some indeterminable time I had crushed a gorged mosquito by the unconscious act of propping my cheek on my fist'. Yet, ironically, what he perceives at this climactic moment of self-creation is a dissolved rather than a unified self: 'Looking into my own eyes, I had the shocking sensation of finding the mere dregs of my usual self, odds and ends of an evaporated identity which it took my reason quite an effort to gather again in the glass' (SM: 176).
13. The mutual implication of chronophobia and chronophilia in Nabokov's autobiography and the novel *Ada* is emphasised by Martin Hägglund's Derridean analysis (2003).
14. Thanks to the cosmopolitan culture celebrated by his parents, Nabokov travelled widely as a child and spent considerable stretches of time abroad in Western Europe. In his early childhood, between 1904 and 1905, for instance, he lived abroad, in Beaulieu, Abbazia and Wiesbaden, for almost

an entire year (SM: 75). He was well used to the *Compagnie Internationale des Wagons-Lits et des Grands Express Européens*, which would convey the family to Biarritz in the south of France. The family also stayed in Bad Kissingen, Berlin and Fiume among other places (SM: 22, 69, 153, 159).

15. As pointed out by Brian Boyd,

> Vyra was one of the three manors around which Nabokov's childhood summers revolved. Although he actually spent more of his Russian life in the family's St Petersburg house, Vyra was always 'home' . . . Since his father had spent his childhood summers at nearby Batovo and his mother hers at Vyra, their excited recollections added a shimmering fourth dimension to a walk through the parks: 'as if come home after years of travel,' they would point out to Vladimir 'the fond landmarks of events enfolded in an impalpable but somehow ever-present past.' (Boyd 1993a: 45; quoting parts of an unpublished chapter of *Conclusive Evidence*)

16. The triangulation of home, absence and nostalgia also underpins the child's proleptic fantasies of exile which Nabokov ironically describes in *Strong Opinions* to highlight their reference to literary topoi romanticising the condition of exile:

> In the first decade of our dwindling century, during trips with my family to Western Europe, I imagined, in bedtime reveries, what it would be like to become an exile who longed for a remote, sad and (right epithet coming) unquenchable Russia, under the eucalipti of exotic resorts. Lenin and his police nicely arranged for the realization of *that* fantasy. (SO: 177–8)

In an unpublished chapter of *Conclusive Evidence*, an earlier version of *Speak, Memory*, Nabokov notes that he 'went through all the sorrows and delights of nostalgia long before the revolution had removed the scenery of his young years' (quoted in Boyd 1993a: 51).

17. Nabokov also underlines the immaterial character of their home when he maintains that 'the nostalgia I have been cherishing all these years is a hypertrophied sense of lost childhood, not sorrow for lost banknotes. And finally: I reserve for myself the right to yearn after an ecological niche: . . . Beneath the sky / Of my America to sigh / For *one* locality in Russia' (SM: 59).

18. The aim of Abraham and Torok as therapists is obviously to liberate patients from their psychic crypts, which is why they subscribe to the cathartic notion that the utterance of certain 'magical' words closely connected with the encrypted secret will dissolve it (1994). In contrast, I would suggest that the crypt actually shields the subject from a traumatic knowledge which would be overpowering if encountered directly and which, similar to the void of trauma, also produces refigurations.

19. See also Michael Wood's reading of *Speak, Memory*, in which he emphasises the gaps and omissions in the portrait of Sergey (1994: 97–8).

20. The entire passage in the letter reads as follows:

> What a joy that you are well, alive, in good spirits. Poor, poor Seryozha . . .! If it were possible to transplant you over here, I think that after struggling along for a year or so you could find something. Your type of profession, diploma, etc., carry a lot of weight here. How do you envisage such a move? You with

your child and husband, or Rostik and E. K. as well, i.e., do you associate the latter with the former – or would the three of you arrive first and would we then join forces to bring over R. and E. K.? I am agonizingly anxious to have them here . . . I shall never forget how we struggled to get out of black 1940 Paris, what nightmarish difficulties they caused us (straight out of *Invitation*), the agonizing procedure of collecting money for the tickets, the 40 degree fever Mityenka had the day of our departure – we bundled him and set out, and Yosif Vladimirovich (who later died over here) and Aunt Nina (who died last year in Paris; Nik. Nik., on his way home from the funeral, was hit by a car and killed) saw us off. (26 November 1945; SL: 60)

21. In my argument that Nabokov's highly stylised text is punctuated by death – and by the death of his father in particular – I am indebted to Brian Boyd's reading of this passage in the introduction of his Nabokov biography. Initially, the church scene seems of a general character, but it actually anticipates 'a precise moment later' in Nabokov's life, 'the day he looks down at his father lying in an open coffin' (1993a: 7). Boyd emphasises the ambivalence underpinning the memory, namely Nabokov's avoidance of mortality, on the one hand, and his compulsive return, on the other hand:

> Even as Nabokov envisages the funeral, he also half-affirms his father's immortality . . . But style cannot charm the facts away: the body still lies there motionless in the church, the candle flames swim because of the tears in young Nabokov's eyes. (Boyd 1993a: 7–8)

In *Speak, Memory*, Boyd concludes, Nabokov time and again 'returns obliquely to his father's death as if it were a wound he cannot leave alone but can hardly bear to touch' (1993a: 8).

22. The passage refers even to a third layer, namely the rescue of the burning *Suvorov* by the *Buynïy* ('Tempestuous'). The destroyer *Buynïy*, commanded by Admiral Nikolay Nikolaevich Kolomeytsev, one of Nabokov's uncles, rescued the commander-in-chief of the Baltic Fleet in the Battle of Tsushima (Straits of Korea) in a traumatic national defeat which concluded the Russo-Japanese War of 1904–5 and triggered the Revolution of 1905. The national hero, that is the uncle in question, was to act as a second in the duel (SM: 147). By aligning his father with the burning flagship *Suvorov* (named after the legendary war hero General Suvorov), Nabokov implicitly elevates him, whom, due to his liberal politics, the 'reactionary press' accused of 'handing over Saint Russia on a plate to World Jewry' (thereby forcing him to challenge the editor of 'the most powerful of the Rightist newspapers' to the duel), to an icon of national history (SM: 147). The 'several lines of a difficult chess combination' probably allude to the game of chess that Nabokov and his father play as they leave Sebastopol for Western Europe on the cargo ship *Nadezhda* (SM: 194). Thus yet another moment of loss is alluded to – and veiled.

23. Writing about his insomnia, Nabokov characterises sleep as:

> the most moronic fraternity in the world, with the heaviest dues and the crudest rituals. It is a mental torture I find debasing. The strain and drain of composition often forces me, alas, to swallow a strong pill that gives me an hour or

> two of frightful nightmares ... but I simply cannot get used to the nightly betrayal of reason, humanity, genius. No matter how great my weariness, the wrench of parting with consciousness is unspeakably repulsive to me. I loathe Somnus, that black-masked headsman binding me to the block ... (SM: 85)

Nabokov adds how as a child he would 'cling to' the light coming from Mademoiselle's bedroom 'since in absolute darkness my head would swim and my mind melt in a travesty of the death struggle' (SM: 86).

24. As Sabine Baumann points out, the Russian title does not specify where otherness is situated, whether in the past, the present or an as yet unknown future (1999: 228). Has the autobiographer emigrated to other shores, or is he addressing a Russian audience on 'shores' which are now perceived as foreign?

25. The passage continues as follows:

> It so happened that I was immediately exposed to the very best in America, to its rich intellectual life and to its easy-going, good-natured atmosphere. I immersed myself in its great libraries and its Grand Canyon. I worked in the laboratories of its zoological museums. I acquired more friends than I ever had in Europe. My books – old books and new ones – found some admirable readers. I became as stout as Cortez – mainly because I quit smoking and started to munch molasses candy instead, with the result that my weight went up from my usual 140 to a monumental and cheerful 200. (SO: 26–7)

Nabokov then goes on to make the point (mentioned earlier) that thanks to this gain, he is 'one-third American – good American flesh keeping me warm and safe' (SO: 27). *Strong Opinions* features several further passages dealing with Nabokov's embrace of his host country (SO: 98, 124, 131, 149).

26. Nabokov's nostalgia for America might be seen in analogy to the nostalgic longing of his Swiss governess. When Nabokov visits her back in Switzerland, she nostalgically longs for Russia, where she always deplored her displacement from her Swiss homeland:

> She spoke as warmly of her life in Russia as if it were her own lost homeland. Indeed, I found in the neighborhood quite a colony of such old Swiss governesses. Huddled together in a constant seething of competitive reminiscences, they formed a small island in an environment that had grown alien to them. (SM: 91)

27. Similar to Nabokov's memoir and his home movie scenario, Salman Rushdie begins his essay in which he coins the notion of the 'imaginary homeland' with a representation of the family home predating the author's existence: 'An old photograph in a cheap frame hangs on a wall of the room where I work. It's a picture dating from 1946 of a house into which, at the time of its taking, I had not yet been born' (Rushdie 1991: 9). By thus framing his reflections on the home, Rushdie indicates that he never actually inhabited the home reconstructed in his memory and imagination.

28. According to Nabokov, 'there's nothing to look at' in Russia:

> New tenement houses and old churches do not interest me. The hotels are terrible. I detest the Soviet theater. Any palace in Italy is superior to the repainted

abodes of the Tsars. The village huts in the forbidden hinterland are as dismally poor as ever, and the wretched peasant flogs his wretched cart horse with the same wretched zest. As to my special northern landscape and the haunts of my childhood – well, I would not wish to contaminate their images preserved in my mind. (SO: 148–9)

29. In a telephone scene, evocative of Nabokov's, Rushdie makes the 'eerie discovery' of his father's 'name, our old address, the unchanged telephone number' in the Bombay directory 'after an absence of something like half my life'. The moment uncannily calls into question the exile's displacement. It appears 'as if we had never gone away to the unmentionable country across the border. I felt as if I were being claimed, or informed that the facts of my faraway life were illusions, and that this continuity was the reality' (1991: 9).
30. In a similar vein, Edward Said identifies the potential of exile in a 'plurality of vision', or what he also calls a 'contrapuntal' awareness (1984: 172).
31. In his reading of the passage, Michael Wood points out that although then seems to be now,

    there are still two scenes, two times and places, even as they seem to (and momentarily actually do) merge. Hence Nabokov's questions ('But what am I doing . . .? How did I get here?'). Time and difference disappear and fail to disappear . . . (1994: 89)

32. Examples for this include the spy thrillers *The 39 Steps*, *The Lady Vanishes*, *Foreign Correspondent*, *Notorious* and *North by Northwest*.
33. In a similar vein, Michael Wood notes that 'haunting is the chief structural effect of *Speak, Memory*'. He also relates this effect to a form of memory which contends that 'nothing is lost, the past is not a foreign country. Then was then and is *also* now' (1994: 86).

Chapter 3

'Aesthetic Bliss' and Its Allegorical Displacements in *Lolita*

Language is what matters in *Lolita* (1955/1958), according to Nabokov, and it is also what my 'exilic' reading of the novel will focus on. In his 1956 postscript, Nabokov describes *Lolita* as 'the record of my love affair' with the English language rather than with the romantic novel (LO: 316). His love declaration can be taken to allude to the fact that *Lolita* came to mark his arrival as an American author, even though the manuscript had initially been rejected by US publishers for fear of prosecution. The novel became a *succès de scandale* through its publication, in 1955, by Olympia Press, a publisher of erotic literature based in Paris, before it appeared in 1958 in the US. In the Russian émigré circles in Europe, Nabokov had already achieved fame as a renowned author of nine novels and numerous short stories. The shift from Russian to English in his writing and the transatlantic move in 1940 not only meant that he had to find an entirely new audience among American readers, but he also felt compelled to discover a new cultural world. 'It had taken me some forty years to invent Russia and Western Europe', Nabokov writes describing the challenge of his two literary careers, 'and now I was faced with the task of inventing America' (LO: 312). Indeed, the three novels that make up his 'American trilogy', *Lolita*, *Pnin* and *Pale Fire* (Wood 1997: 162), are firmly grounded in his re-invention of American culture. *Lolita* is clearly not the text of a foreign, but of an American writer, and its references to the details of American myths of everyday culture – advertisements, movies, motels, teenagers – and the freeplay of signifiers and intertexts already adumbrate American Pop Art and American postmodern literature. The fact that the success of Nabokov's 'first' American novel would allow him to resign as a professor at Cornell and move to the Grandhotel Montreux Palace in Switzerland is not entirely paradoxical, but signals his individual version of the American Dream.

Apart from his development of a new cultural idiom, Nabokov's emphasis on his linguistic romance can also be understood as an aesthetic comment underscoring that *Lolita* is first and foremost a text about the erotics of language. As often noted, the novel develops an elaborate network of numerous textual allusions and parodies, including references to texts by Dante, Poe and Mérimée.[1] At the same time, there is an abundance of linguistic puns, rhymes and alliterations emphasising the allure of Nabokov's re-invented English. While addressing the figure of Lolita, the linguistic outburst in the famous opening of the novel, for instance, anticipates the sensual pleasure of language that will permeate the text as it demonstrates how the physical articulation of the central signifier 'Lo-lee-ta' involves 'the tip of the tongue taking a trip of three steps down the palate to tap, at three, on the teeth. Lo. Lee. Ta' (LO: 9). By foregrounding both its visceral materiality and textual quality, Nabokov's novel, however, not only pays homage to language and literature. His writing also shows how things become transient, elusive and overdetermined as they are re-created in and through language. In fact, I claim that it is in its treatment of language that *Lolita* is a profoundly 'exilic' text. It is not just that the novel deals with displacement on a thematic level, which is something it shares with many other texts by Nabokov, including his early novels set in Russian émigré circles, and also *The Real Life of Sebastian Knight*, *Pnin* and *Pale Fire*. After the inheritance of '*mon oncle d'Amérique*' (LO: 27), Humbert moves to the United States, where the cultural emigrant embarks on frantic migrations. In addition to that, *Lolita* marks an aesthetic dislocation, especially in the way in which it valorises poetic language and imagination.

There is a curious correspondence between *Lolita* and the autobiography *Speak, Memory* discussed in the previous chapter, although Nabokov, well known for his 'strong opinions', seeks to draw a firm line of separation between his autobiographical text, on the one hand, and his fictional text, on the other. While he describes *Speak, Memory* as 'strictly autobiographic', he insists that 'there is nothing autobiographic in *Lolita*' (SO: 77). Yet the two texts do have important aspects in common. *Lolita* not only follows figurations of nostalgic memory already at stake in the previous text, but also shares its obsession with and fascination for poetic language and re-creative imagination. Within a fictional space, the novel thus renegotiates concerns and issues already prefigured by the autobiographical text, notably questions having to do with the ways in which aesthetic texts hook into the world, and how they negotiate mortality, loss and geopolitical displacement as moments which curtail and set limits to the individual and its imagination. While *Speak, Memory* seeks to undo the impact of a cataclysmic history in and through poetic language, the textual 'flight' into aesthetic enjoyment appears to be even more pronounced and the referentiality even more oblique in the fictional novel *Lolita*. Foregrounding the pleasure afforded by poetic language, the novel implicitly gestures towards the aesthetic limits also at stake in the autobiography. As I will show in this chapter, Humbert Humbert's solipsistic narrative excludes finitude and the position of the other, while Nabokov's writing performs the impossibility of poetising the experience of exile.

Nabokov affirms his privileging of poetic language over notions of referentiality time and again. In his postscript to *Lolita*, he embraces literariness as emphatically as he rejects 'topical trash or what some call the Literature of Ideas': 'For me a work of fiction exists only insofar as it affords me what I shall bluntly call aesthetic bliss, that is a sense of being somehow, somewhere, connected with other states of being where art (curiosity, tenderness, kindness, ecstasy) is the norm' (LO: 314–5). In a similar vein, 'aesthetic bliss' is also foregrounded when he describes the pleasure he derives from the writing process and hence from the shaping of language. 'The book I make is a subjective and specific affair. I have no purpose at all when composing my stuff except to compose it. I work hard, I work long, on a body of words until it grants me complete possession and pleasure' (SO: 115). While Nabokov may distance himself from his brilliantly well-read but deluded protagonist in almost all other respects, the author and narrator meet in their embrace of poetic language. They both work 'on a body of words' granting 'possession and pleasure'. In his narration, the *auteur manqué* Humbert Humbert can be seen to continually caress the texts and cultural discourses that feed his linguistic *feu d'artifice*. Eclipsing the real body of the girl Dolores Haze with his search for '*le mot juste*' (LO: 47), the narrator of *Lolita* is in love with language and literature more than anything else. The textuality of his narration allows a completely free-floating self-fashioning of his persona – for all we know, he may have made up his entire story. Yet, as argued by Elisabeth Bronfen, the novel can also be seen to trace how this entirely self-referential economy screens off any reference to a world outside his image repertoire (1992: 371).

Humbert Humbert's claim that 'this book is about Lolita' is at once affirmed and undercut by the closed circularity of his narrative, which equally begins and ends with the invocation of the name 'Lolita' (LO: 253, 9, 317). His memoir does, indeed, revolve around Lolita – but as a signifier of his poetic fantasy rather than as an independent person. Her real body is put under erasure as Humbert Humbert and his apostrophes turn her into a literary trope, namely the muse and beloved as a source of poetic inspiration.[2] The implications of this aesthetic figuration are paradigmatically played out in his renaming of Dolores Haze. In eliding her full name, Humbert Humbert deprives her of her particular position in the social symbolic network, emphasising instead her status as a literary creation. His diminutive 'Lolita' also literally overwrites the pain implicit in her first name 'Dolores' more than her own Americanised abbreviation 'Dolly' and her mother's brisk 'Lo'. By analogy, the poetisation of his overall rhetoric can be said to be insidiously immune against the pain it actually inflicts on Dolores Haze as it elides her subject position. As a protagonist 'on the move', Humbert Humbert performs not only a geographical flight in his hyperactive travelling across the topographical terrain of the United States following his emigration from Europe; he also enacts a flight from referentiality that is first and foremost textual. Or put differently, it is to take refuge from the other, death and pain as that which sets limits to and thus curtails his individual imaginary that he turns to the 'masturbatory' solipsism of his language.

My reading of *Lolita* will focus on precisely this process, namely how the novel's aesthetic textuality effaces referentiality by poetising both the world and the self. By reinserting the question of referentiality into the critical analysis, I intend not to reduce the novel to historio-cultural contexts, but to trace the implications of its aesthetics. As we shall see, *Lolita* does gesture towards a referential vanishing point, mainly through the body, pain and subject position of Dolores, which are eclipsed by Humbert Humbert's solipsistic rhetoric. Yet, while the violence of this aesthetic closure is played out on the diegetic level, its consequences, I claim, are not reflected with respect to the novel's overall poetics. On the one hand, the novel and its implied author do distance themselves from the narrator Humbert Humbert and his erotic obsession, for example by textually framing his confession with the mock preface of the alleged editor John Ray Jr and Nabokov's own postscript. On the other hand, the novel discloses a complicity by embracing the 'aesthetic bliss' which it also attributes to its first-person narrator.

The crux of the novel is precisely that its narrative levels and voices cannot always be clearly distinguished, especially when it comes to the question of aesthetic language. At first sight, *Lolita* seems to celebrate the infinite possibilities of a buoyant playfulness exclusively ruled by language. Yet it can also be seen to refer to the sadness of a situation in which 'I have only words to play with' (LO: 32). On some level, this is not only Humbert Humbert's predicament but also Nabokov's own tragedy. As argued in my reading of *Speak, Memory*, language may be empowering in mitigating the impact of exile by poetic means. The exclusive emphasis on poetic language, however, also points to a blind spot in Nabokov's project, namely the difficulty – or even impossibility – of transforming the referentiality of exile into the artistic text.

Undoubtedly, one needs to be cautious when bringing to bear notions of referentiality and experience onto the analysis of a non-mimetic piece of fiction. Again, I am not suggesting that the novel could or should depict a historical reality. Rather, I argue that the very aesthetics of the novel puts into question any image of Nabokov as a happy expatriate as it points to the impossible textual integration of what Fredric Jameson (1981) would call the painful impact of history.

In tracing this passage from playfulness to sadness, it is helpful, given the novel's seemingly all-embracing ironic stance, to distinguish between (at least) two larger categories of irony, which are produced by different positions and narrative levels and could be described as textual or structural irony and allegorical or sublime irony respectively.[3] Structural irony is signalled by the implied author, who, as already mentioned, invokes ironic distance in his attempt to dissociate himself from the problematic perspective and perception of the unreliable first-person narrator.[4] Textual or verbal irony, in turn, is celebrated both by Humbert Humbert and the text at large as they invoke a plethora of allusions. Their protean character produces an unstable, hovering quality of signification that is not anchored in any one of the textual references. Humbert Humbert plays with our readerly expectations raised by his use of intertextual allusions, but he also tries to make us complicitous with his perspective as he refers us to his ironical treatment of both other figures and himself. Moreover, the novel not only abounds with references to romantic texts, but also has recourse to romantic irony. In other words, it invokes a textual mirage only to reveal that the narrator Humbert Humbert and the fictional world of the text as a whole are fabrications created and shaped by the author Nabokov, who ultimately pulls the strings. As the addressees of these various forms of irony, readers are called upon to participate in the construction of the text's meaning, while they are also reminded time and again that they may be letting themselves be taken in by false leads. The novel thus offers a plurality of entrances, but all of them are potentially undermined by the slippage of irony.

Nevertheless, it appears as though not the entire text were subject to verbal, structural or romantic irony. Or put differently, irony of this type does not work in all respects and on all levels. Something appears to elude it, and this is where a different kind of irony may be seen to unfold. To be more precise, ironic distance appears to break down as a result of a slippage among narrative voices all of which hold on to language in a similar way. One could, therefore, ask whether this is the blind spot of the text, its point of fracture. In other words, is this the moment in which exilic displacement writes itself into the text, the plane of referentiality which cannot be caught up with but which catches up with the novel? This would mean that *Lolita* is not just a 'travelling' text as it shuttles back and forth between multiple textual references such as the literary 'high' canon, popular culture, road novels and movies. Rather, it also entails a tropological displacement or 'alien voicing' (Seidel 1986: 14) of allegory which, in analogy to the traumatic void encrypted in *Speak, Memory*, refers to a moment that can be neither directly narrativised nor textualised. Hinting at a breakdown of symbolic representation, the text could, therefore, be said to turn around the impossibility of transforming exilic experience into an all-aesthetic project.

It is precisely in the sense of such an elusive referent that it makes sense to speak of an allegorical or sublime irony. In other words, there is a form of irony we may be able to perform as critics as we reinsert the question of referentiality into the aesthetic stance and thus point to an allegorical discrepancy the text itself necessarily has to remain blind to. The secret sadness subtending Nabokov's writing resides in the fact that exilic experience has to be left out in his poetisation and, as a result of this exclusion, returns on another level. In order to analyse the text's antagonism between flippant playfulness and tragic sadness in more precise terms, my discussion will focus on three areas, namely (1) the nostalgic tropes that characterise Humbert's childhood romance, (2) the way in which the narrator relocates and dislocates himself in the textual process and, finally, (3) the manner in which narratorial and authorial levels converge on aesthetic language.

Childhood Romance

Lolita reveals a discrepancy in the way in which the text proliferates and develops into many directions at once and, at the same time, comes to a stop by embracing art as well as valorising Humbert Humbert's nymphet fiction. From the beginning, the novel emphasises its overdetermined textuality not only by invoking a multiplicity of signs, texts and images, but also by performing protean shifts between them. Each of the many genres and discourses introduced by the first-person narrator Humbert Humbert refers to another role he fashions for himself. Awaiting his trial for the murder of the playwright Clare Quilty, the rival he deems responsible for Lolita's elopement, he sets out to write a testimony so as to justify himself to an imaginary jury he repeatedly addresses. Designed 'to save not my head ... but my soul' (LO: 308), his narrative, however, also alludes to the spiritual and autobiographical genres of the memoir and confession. Moreover, his writing seeks to immortalise Lolita as the signifier of his art, thus not only producing a belated 'love letter', but also an artistic text bound to produce fictions. By providing him with myriad masks – Humbert Humbert is a criminal, victim, sinner, penitent, lover, madman and artist – these discursive manipulations and generic displacements render both him and his narration iridescent and elusive. In the same way, his ludic text draws on a plethora of disparate and even incompatible intertexts ranging from the literary canon, including Poe, Keats, Dante, Mérimée, to the popular culture of postwar America, its movies and magazines. It is not by accident that Nabokov's protagonist narrator should be a literary scholar. He is aware of, and thus ironically debunks, the cliché-ridden character of many of the textual tropes and genres he quotes and, in already invoking interpretative models, his allusions also seem to forestall and undermine almost any interpretation the reader may think of. By thus continually shifting between his intertexual and generic references, Humbert Humbert's narration makes sure that the reader can 'inhabit' none of them.

Similarly the mock foreword by the alleged editor John Ray Jr PhD multiplies the novel's irony and textuality by playing with the expectation that editorial comments put texts into perspective and vouch for their authenticity. As suggested by Nabokov's authorial inscription in the anagram Vivian Darkbloom, which is also the name of the mistress of Clare Quilty and of the author of the forthcoming biography 'My Cue', the preface does give signals, clues and cues to the readers, some of them correct, others not to be trusted. Thus the editor John Ray Jr provides us with the crucial information that by the time of the text's publication, both Lolita and Humbert Humbert are dead. Yet his conclusion that 'no ghosts walk' is proven wrong as their death effectively enhances the textual quality of the narrative and their status as textual constructions. Then again John Ray Jr maintains that the story has a real basis, but fact and fiction come to be blurred when he points out that some of the names have been changed, that identities have been suppressed and that he himself has corrected certain clues and 'signposts', thus obscuring the direction of Humbert Humbert's text. Most important of all, John Ray Jr characterises Humbert Humbert's 'remarkable memoir' as a psychological 'case history' destined to become 'a classic in psychiatric circles' (LO: 3–5). In so doing, he introduces yet another genre, which allows him to fashion a coherent story with a moral code – and for which the novel ridicules him as an obtuse commentator. Not only will Humbert Humbert repeatedly poke fun at the genre by making up case histories of his own, but all of a sudden, towards the end of the foreword, another voice emerges. This voice cannot be the editor's but must be the implied author's as it shifts focus to the aesthetic as that which eludes Ray's psychological and moral discourses, and says about Humbert Humbert's writing: 'how magically his singing violin can conjure up a tendresse, a compassion for Lolita that makes us entranced with the book while abhorring its author!' (LO: 5).

The preface thus already introduces the aesthetic as the discourse and trajectory that will never be undermined in the course of the novel. While I will discuss the convergence of Humbert Humbert and Nabokov on the question of aesthetic language in the final part of this chapter, I want to propose here that the textual surfeit and slippage of Humbert Humbert's narrative come to be paradoxically arrested by his textual nymphet. As the one and only aspect of his narrative that he never questions, Humbert Humbert's nymphet fantasy scenario gives rise to a compulsion that is comic. The scenario reveals him to be the prisoner of his own fantasy and fiction, and it also marks the point where his narrative undermines itself. While putting everything else into question, he does not seem to be aware of the fact that he may deceive himself more than his addressees. Yet, over and beyond producing comic effects, his compulsion also reveals the 'exilic' implications of his art and narrative. His French Riviera love for Annabel Leigh, 'a lovely child a few months my junior' (LO: 12), which he presents as the prehistory and cause of his obsession with nymphets in general, and Lolita in particular, is explicitly modelled on Edgar Allan Poe's 'Annabel Lee'. In Poe's elegiac poem, the lyrical subject mourns the premature death of his beloved in 'this kingdom by the sea' and, in so doing, poetically invokes the plenitude of their remote childhood love 'that was more than love' (1977: 632–4). From the start, Humbert Humbert's childhood romance is, therefore, refracted by its re-enactment of a literary precursor text. At the same time, I want to argue that his narrative is 'exilic' in reworking notions of loss, absence and aesthetics. It enacts the idea that it is the loss and/or absence of something that inspires the artist and produces the aesthetic, but also the conundrum that while countering loss, aesthetic representation may produce ever more transcience and absence. It is in this sense that Humbert Humbert's romance can be said to follow a logic that is exilic. It presents an act of re-creation which does not have any stable frame of reference – a fact that Humbert Humbert seeks to cover up in his compulsive (and violent) nostalgia.

Humbert Humbert's narrative rests on his *idée fixe* that the 'foreplay' of his nymphet obsession is to be found in his childhood love. 'There might have been no Lolita at all', he speculates at the beginning of the text, 'had I not loved, one summer, a certain initial girl-child' (LO: 9). His seaside encounter as a thirteen-year-old with Annabel Leigh produces a singular passion, which, however, remains unconsummated since their second and final erotic rendezvous is disrupted by two bathers – 'and four months later she died of typhus on Corfu' (LO: 13). If his nymphet fiction goes back to this childhood romance, his Annabel Leigh repeats Poe's Annabel Lee. On the one hand, the re-enactment of a literary text undercuts his narrative by troubling any notion of stable origin. On the other hand, it is to endow his childhood romance with an elegiac echo that Humbert Humbert repeats the previous script and the literary precursor – the dead beloved and muse in 'Annabel Lee', who was inspired by Poe's real child bride Victoria Clemm and her early death and who, in turn, inspires Humbert Humbert's Annabel Leigh: 'That little girl with her seaside limbs and ardent tongue haunted me ever since . . .' (LO: 15). The literary resonance of the re-enacted elegy provides both his childhood romance and later obsession with a backdrop of loss and nostalgia, while the multiple deaths of Annabel (as the real Clemm, the beloved in the poem and the one in Humbert Humbert's childhood) allow him to fashion the nymphet as a figure that is from the very start literary and textual.

The fact that Humbert Humbert 'commemorates' a previous literary text suggests that his childhood romance may be one of his 'pure classics in style', just like the 'fake "primal scenes"' with which he teases his psychiatrists in 'robust enjoyment' (LO: 34), or the counterfeit affairs which he makes up for Charlotte Haze – 'I also had to invent, or pad atrociously, a long series of mistresses for Charlotte's morbid delectation' (LO: 79). Yet, if the Annabel story is one of his fakes, it is fabricated to deceive himself. While thinking about the cause of 'the rift in my life' giving rise, or rather arousing, his 'excessive desire' for under-age girls (LO: 13), Humbert Humbert appears to consider infinite possibilities:

> When I try to analyze my own cravings, motives, actions and so forth, I surrender to a sort of retrospective imagination which feeds the analytic faculty with boundless alternatives and which causes each visualised route to fork and re-fork without end in the maddeningly complex prospect of my past. (LO: 13)

All of a sudden, however, Humbert Humbert rejects the 'boundless alternatives' in favour of one single genealogy. Cautious in the beginning, he is now 'convinced . . . that in a certain magic and fateful way Lolita began with Annabel' (LO: 13–14). His compulsion thus appears to be sparked by a nostalgia, which is never undermined by his narration but which instead serves as a reassuring remedy and deception. Although his sense of loss lacks any stable frame of reference – it is unclear where it originates – the nostalgic framework posits a point of origin both in the form of a meaningful explanation and a prior state of wholeness.

Humbert Humbert's childhood romance not only operates as a fantasy about the origin of his desire. Given the imaginary trajectories it inspires, the Annabel romance also marks the origin of his fantasy work. Even though it is presented as only one possible story among 'boundless alternatives', Humbert Humbert takes his childhood love to form the determining cause of his obsession. Yet what kind of 'origin' does his narrative construct? What alternative narratives or economies may be displaced or covered up by his childhood romance? Like the classic family romance discussed by Freud, Humbert Humbert's memoir elevates a childhood past in nostalgic fashion. At the same time, his fantasy signals, like the Freudian scenario, that something is 'out of place'.

Significantly enough, the romance episode does not end with 'the shock of Annabel's death' (LO: 14). As noted by Lucy Maddox, the narrative sequence departs from the chronological story-line (1993: 80). The rhetorical implications of this change are worth noting. When narrating his singular childhood love, including the desperate erotic exchanges under the prohibitive law of the adults, the thwarted final sexual union and Annabel's sudden death, Humbert Humbert notes: 'I have reserved for the conclusion of my "Annabel" phase the account of our unsuccessful first tryst' (LO: 14). As a result, the 'ache' that 'remained with me' is attributed to erotic desire and its thwarted satisfaction rather than her death (LO: 15). Although the intimate *tête-à-tête* is eventually disrupted by 'her mother's voice' (LO: 15), the scenario offered by way of conclusion is one of bliss. In contrast to the second love scene, which is described earlier in burlesque terms – 'with somebody's lost pair of sunglasses for only witness' and 'two bearded bathers, the old man of the sea and his brother . . . with exclamation of ribald encouragement' (LO: 13) – before it is then cut short by the abrupt reference to Annabel's death, the first encounter is evoked in lyrical fashion.[5] Both the nocturnal mimosa grove setting and Annabel's expression are said to be 'dreamy and eerie' (LO: 14); the scene appears to brim with the generous exchange of pleasure promising an even greater climax:

> My darling would draw away with a nervous toss of her hair, and then again come darkly near and let me feed on her open mouth, while with a generosity that was ready to offer her everything, my heart, my throat, my entrails, I gave her to hold in her awkward fist the scepter of my passion. (LO: 15)

In a similar vein, the passage leading up to this scene emphasises the singular matching of the youthful lovers: 'The spiritual and the physical had been blended in us with . . . perfection . . . Long before we met we had had the same dreams. We compared notes. We found strange affinities' (LO: 14). Instead of the separation signalled by the various disturbers of love and then, irrevocably, by Annabel's death, the romance thus highlights blissful wholeness.

A related displacement of mortality also occurs with respect to the mother's death. Humbert Humbert opens his childhood episode with the announcement that he is 'going to pass around in a minute some lovely, glossy-blue picture postcards' (LO: 9). Presumably depicting his childhood home, the French Riviera hotel owned by his father, these 'glossy-blue' representations serve as pictorial correlates of the overly positive terms in which he advertises his childhood as a prolonged vacation in a protected environment:

> I grew, a happy, healthy child in a bright world of illustrated books, clean sand, orange trees, friendly dogs, sea vistas and smiling faces. Around me the splendid Hotel Mirana revolved as a kind of private universe, a whitewashed cosmos within the blue greater one that blazed outside. From the aproned pot-scrubber to the flanneled potentate, everybody liked my, everybody petted me. (LO: 10)

The adjectives used by Humbert Humbert – 'bright', 'clean', 'friendly', 'smiling', 'splendid' – describe the home as a flawless site. While casting the home as a product of phantasmatic idealisation, their hyperbolic optimism also suggests that there might be something amiss with Humbert Humbert's 'whitewashed cosmos'. It is not just that contrary to the home's traditional encoding as a site of intimate privacy and belonging, Humbert Humbert's 'private universe' is a semi-public sphere, peopled by hotel guests. Even more importantly, the home's ambivalence is heightened when just before the assertion of his having been 'a happy, healthy child', we learn in passing about his 'very photogenic mother', who 'died in a freak accident (picnic, lightning) when I was three', and Aunt Sibyl, the poet, who replaces her and then correctly predicts her own death (LO: 10). Similar to the narrative sequence of the 'Annabel phase', Humbert Humbert's imagination replaces his allegedly 'cheerful motherlessness' first with the phantasmatically idealised family home and then by the textually inspired Annabel figure (LO: 11).

Closely connected to a displacement of death, Humbert Humbert's imagination plays a literary game of lost and found, in which absence is substituted by narratives and representations. In tandem with poetic imagination, his childhood romance displaces death with erotic desire, loss with a romantic text. By replacing the maternal object with Annabel, the family romance as a whole and the narrative of a missed erotic chance in particular promote the idea that the paradise of plenitude and perfection could potentially be (re)gained. The imitation of a literary love story obscures death as the cause and origin of Humbert

Humbert's sense of loss and absence. At the same time, Humbert Humbert's ironical textual surfeit is arrested by the nostalgic figuration it invokes with the Annabel episode. It is precisely to enact a paradisiacal origin that his narrative excess gets hooked on this particular version of the family romance. The nostalgic narrative supports the reassuring idea that lack and desire ('the rift in my life') can be traced back to a particular moment of emergence. By tracing his nympholepsy to the thwarting of a first act of recuperation, Humbert Humbert gives lack and hence desire an ineluctable cause and origin.

Humbert Humbert's narrative situates wholeness and perfection not just in the past, but above all in the register of the imaginary. His childhood romance can be seen to signal a flight into poetic imagination because it marks the re-finding of a previous text, and also because it encodes Annabel as a figure who is textual and imaginary from the beginning. Also characterised as an affair of the imaginary is the obsession it triggers. Humbert Humbert's very definition of the nymphet situates her as the product of his extraordinary perception, as the figment of his imagination. As he points out, one has to be 'an artist and madman, a creature of infinite melancholy' in order to discern the 'ineffable signs' that distinguish a nymphet from ordinary girls (LO: 17). Both his textually inspired romance and his nymphet fiction function as a disavowal of any imaginary curtailment.

Even more to the point, Humbert Humbert's imagination 'erects' itself against a facticity that could be circumscribed with Elisabeth Bronfen as a configuration of 'materiality, maternity and mortality' (1992: 376). Following the demise of the mother, which points to the fact that the life-giver is inevitably also a death-bearer, Humbert Humbert's narrative consistently comes to link maternity to bodily materiality and mortality so as to deflect death onto the (m)other. It is not by coincidence that his text has all the mother figures killed with a vengeance. No less dramatic than the 'freak accident' in which his mother dies, Charlotte Haze is run over by a car, while his first wife Valeria and Dolly Schiller both pass away in childbirth, that is at the very moment they become mothers. The deflection of mutability and death onto the maternal body is crucial because, by way of contrast, this leaves the nymphet untainted. Not (yet) falling under the fatal function of maternal reproduction, her prepubescent figure serves as a fetishistic signifier. It is over her body, turned into a trope of purity and perfection, that Humbert Humbert's imaginary recovers a retroactive plenitude.

The mythical figuration of the nymphet is evident when Humbert Humbert determines her age limits with '"nine" and "fourteen" as the boundaries – the mirrory beaches and rosy rocks – of an enchanted island haunted by those nymphets of mine and surrounded by a vast, misty sea' (LO: 16). In conjuring up an 'intangible island of entranced time' (LO: 17), he transports the nymphet into a realm that is situated beyond finitude. In much the same way, the passage of time and the mutability it implies seem to be suspended when Humbert Humbert sees Lolita for the first time. In Charlotte Haze's New England backyard, he perceives not Dolores but 'my Riviera love': 'the same child – the same frail, honey-hued shoulders, the same silky supple bare back, the same chestnut head of hair'. His 'passionate recognition' means that historical time completely evaporates: 'The twenty-five years I had lived since then, tapered to a palpitating point, and vanished' (LO: 39). Time seems to be arrested because he conflates the two girls, but also because his claim that 'my discovery of her was the fateful consequence of that "princedom by the sea"' (LO: 40) follows the myth of love at first sight, in which a contingent encounter is refigured as a fateful necessity (Dolar 1996: 131–3).

Not only does Humbert Humbert's nymphet fiction, in its conflation of Annabel and Lolita, rest on a mis-recognition. His attempt to romantically resurrect a seemingly eternal past is, in fact, self-defeating. His privileged object does not elude temporality; on the contrary, the nymphet is marked by a singular evanescence. Characterised as a 'little deadly demon', she embodies an 'elusive, shifty, soul-shattering, insidious charm', while her 'fey grace' encodes her as a precarious creature portending death and fated to die (LO: 17). Because nymphets can never grow up, they 'die' as soon as they turn into sexually mature women, who are described by Humbert Humbert as 'the coffin of coarse female flesh within which nymphets are buried alive' (LO: 175). The nymphet thus undergoes many deaths, including the figurative death brought about by the inert stasis of Humbert Humbert's textual nostalgia as it seeks to re-create Dolores as an image of perfection in which he can mirror himself. In his endeavour to break 'her spell by incarnating her in another' (LO: 15), the spectral phantom of Annabel comes to subsume the body of Dolores Haze, and even as 'this *nouvelle*, this Lolita, *my* Lolita, was to eclipse completely her prototype' (LO: 40), Dolores remains overwritten by the signs and texts which feed his nostalgic nymphet fiction.

All of this could be summarised by saying that in his obsession with Lolita, Humbert Humbert's childhood romance is 'twisted' into a form of perversion. Yet what makes his scenario perverse is not his nympholepsy, which he calls in turn a 'perverse delight' (LO: 17), 'my criminal craving' (LO: 23) as well as 'my degrading and dangerous' desire (LO: 24). Rather, his perversion plays itself out as a conservative structure which underpins his nostalgic narrative. Remarking that 'perversions are never what they seem to be', Louise Kaplan points out that 'the pervert is rigid and conservative' (1991: 42). Subversion and transgression are, in other words, deceptive because the perverse script imposes coherence and continuity by performing a fixation of desire. Its point is a disavowal of any lack and loss – as shown by the endeavour of Humbert Humbert's imaginary to stave off any curtailment implicit in imperfection and finitude.

Humbert Humbert's fetishistic fixation may be debunked by Nabokov as a comic compulsion. Indeed, Humbert Humbert himself is well versed in the literature on the subject and pokes fun at the psychoanalytical models partly rehearsed in my reading. Yet Humbert Humbert's irony does not pertain to his nostalgia. By embracing an imaginary that is hooked on a literary past, Humbert Humbert desires the world to mirror his nostalgic memory. Or put differently, his nostalgia is primarily a longing for texts, which he tries to impose onto the other and the world. While the nostalgic theme and structure of *Lolita* hark back to *Speak, Memory*, the novel demonstrates how the nostalgia of its protagonist narrator goes awry. Unlike Nabokov's autobiography, Humbert Humbert's memoir does not sustain a longing for the absent, but instead seeks to realise a notion of wholeness retroactively inspired by a literary text. Not only does Humbert Humbert invoke the rigidity of the perverse structure in order to deflect any responsibility for the 'fateful' compulsion he obeys. But his obsessive repetition of a scenario based on an earlier script also has violent implications. The 'pain and horror' (LO: 125) of his nymphet fiction are the result of the very rigidity and nostalgia with which he seeks to re-enact a textual memory. It is not only the imaginary of a literary past but also a nostalgic stasis and, eventually, a fatal rhetoric that he projects onto a present which eludes him in both comic and sad ways.

This avoidance of knowledge, implicit in Humbert Humbert's nostalgic imagination, is at the very core of the readings Stanley Cavell proposes for Shakespearean tragedy. Shakespeare's protagonists, he points out, tend to stave off their finitude by positing the other as a stake of perfection. Othello, for instance, denies his imperfection, which is implied by the impossibility of fully knowing the other, by transforming Desdemona into an image of purity (Cavell 1987: 125–42). Not only do his disavowal and image-making eventually result in the literal production of a corpse. The denial of imperfection, Cavell argues, means a failure to acknowledge the other in her difference and separateness (1987: 138). A similar argument can also be made with respect to *Lolita*. As the next part of the chapter will argue, Humbert Humbert's rhetoric not only turns Dolores Haze into a figural corpse. The particular 'exile' which Humbert Humbert subjects himself to emerges as the fact that his imagination cannot acknowledge the world and the other in their difference and separateness.

Textual Relocations

The 'tombal jail' in which Humbert Humbert composes his confession can be understood metaphorically (LO: 109). Not only will he die in the 'tomb' where he writes his text and thus transforms Dolores into a textual trope, but he is also from the very beginning caught up in the 'jail' of his language and imagination. In what follows I will trace the solipsistic rhetoric that underpins Humbert Humbert's re-creation of the world through literary texts and tropes. What are the effects and consequences of his poetisation of the world through a seemingly boundless proliferation and freeplay of signs and images? What does its texual surfeit displace, and how does it impinge on the positions of separateness and difference that exist beyond his solipsistic image repertoire? As I shall argue, the free-floating economy of language, texts and images invoked by Humbert Humbert's desire to 'fix once for all the perilous magic of nymphets' performs an aesthetic closure that both avoids and excludes referentiality, the other and the body (LO: 134). Blind to the world in which he finds himself, Humbert Humbert cannot acknowledge the separateness of the other and thus forces his deluded imagination and narrative focalisation onto Dolores. The 'exilism' in *Lolita*, I want to argue, consists of the violent ways in which Humbert Humbert imposes his poetisation onto the world and thus inflicts pain both on the other and himself.

To illuminate what is at stake, I propose a brief excursion to *Pnin*, which thematises a different relation between exile and language. There is much in the story of Pnin to suggest a figuration of exile far more tragic and violent than Humbert Humbert's. Pnin himself is said to have been displaced first by the Russian Revolution and then by Hitler Germany; his fiancée Mira was murdered in the concentration camp of Buchenwald. The novel is, in fact, one of Nabokov's texts that are most explicit in their reference to a catastrophic history. While *Bend Sinister* and *Invitation to a Beheading* both comment on (historically non-specific) systems of totalitarianism, *Pnin* takes the Holocaust as its traumatic centre. Having found a position as a professor of Russian studies at an American college, Pnin repeatedly suffers from cardiac spasms, 'something like a heart attack, which is perhaps an attack of history'

(Wood 1997: 169). The survivor tries to forget: 'In order to exist rationally, Pnin had taught himself, during the last ten years, never to remember Mira Belochkin . . .' (P: 112). Yet, in his memory flashes, the present turns into the past; Mira is still alive and continues to die because he does not know how she was killed. 'And since the exact form of her death had not been recorded', the narrator notes, adopting Pnin's perspective, 'Mira kept dying a great number of deaths in one's mind, and undergoing a great number of resurrections, only to die again and again . . .' (P: 113).

Pnin dotes on gadgets he first discovers in America. Yet the mythical signs of his host country escape him not only because he brings the wrong codes to bear on his readings, but also because, as a survivor haunted by the past, he continues to see too much referentiality. 'I do not understand what is advertisement and what is not advertisement' (P: 50), Pnin remarks, and when Joan Clements explains to her roomer that in an advertisement with the 'very clever . . . combination of two ideas – the Desert Island and the Girl in the Puff', the 'puffs' stand for the projected thoughts of the figures, he sadly refers to the atomic bomb explosion he sees instead (P: 50–1). Yet, even though Pnin is not in control – neither of the past, nor the language of his host country, nor the narration of his story – the novel represents a comparatively happy figuration of exile and an optimistic take on immigration. Most important of all, Pnin feels at home where, in fact, he is not. Many of his misadventures are the result of cultural misunderstandings and misreadings. Their consequences are sad and serious, for example when Pnin is sent to Ellis Island because he does not fully understand the question the immigration officer is asking him, as well as cruel and comic, for example when Cockerell, one of his colleagues at the college, impersonates the funny foreigner so as to ridicule his language and gestures. At the same time, the novel maps a cultural space in which several positions can co-exist, 'an America which still offered a home to the world's homeless' (Wood 1997: 163). Pnin is clearly mistaken in his belief that he is in command of cultural codes, but he may be correct in his assumption that even though his English remains weird and continues to be ridiculed by the culturally arrogant, he will indeed be an American in 'two–three years' (P: 31).

The novel shows, among other things, how Pnin's being so much at home with himself leads to a 'Pninification' of his world. The idiosyncracy of his perspective is, however, very different from the type of delusion that other Nabokov characters are subject to in *Lolita*, *Despair* and *The Eye*. Most important of all, Pnin does not – and cannot – impose his perspective on others because he neither controls the narration nor dominates the focalisation of his story as Humbert Humbert does. Hardly fluent and certainly not eloquent in the language of his host country, Pnin stands in stark contrast to the narrator of *Pnin* and his brilliant English. In the final chapter, the elusive voice of the narrator all of a sudden turns into a personified first-person narrator, a lepidopterist and renowned Anglo-Russian author sharing Nabokov's initials. Not only the fact that V. N. appears to be the more successful and assimilated immigrant is important – he has just been invited to join the English Department, while Pnin loses his position since Waindell College no longer regards Russian as a culturally significant language. The sudden emergence of the narrator's snobbishly arrogant upper-class persona also suggests that his presumably omniscient and objective narration has been biased and condescending all along.

Despite the narrative authority and cultural power of the narrator, one might argue that in analogy to the co-existence of cultural positions, the aesthetic space of the novel also includes and maintains several textual perspectives. Thus, for example, Pnin disagrees with V. N.'s rendition of events, which suggests that there may be errors in the narratorial fiction of the latter. Moreover, shortly after the arrival of V. N. at Waindell, Pnin finds an exit as he literally escapes and eludes him and his narration. Towards the end of the novel, V. N. is on his way to Cockerell when he suddenly sees Pnin with his dog in 'a small pale blue sedan' packed with his belongings. Because Pnin does not notice him, V. N. hopes to 'catch him' at the next traffic light. He hurries and has 'another glimpse of my old friend' (P: 159). Yet the very next moment, the light turns green and Pnin and his dog disappear – to elude him for good:

> From where I stood I watched them recede in the frame of the roadway . . . the little sedan . . . spurted up the shining road, which one could make out narrowing to a thread of gold in the soft mist where hill after hill made beauty of distance, and where there was simply no saying what miracle might happen. (P: 160)

When, at the very end of the novel, the narrator V. N. arrives at Cockerell's house, Cockerell begins recounting one of Pnin's mishaps. As the attentive reader notices, Pnin's cruel imitator has gotten the details of his anecdote all wrong. Rather than on Pnin, the joke is thus on Cockerell and perhaps also the narrator.

In comparison with the narrator and the protagonist in *Pnin*, Humbert Humbert is far more empowered than either one of them. Since he controls both narrration and focalisation, his perspective is far more hermetic and claustrophobic than V. N.'s position and, compared to Pnin, he is really in command of a great range of cultural texts and images as well as his own eloquent English. The power and monopoly of his language and imagination are precisely the problem, as they leave no room for escape, neither to Dolores Haze nor to Humbert Humbert himself. In fact, he keeps translating her into a textual trope after she runs away from him and also after she refuses to return to him. As this part of the chapter will demonstrate, Humbert Humbert's texts and images de-animate her by superseding her presence and position. Unlike Mira's continual dying, Lolita's demise is the result not of a traumatic memory, but of a violent rhetoric.

In contrast to Pnin, Humbert Humbert presents himself as a master of myth. If the former cannot but read referentially, the latter not only refuses to acknowledge the existence of a world outside his text and image repertoire but also violates and depletes it by virtue of his free-floating language. This means that in contrast to Pnin, who may not properly function in a culture that heavily relies on mythical meanings, Humbert Humbert's language blends into the very principles of myth. According to Roland Barthes (2000), mythical speech appropriates and depletes the particular, the historical by transforming it into the general, the universal. Myth can be everywhere, and the only viable method to counter myth, Barthes argues, is to mythify already existing myths. However, when Humbert Humbert quotes literature and popular culture, texts and images which are already mythical, his gesture is not one of demythification. Rather, he invokes mythical signs and tropes to graft them onto the other, the body, the world, which are thus at once aestheticised and depleted. It is only at the level of the implied author and the novel as a whole that this mythical depletion is self-consciously articulated. More specifically, *Lolita* refers us to a dislocation in Humbert Humbert's language and imagination by tracing the discrepancy between his tropes and the world.

As a text about language and imagination, *Lolita* deals with exilic effects that are specifically literary. In fact, the figuration of exile played out in the novel would not be possible in cinema. Film does not lend itself to a solipsistic convergence of narration and focalisation as we find it in Nabokov's novel because the cinematic medium always works with the co-existence of several audio-visual tracks and channels, the physical presence of characters as well as the undeniable difference between their positions and 'voices', none of which can completely dominate the film narrative. Discussing Stanley Kubrick's cinematic rewriting of Nabokov's novel, Robert Stam points out that the 'discursive power' which unreliable character-narrators can have in novels is 'almost automatically relativized by film' (2005b: 232). The narrator in a novel controls the linguistic discourse as the one and only medial channel, even though his narration and self-presentation may be undermined by the ironical distance of the implied author. The narrator in film may also partly control the verbal track – through voice-over – but his control is challenged by numerous other cinematic features, above all by the multiplicity of medial channels and the predominantly visual means of storytelling (Stam 2005b: 231–2). In the novel, Humbert Humbert claims to have 'safely solipsized' Lolita (LO: 60). The medium of film, on the other hand, makes it impossible for him to subsume her, or any other figure, under his solipsistic imagination.

While a detailed comparison would go beyond the scope of this book, it will suffice to point out that Kubrick's *Lolita* pursues a project entirely different from that of Nabokov. Not only does Kubrick, in the first film he made as an American director in Britain, re-create America, the country Nabokov 'invents' in his novel to become an American writer. He also shifts away from Nabokov's reflection on language and imagination as well as the artificiality the novel displays as a linguistic artefact so as to turn instead to a mimetic mode of representation. By casting the resilient and assertive star Shelley Winters in the role of Charlotte Haze, Kubrick gives her figure an emotional space, presence and resonance which she does not possess in the novel. Her character thus undercuts the monopoly held by the mythical speech and delusion of Nabokov's Humbert Humbert, whom Kubrick has played by a hardly self-assured James Mason. Moreover, the film takes seriously the claim made by Nabokov's Humbert Humbert that 'this book is about Lolita' (LO: 253) by also putting emphasis on the separate individuality of Dolores Haze, and thus on what escapes Humbert Humbert's narration and focalisation in the novel. As a result, Kubrick's cinematic characterisation of Dolores (Sue Lyon) works against Humbert Humbert's definition of Lolita as a mythical signifier.

In contrast to the film, the mythical trajectory forms the very linchpin of the novel. Nabokov's *Lolita* explores how in certain literary tropes, art feeds on the other's death, and how in Humbert Humbert's textual treatment of Lolita, referentiality at once vanishes and returns. In a sense, Humbert Humbert is always already moving towards the mythical textuality he finally produces in his 'tombal jail' awaiting his trial for the murder of Clare Quilty. As already indicated by his textually inspired childhood romance, he represents a figure who desires and remembers the texts he has absorbed in his reading. Likewise, the overabundance of discourses and images provided by these texts and nurturing his artistic potency allows him to fashion himself in a seemingly free-floating manner as he seeks to turn the world, and particularly Lolita, into an enduring trope of his aesthetic power. In order to immortalise her and, above all, provide himself with a lasting signature, he claims an imaginary realm beyond any referentiality, mutability and mortality, which becomes evident not least in its rivalry with maternal reproduction – 'in a sense, I was always "with Lolita" as a woman is "with child" . . . ' (LO: 107).

Humbert Humbert presents himself as a deft linguistic juggler in control of his creation and the representations that it feeds on. Yet his textual relocations also have precariously dislocating effects. On the one hand, he may be empowered by a freeplay of language and a myriad of allusions, while on the other hand he is also subsumed by his multiple citations. Not only is his effort to translate Lolita into a stable trope of his creation, and thus to capture and 'fix' both the 'perilous magic of nymphets' and his 'excessive desire', undermined by the incompatibility of the many textual references he quotes, but his ironic attitude towards the clichés imitated by his text also reverts into a textual form of homelessness. As a flippant parody parrot, he can only appear in the frame of the always-already written so that he is spoken by hybrid quotations which are at once alien and all he possesses. One could therefore speculate on the pain and despair that may be caused by the fact that the archive of received ideas and words constitutes the only language available to him – a mythical language, moreover, which does not adequately match the anguish of his *mal de coeur*. It thus appears to be the very freeplay of his language that signals his dislocation and his distance from the world. As Humbert Humbert remarks at one point: 'I have only words to play with!' (LO: 32).

Like his nostalgia, Humbert Humbert's exile appears to be first and foremost a textual affair. The line of flight in his textual relocations both echoes and depletes American culture. After all, the country he migrates to has always been conceived as the foundation of a new Eden based on Biblical texts. Moreover, when he journeys towards his re-creation of a childhood paradise based on the nostalgic Annabel script, he also travels through a country which has literally been on the move ever since the arrival of the first pilgrims and immigrants, settlers and pioneers. More specifically, he can also be seen to pursue a tradition of escapism that is specifically American: a line of flight that typically allows a male figure to escape from the feminine facticity of the social community and the domestic home.[6] Yet, in leaving behind the suburban home of Charlotte Haze after her death for the road and the motel, he simultaneously exiles himself from referentiality. In fact, one could say that his recourse to a textuality which translates everything into clichés and stereotypes constitutes his particular form of dislocation. The itinerary of his first year-long American journey with Dolores reads like an assemblage of signifiers that celebrates language in its poetic materiality but is otherwise empty.[7] Retrospectively, the narrator observes how the 'joy-ride' left nothing but a representational residue in the form of tattered map and guidebook material:

> We had been everywhere. We had really seen nothing. And I catch myself thinking today that our long journey had only defiled with a sinuous trail of slime the lovely, trustful, dreamy, enormous country that by then, in retrospect, was no more to us than a collection of dog-eared maps, ruined tour books . . . (LO: 175–6)

The passage may be tinged with a certain sadness or regret caused by this emptiness, but even though this registers, Humbert Humbert's text does not reverse its trajectory of representational closure.

Of course, one could follow Humbert Humbert's memoir on its own terms, namely as an example of pure artifice. But this would mean to overlook what his textuality cannot but leave out. At the risk of inviting speculation into my reading, I want to argue that the always-already written material may be invoked as a cover-up. Obviously this cannot be proven literally – if Humbert Humbert's language is designed as an escape into the imaginary, referentiality forms the vanishing point of his memoir and as such is conveyed only as absence. Yet, although referentiality cannot be directly located within the diegesis of his memoir, Humbert Humbert's flight may be traced on the rhetorical level. In a sense, his compulsive travelling finds an aesthetic correspondence in the frantic production of narratives as well as a surfeit of language, whose hyperactive restlessness can be read as a rhetorically significant gesture. In other words, it appears as though, by incessantly migrating from discourse to discourse, from intertext to intertext and, during his travels, from state to state, from coast to coast, the narrator is propelled not only by his paranoia that he is being pursued by Clare Quilty, but also by a search for '*le mot juste*' and a flight into the imaginary, both of which enact an avoidance of the real. It is precisely by moving towards a text which always emphasises its self-referentiality that his hyperactive travelling points to what it seeks to avoid.[8]

The consequences of this imaginary escape are most palpable in the way in which cultural texts and images come to supersede and hence efface the other, its body and subject position. To be more precise, the double articulation of Humbert Humbert's textual flight plays itself out most prominently in its translation of the American pre-teen Dolores Haze into the textual signifier Lolita as well as the violence that attends this process of textualisation. In turning her into the sign and anchoring ground for the text of his desire, Humbert Humbert not only establishes and aggrandises his aesthetic control over the other's textual

'Aesthetic Bliss' and Its Allegorical Displacement in Lolita 107

disembodiment but simultaneously effects a vanishing of referentiality. As Elisabeth Bronfen points out in her analysis, the narrator's attempt to immortalise Lolita as the muse of his creation rests on a paradoxical rhetorical killing, which is reinforced by the fact that in translating 'the ungraspable soma to the controllable sema . . . his imaginary compulsively returns to feminine figures of death' (1992: 373). Literally overwritten by texts about dead women such as Poe's Annabel Lee, Mérimée's Carmen or Dante's Beatrice, Dolores Haze comes to be figuratively de-animated. Yet, even as the text's rhetorical killing puts Dolores's real presence under erasure, it 'inevitably also articulates the real subject position of the effaced child-bride Dolores Haze, though only uncannily, as a presence in absence' (Bronfen 1992: 371). In analogy to Bronfen's reading, I want to argue that it is precisely through the textual erasure of Dolores that referentiality does return, albeit in an oblique manner.

As is also noted by Elisabeth Bronfen (1992: 375), Dolores Haze is the first and only nymphet that Humbert Humbert can touch, whereas all the previous nymphets could be possessed as objects of his sight alone. It is not only that '*this* Lolita, *my* Lolita, has individualized the writer's ancient lust . . .' (LO: 45), thus allowing his scenario to feed on her particularity. At the same time, the tangible nymphet introduces the issue of her particular presence, which the mythic image depletes even as it is also nourished by its specificity. Thus, as he reaches his masturbatory climax with a seemingly ignorant Dolores on his pyjama lap on a Sunday morning in the Haze living room – the first explicit sexual encounter that prefigures the rape scenarios of their 'joy-ride' – he makes himself believe that he has enjoyed an image created by himself.

> Lolita had been safely solipsized . . . What I had madly possessed was not she, but my own creation, another, fanciful Lolita – perhaps more real than Lolita; overlapping, encasing her; floating between me and her, and having no will, no consciousness – indeed, no life of her own. (LO: 60–2)

On the one hand, Humbert Humbert's invocation of 'another, fanciful Lolita' allows him to claim that he has interfered with an image, not a body, that in fact no violation has been committed: 'The child knew nothing. I had done nothing to her' (LO: 62). On the other hand, he not only abuses a real body, but as the passage underlines, the mythic image arousing him requires the de-animation, even negation of the real presence and subject position of the other, who has 'no will, no consciousness – indeed, no life of her own'. To project Lolita 'as if she were a photographic image rippling upon a screen' (LO: 62) means not only to 'strip' her of her particularity but to deprive her of any individual subjectivity and 'voice' because they exceed the solipsistic parameters of his imaginary domain. Superseded in his imaginary by a creation 'more real' (LO: 62), Dolores lacks a life of her own, because Humbert Humbert effaces and hence violates what does not fit his 'masturbatory' solipsism. As a consequence, her body is doubly violated, physically – 'there seemed to be nothing to prevent my muscular thumb from reaching the hot hollow of her groin . . .' (LO: 61) – as well as figuratively, that is by her transformation into a free-floating mythical signifier. The physical violence inflicted is thus reinforced by the violent closure of Humbert Humbert's imagination.

Resting on 'the hermetic vision of her which I had locked in' (LO: 123), Humbert Humbert's creation turns the elusive other into a seemingly stable sign and anchoring ground for the text of his desire. It is as an empty signifier deprived of its bodily presence that Dolores is made to nourish a narcissistic allegory of his desire as well as his creative potency – 'my own passion . . . the eternal Lolita as reflected in my blood' (LO: 65). In fact, Humbert Humbert makes a claim for her possession early on in the opening lines – 'Lolita, light of *my* life, fire of *my* loins. *My* sin, *my* soul' (LO: 9; my emphasis). While the figure of apostrophe is traditionally understood to address an absent and/or dead being so as to make it present and alive, the dialectic between the animate and the de-animate is inverted in Humbert Humbert's address. His aesthetic animation of Lolita requires the rhetorical de-animation of Dolores.[9]

As it fondles the literal materiality of language, his invocation can also be taken to illustrate that the actual girl is turned into a dead letter. The textual corpus that inspires his memoir effectively turns her into a figural corpse. As a re-creation of the many literary figures of death making up his image repertoire, she comes to be eclipsed by the texts that are re-written over her body. Referentiality fades together with her presence and pain as she is supplanted and effaced by a plethora of texts and images which Humbert has incorporated and which she is made to mirror for him in a narcissistic fashion. One could consequently ask to what extent the rhetorical translation of Lolita into a trope of language, literature and imagination discloses an ambivalent desire not only for the immortality of an image but also the death of the other. That Humbert Humbert's memoir may be conceived as a double-edged *mise-en-scène* of a fear of mortality and a desire for de-animation is underscored not least of all by the numerous textual references to Carmen and her lover's desire to shoot her.

At the same time, it is important to note that this necrophiliac strand is first and foremost a consequence of Humbert Humbert's thanatopoetics and the way in which it works as a 'killing agent'. Contrary to the contention of John Ray Jr in his foreword that 'no ghosts walk' (LO: 4) after the death of the text's protagonists, Humbert Humbert's memoir is at once inspired and haunted by textual revenants and corpses. As stipulated by the narrator, its 'publication is to be deferred' not only until after his own demise but until Lolita's as well so that her invocation is, from the beginning of the text, inscribed by the proleptic prefiguration of her death (LO: 308). While executing death as a trope and as a parody of other texts featuring dead women, his memoir also anticipates actual death, which will complete his metaphorical killing.[10] In fact, the text circles around death in an ambivalent way. Humbert Humbert explains that even though he is 'in love with Lolita forever', he knows that with only two years of her nymphet existence left, she is not going to 'be forever Lolita' (LO: 65). It is therefore to transcend the body, its imperfection and finitude that together with Humbert Humbert's signature, the text seeks to preserve '*that* Lolita, *my* Lolita' (LO: 65). Yet paradoxically enough, the very textuality of Humbert Humbert's writing engenders what it seeks to overcome. In excluding absence and death, it re-inserts them on another, rhetorically fatal level. In fact, the text appears to be caught up in its (im)mortal imagination. While it concludes with an invocation of 'the refuge of art . . . the only immortality you and I may share, my Lolita' (LO: 309), its first sentences already address Lolita as a mythical signifier, underlining the at once hermetically sealed and rhetorically fatal gesture of aesthetic (im)mortality.

Following this argument, we could say that Humbert Humbert 'misses' Dolores in a double sense. When she succeeds in physically escaping during their second American tour, he mourns her absence. While attempting to re-present her in her elusiveness, he produces images that are more free-floating than ever and, having no longer any body to ground them, completely elude his control. However, as I have been suggesting, he also 'misses' her from the very beginning because in subsuming the actual girl under his imaginary, he consistently elides her presence and subject position. She is bracketed both by his linguistic loquacity and textual excess, which overwrite her in a proliferating way, while they also lock her into aesthetic closure. The only level at which they meet, but which he significantly cannot acknowledge, is physical rape. Moreover, the elision of referentiality not only results in the pain inflicted on the other, but it may also be a violent act Humbert commits against himself. Even though he never grasps the full impact his imaginary has on the other, pain does register at some level. Indeed, his imaginary solipsism is increasingly disturbed when the repression of referentiality effects an uncanny return of 'pain and horror' (LO: 125). Or, as Humbert puts it towards the end of the first part of his narrative, after death has removed his wife Charlotte Haze as obstacle and after he has for the first time physically penetrated his stepdaughter: 'The realization of a lifelong dream had . . . overshot its mark – and plunged into a nightmare' (LO: 140).

Designed to keep referentiality at bay, Humbert Humbert's textual imaginary nevertheless articulates a return of the real – yet only if as readers we are willing to engage with the discrepancies between his textuality and its exclusions. With my negotiated reading, I want to draw attention to the ways in which the novel points to the costs of this imaginary escape and the concomitant exclusion of referentiality by playing out the both violent and fatal side effects of this rhetoric. Like any act of effacement, Humbert Humbert's textuality inevitably gestures towards what it obliterates. The novel underscores the solipsistic imaginary of its narrator by virtue of its rhetorical closure, which means that referentiality is rendered 'present' in the form of a textual gap or lacuna. With respect to Dolores, one could therefore say that the text obliquely inscribes her subject position so as to 'make it appear as having disappeared'.[11] She becomes visible as absence in Humbert's imaginary, which cannot but point to the process of her disappearance.

Paradoxically, her subjectivity makes an oblique return precisely in and through its effacement. In seeking to overlook her presence – 'it was always my habit and method to ignore Lolita's states of mind' (LO: 287) – Humbert Humbert cannot fully negate the discrepancy between the mythical image he has created, on the one hand, and the actual girl, on the other hand. Whether deliberately or unwittingly, he repeatedly describes how her pain articulates itself as he tries to ignore it, thus for instance in 'her sobs in the night – every night, every night – the moment I feigned sleep' (LO: 176). There are some rare moments in which he appears to acknowledge that she occupies a fantasy space beyond his narcissistic imaginary, 'an outside world that was real to her' (LO: 284). In one scene in particular, her perspective makes an anamorphic appearance in his otherwise hermetic imagination: 'I happened to glimpse from the bathroom, through a chance combination of mirror aslant and door ajar, a look on her face . . . that look I cannot exactly describe . . . an expression of helplessness . . .' (LO: 283). In this multiple refraction of perspectives, her pain and particular difference return with a vengeance. Even as he translates this knowledge into another cliché, the enigma of the innocent lost waif, Humbert is, at least temporarily,

> struck . . . that I simply did not know a thing about my darling's mind and that quite possibly, behind the awful juvenile clichés, there was in her a garden and a twilight, and a palace gate – dim and adorable regions which happened to be lucidly and absolutely forbidden to me . . . (LO: 284)

While causing collateral damage, no rhetorical depletion or effacement can ever be complete. Even as the signifier Lolita effects a vanishing of the real girl, it needs nourishment from the mythically appropriated body so that the rhetorical death of the latter is, as Roland Barthes would put it, 'a death with reprieve' (2000: 103). Made to give sustenance to Humbert Humbert's 'Lolita', Dolores is put at a distance as a 'speaking corpse'. Yet it is over her real body and subject position that referentiality returns to trouble and destabilise Humbert's narcissistic fantasy. His feeling after first raping the twelve-year-old as if she were 'the small ghost of somebody I had just killed' (LO: 140) not only alludes to the mythical reincarnation and nourishment of his old and his new love, Annabel and Lolita, through the rhetorical murder of Dolores. It also anticipates a reverse process, namely how the rhetorically as well as physically violated other comes to haunt and disturb his imaginary, thus insisting that he has indeed, in her words, 'torn something inside her' (LO: 141).

While Humbert both violates and negates her subject position, Dolores embodies an individual separateness which cannot fully be subsumed by his textual imaginary. Even if only *ex negativo* – that is, by taking up the locus of absence – she does inscribe his text with a position of her own, a corrective both to his deluded fantasy and his hyperactive logorrhea. Pointing to the discrepancy of his mythical image and herself, her figure further signals the incompatibility of their imaginary domains. While Humbert is, from the very outset, moving along his search of textual stereotypes and clichés, the desire of the American preteen travels towards celebrity, especially on their second cross-country journey, and, in so doing, articulates her independence, or at least divergence, from his image repertoire. In addition, her growing resistance and ultimately her escape in the second part of the novel signal not only that she partly eludes his control and closure, but also that she does not reciprocate his scenario. Her contradiction thus undermines his endeavour to immortalise himself as artist and lover.

The closure of Humbert Humbert's imaginary is also destabilised as Dolores embodies an awareness of vulnerability, which he seeks to displace in his textuality. Even as he views and distances matters as parody – by, for example, referring to their life as a 'parody of incest' (LO: 287) – and, in so doing, trivialises her pain, Humbert Humbert nevertheless has to gesture towards the 'real' Dolores as well as the painful knowledge that she broadcasts to him in her awareness of death. 'You know', he at one point overhears her say, 'what's so dreadful about dying is that you are completely on your own' (LO: 284). While the separateness of Dolores is put at a distance in much of Humbert's loquacious text, it becomes unavoidable during their last conversation. Visiting her several years after her flight, he immediately notices her metaphorical death as nymphet. 'The death I had kept conjuring up for three years was as simple as a bit of dry wood. She was frankly and hugely pregnant' (LO: 269). Yet, in contrast to his figurative invocation of death, Dolly, alias Mrs Richard F. Schiller, brings back the body of facticity. Her smoking gestures appear to resurrect her dead mother: 'Gracefully, in a blue mist, Charlotte Haze rose from her grave' (LO: 275). Obviously Dolly cannot know that her motherhood will become synonymous with mortality – as stated in John Ray's foreword, 'Mrs "Richard F. Schiller" died in childbed, giving birth to a stillborn girl . . .' (LO: 4). Nevertheless she can be seen to affirm facticity by moving towards the symbolic of the family triad as well as towards the curtailment of fantasies and desires implicit in the domestic everyday that Humbert's imaginary has been escaping all along. Indeed, her uncompromising 'no' when he asks her to 'come to live with me, and die with me' (LO: 278–9) can be read as an explicit rejection of his fiction, and it also repeats the interruption of the childhood love which his scenario was supposed to recuperate.

As often noted, *Lolita* gestures towards ethical recognition.[12] In fact, there is a brief moment during their last encounter in which Humbert Humbert seems to both love Dolly beyond her past nymphage and acknowledge her in her separateness: 'I looked and looked at her, and knew as clearly as I know I am to die, that I loved her more than anything I had ever seen or imagined on earth, or hoped for anywhere else' (LO: 277). One could speculate that introducing a pause into his textual proliferation, this volatile acknowledgement may endow his retrospective narration with a moment in which he appears to register the discrepancy between his narcissistic imaginary and the world of her fantasy space. Yet his recognition appears to be temporary and highly selective at best. In fact, I would emphasise that in the end, Humbert Humbert is shown to be permanently caught up in his imagination and, above all, in his attempt to aestheticise the world and the other in his 'refuge of art' (LO: 309).[13] Having forever lost her, he returns to his mythical signifiers denoting 'my Lolita' and, by thus aesthetically idealising her, propels her both prematurely and irrevocably into an aesthetic beyond. As mentioned earlier, he concludes by paying narcissistic homage to his aesthetic discourse as 'the only immortality you and I may share, my Lolita' (LO: 309). By once more echoing the privileged signifier 'Lolita', which already opened his text, Humbert Humbert's ending epitomises how his language literally overwrites the other. As he enters his imaginary realm for good, it is only as its ground and vanishing point that we can insist – together with Dolly Schiller – on a violently elided plane of referentiality.

Language to Infinity

Another of Nabokov's would-be artists, Hermann Karlovich in *Despair*, plans to create his masterpiece by committing a perfect crime. His artwork is flawed in several respects. It hinges on the resemblance between himself and his double, the tramp Felix, but after his execution of the murder, nobody recognises him in the corpse of the killed 'double'. Moreover, the literary doubling of his murder, which he intends to create in the form of a detective tale to prove his genius, also fails. In fact, Hermann Karlovich's mistake manifests itself not only in his deluded mis-recognition and in the self-sabotage of his plot when he overlooks a crucial clue and piece of evidence, but it is also highlighted by an authorial persona. While not participating in the diegesis but repeatedly addressed by him, this authorial voice forces Hermann Karlovich to destroy the symmetry of his text by adding another chapter and, in so doing, triumphs over his artistic limitations. Like *Despair*, *Lolita*, too, explores ways in which art can go awry – if the artist is deluded, if he forces his limited (and limiting) perspective onto the outside world. In this final part of the chapter, I want to turn to the implications which aesthetic language has in *Lolita* as a novel in which the narrative levels are not as clearly separated as in *Despair*. How can we describe the relation between the author and his first-person narrator in their joint valorisation of aesthetic language and imagination?

As I have been arguing, Humbert Humbert's exile is first and foremost a result of his flight into language as well as the blindness and violence with which he superimposes his imagination onto the other. If ethical recognition ever occurs on his part, it is definitely revoked in his final (im)mortalisation of Lolita at the end of the novel. Though not as literally as Hermann Karlovich's murder of his double, he kills Dolores through the rhetoric of his art. The discrepancy at stake in his violent conflation of an imaginary figure with the presence of a real body is both occluded and revealed in his text by a tropological movement or allegorical displacement. Given the violence and blindness of his nymphet allegory, the question arises how the narrator and his aesthetic language are framed by the novel and its 'aesthetic bliss'. To what degree are the effects of his language self-consciously reflected by the overall poetics of *Lolita*? How far does Nabokov's irony reach, and how stable is his distance? Could we say that in analogy to the nymphet fiction as the one area which Humbert Humbert never questions in his narrative, aesthetic language forms the one domain which is not subject to the irony of Nabokov's novel? All of this means to ask whether the novel itself harbours a blind spot, a moment in its treatment of Humbert Humbert's language which is allegorical in so far as it cannot be reflected and articulated. To explore the implications of this gap will be the aim of my allegorical reading in this final part of the chapter. More specifically, I want to argue that in analogy to the discrepancy that haunts Humbert Humbert's memoir, the text produces an 'alien voicing' among its narrative levels, an allegorical displacement which constitutes the novel's figuration of exile.

There are several ways in which the implied author Nabokov signals his distance from his limited protagonist and narrator. With its homage to imagination, nostalgia, literature and language, Nabokov's *Lolita* features some of the themes and concerns most deeply invested in his oeuvre, especially but not only in his autobiographical text.[14] While his oeuvre may at times seem to compulsively repeat themes of memory and nostalgia, the fiction text refigures them with a difference. If, as argued in the previous chapter, the aesthetics of *Speak, Memory* is inspired by a stereoscopic vision that oscillates incessantly between the past and present, between here and there, the novel has its protagonist's perspective focused on a hopelessly ossified nostalgia. Not possessing the mobility of his creator, Humbert Humbert is shown to counter a lack and lacuna by holding onto a nostalgic rigidity. By demonstrating how the narrator subsumes the other under his imaginary domain, the novel traces the painful consequences that his childhood romance and textual affair have for Dolores Haze, whose suffering Nabokov sympathetically referred to as 'my little girl's heartrending fate' (SO: 25).[15] While following cherished themes, Nabokov criticises his problematic narrator and the destructive effect of his nostalgic compulsion.

Moreover, the implied author signals time and again that the protagonist narrator is not master of his own writing. Humbert Humbert unwittingly points to contradictions and discrepancies in his textual self-fashioning, while his hyperbolic gestures and his claim to artistic omnipotence are ironically debunked by Nabokov's emphasis on his superior aesthetic control. His cameo appearances in his anagrammatic alias 'Vivian Darkbloom' (LO: 4, 31, 221), for instance, point to a whole plane of puns and games which the narrator is unaware of and which, similar to Hitchcock's cameos, serve as a self-reflexive means to point out to the reader the presence of a master manipulator – the one and only truly accomplished artist – operating at another level. In fact, the novel's structural irony is predicated on the existence of different narrative levels. It is by virtue of their separation that the implied author can point at the ethical and artistic shortcomings of his narrator and ironically distance himself from his self-deceptions.

There is, however, one aspect at the very core of *Lolita* that is not subject to the irony of the implied author. Indeed, it appears as though in analogy to the textual nostalgia which Humbert Humbert cannot ever undermine, 'aesthetic bliss' represents the one area which Nabokov needs to hold on to at all costs. Because the author and narrator converge on language, there is a murky alignment, a curious overlap between the various narrative levels, as if the novel did not – and indeed could not – clearly separate them. Or put differently, the distance between the implied author and the narrator breaks down because the novel exempts language from its far-reaching irony. Humbert Humbert's text may be framed both by John Ray Jr's foreword and Nabokov's (later) postscript. Yet, in the former, an authorial voice apart from the ridiculed editor foregrounds the aesthetic quality of Humbert Humbert's text and, in the latter, Nabokov affirms 'aesthetic bliss' as the defining feature of the literary and its enjoyment, thus putting into question any ironical distance from 'the refuge of art' embraced by Humbert Humbert. If the narrator celebrates a love for texts and language, this holds even more for Nabokov. Both as author and critic, he repeatedly reminds us of the primacy of 'style' and 'art' as 'the only thing that really matters in books' (LL: 138). He declares that 'my main desiderata' are 'style and a rich vocabulary' (SL: 42) and accordingly asks the reader to pay microscopic attention to textual details and their combination as they 'yield the sensual spark without which a book is dead' (SO: 157). As readers, we are inevitably drawn into the hybrid wealth of the vocabulary and wordplay of *Lolita*, the acme – together perhaps with *Pale Fire* – of Nabokov's writing. It would be difficult not to read the novel as a love affair with the English language, as Nabokov describes one of his linguistically most elaborate and flamboyant texts, 'a special favorite of mine' (SO: 15).[16]

Rather than focusing on the pleasure of the text alone, I want to ask whether in its aesthetic embrace, the novel may be said to follow a movement similar to Humbert Humbert's memoir. Could we say that what is performed in both cases is a flight into language, a withdrawal into textuality? In *Lolita*, I have been arguing, Nabokov traces the violent costs of textual tropes. He offers a sustained reflection on the de-animation at stake in language and writing in general and on a particular mythical configuration, prevalent in the romantic texts quoted by Humbert Humbert, in which writing empowers itself via the death of a usually feminine other. If, on the part of the protagonist, recognition remains temporary, Nabokov's novel offers an ethical comment on literary language. Oddly enough, however, Nabokov's reflection remains limited to Humbert Humbert's text. It does not pertain to the lacunae of his own writing, nor is it related to the valorisation of aesthetic language in his overall poetics. If, in the case of the narrator, there is always the ironical corrective of another narative instance, the author presents himself as the ultimate controller, whose position cannot be subject to any deconstruction within the novel itself. Yet, since the text criticises Humbert Humbert's language and yet continues to embrace 'aesthetic bliss', it harbours an unresolved discrepancy. As a consequence, Nabokov's novel appears to be haunted by a blindness to his own aesthetic investment, which correlates with Humbert Humbert's retreat into aesthetic language and perhaps also his wilful blindness to its violent exclusions. This then is the allegorical discrepancy or irony which escapes the novel but which we may be able to perform as critics.

If, indeed, the blind area of Nabokov's aesthetics is his unconditional embrace of language, what does it exclude and/or cover up? In the proliferating language of Humbert Humbert's text, I have been arguing, facticity re-emerges even as it forms the vanishing point from which the protagonist runs away as he ventures on his hyperactive journey both across the United States and through the literary archive. Could an analogous argument also be made with respect to the aesthetic language of Nabokov? Could one argue that Nabokov's aesthetics enacts a withdrawal to textuality which severs referential links in analogy to Humbert Humbert's elision of the other, its body and subject position? Does Nabokov's language perhaps not only veil but also reveal what it is pitted against?

Lolita teems not only with intertextual allusions and aesthetic patterns, but also with a doubling and mirroring of sounds and words, which foreground the poetic function of language. Evoking an enjoyment of language beyond semantic meaning, they reverberate in the wordplay of sequences such as 'drumlins, and gremlins, and kremlins' (LO: 33–4). Over and above Humbert Humbert's dual name and his double Clare Quilty, analogous reduplications are reproduced by the mirroring of textual details such as the repetition of the number in the Ramsdale address ('342 Lawn Street') in the hotel key at The Enchanted Hunter hotel (LO: 118). Withholding any definite 'key' to their signification, the spectacular play of verbal and textual cross-references enhances the novel's freeplay of language, which privileges the signifier over the referent.

By thus turning upon itself in self-referential fashion, Nabokov's language can be said to follow Michel Foucault's notion of a 'language to infinity' (1977). As argued by Foucault, modern literature begins at the moment in which language becomes its own mirror. Its writing 'automatically dictates that we place ourselves in the virtual space of self-representation and reduplication' because, rather than referring to an *hors-texte*, it self-reflexively points to itself (Foucault 1977: 56). Yet, as Foucault underlines, self-reflexive language redoubles itself in order to erect an 'infinite space' against finitude, the limit posed by death. 'Headed toward death, language turns back upon itself; it encounters something like a mirror; and to stop this death which would stop it, it possesses but a single power: that of giving birth to its own image in a play of mirrors that has no limits' (Foucault 1977: 54). The textual patterns of *Speak, Memory*, I have argued, seek to undo loss, while they also remain haunted by it. Similarly, the overdetermined language of *Lolita* can be said to create an infinite hall of virtual mirrors, which is simultaneously pitted against and directed towards the the real impact of Nabokov's exile.

The novel's numerous references to the popular culture of the American postwar period form a feature that is both prominent and overdetermined. Humbert Humbert's memoir refers ever and again to signs and images circulated by advertisements, magazines and movies. Charlotte Haze, for instance, is introduced as 'a weak solution of Marlene Dietrich' (LO: 37), and Lolita's room is decorated with advertisement and fan images: 'A full-page ad ripped out of a slick magazine was affixed to the wall above the bed, between a crooner's mug and the lashes of a movie actress' (LO: 69). While he valorises the literary clichés he quotes, Humbert Humbert is at once attracted and repulsed by the representations of popular culture, which he aligns with Lolita as the person 'to whom ads were dedicated: the ideal consumer, the subject and object of every foul poster', because 'the words "novelties and souvenirs" simply entranced her by their trochaic lilt' (LO: 148). Yet what he attributes to her taste for the banal and the trivial is also Humbert Humbert's very own soft spot. After all he, too, is intrigued by the 'lilts' of poetic language – as is Nabokov. Discussing the 'musicals, underworlders, westerners' which he watches together with Dolores, Humbert remarks that the musicals promulgate a mythical fantasy of success by invariably ending with 'a show-crazy girl' and 'her apotheosis on fabulous Broadway', that the 'underworlders' feature 'pathologically fearless cops', and – after displaying 'a plethora of pain' – the westerns conclude with 'nothing to show but the rather becoming bruise on the bronzed cheek of the warmed-up hero embracing his gorgeous frontier bride' (LO: 170–1). His description may dismantle these myths of health and happiness as 'an essentially grief-proof sphere of existence wherefrom death and truth were banned' (LO: 170). But at the same time they overlap with the gesture of his own mythical language, which moves towards a comparable 'grief-proof sphere'. In criticising the depletion at stake in popular myths, he may have more in common with them than he is willing to admit.

While the protagonist's reference to popular culture works in analogy to the literary tropes that feed his own mythical language, its role in the novel as such is more difficult to ascertain. What are the effects of this mythical and yet historically specific language so central to Nabokov's 'invention' of America? What does it do apart from endowing the novel with a cultural setting or, in Nabokov's words, with 'such local ingredients as would allow me to inject a modicum of average "reality" . . .' (LO: 312)? In the novel, historical events hardly ever surface. But when they do, they refer to the memories of a catastrophic history. Humbert Humbert emigrates when 'the gloom of yet another World War had settled upon the globe' (LO: 32); Dick Schiller's deafness is traced to his being a 'veteran of a remote war' (LO: 273), and his friend Bill 'lost his right arm in Italy' (LO: 275); Humbert Humbert's nightmares, finally, disturbingly evoke 'the brown wigs of tragic old women who had just been gassed' (LO: 254). All the more striking in the few isolated appearances they make in the text, these passages refer to the very real horror of the recent past as though they could be integrated neither into the virtuoso surface of Humbert Humbert's language nor into the stylised images of popular culture he quotes. Their effect is one of rupture – similar to Pnin's attacks of history and the passage in which the survivor sees an atom bomb explosion where the other figure insists on the mythical meaning of 'something much funnier' (P: 51). Are we to read the references in *Lolita* to popular culture together with the two interpretations of the advertisement in *Pnin*, which suggests that the smooth artificiality of mythical images circulated to advertise the hyperbolic optimism of the postwar, post-Holocaust and post-Hiroshima era is grounded on the very real horror of the recent past? Does Nabokov invoke popular culture as a symptom of a culture that refuses to look at trauma and attempts instead to cover up the disturbing memories of surviving immigrants? Does the novel's citation perform how history both vanishes and returns – in American popular culture and in Humbert Humbert's mythical language? Or is Nabokov's novel itself haunted by referentiality as an unspeakable limit, a disturbing knowledge of catastrophes survived? Does the novel's extensive use of irony and parody serve as an apotropaic manoeuvre to keep this disturbing knowledge at a safe distance? Is there a covert complicity with the myths of 'healthy' happiness and successful self-fashioning so prevalent in the postwar period?

'Aesthetic Bliss' and Its Allegorical Displacement in Lolita   119

On some level, Nabokov appears to be aware of the discrepancies of his text. But he nevertheless moves in the direction of 'aesthetic bliss'. Following Fredric Jameson's vocabulary, his language can be said to 'carry the Real within itself as its own intrinsic or immanent subtext' (1981: 81). His writing creates a textual surplus, a redoubling of language to infinity, which covers up a gap – namely the impact of dislocation, loss and exile. As argued in detail in my reading of *Speak, Memory* in the previous chapter, the aesthetic language embraced by Nabokov functions as a protective ploy, not only in its exuberant playfulness but also because it provides the exiled writer with an empowering 'new world to rule' (Said 1984: 167).

In a similar vein, Nabokov's loss of the mother tongue appears to serve as a protective fiction. The forced abandonment of Russian in his writing represents his privileged narrative of exile, and it is also the only form of loss explicitly referred to in the novel's postscript. Nabokov opens his comment with an 'autobiographic device', the ironical hint that the following 'may strike one – may strike me, in fact – as an impersonation of Vladimir Nabokov talking about his own book' (LO: 311), but ends on an unusually personal and urgent note. Immediately after his overt description of *Lolita* as the record of his love affair with the English language, he suddenly shifts to his abandonment of Russian, which he describes as his personal affair and no one's business. Yet, although 'I feel my voice rising to a much too strident pitch', he nevertheless appears compelled to write about it.

> None of my American friends have read my Russian books and thus every appraisal on the strength of my English ones is bound to be out of focus. My private tragedy, which cannot, and indeed should not, be anybody's concern, is that I had to abandon my natural idiom, my untrammeled, rich, and infinitely docile Russian tongue for a second-rate brand of English, devoid of any of those apparatuses – the baffling mirror, the black velvet backdrop, the implied associations and traditions – which the native illusionist, fractails flying, can magically use to transcend the heritage in his own way. (LO: 316–17)

Michael Wood argues that by shifting from the Russian mother tongue to a 'fabulous, freaky, singing, acrobatic, unheard of' re-invention of the English language, Nabokov's prose writing signals a 'horrible self-deprivation' (Wood 1994: 5, 3). Nabokov, Wood further points out, did not actually lose his native language but enacted 'a voluntary miming . . . the worst loss he could imagine for a writer, stylistic exile without end' (Wood 1994: 4). The linguistic exile Nabokov foregrounds in the postscript is, 'symptomatically, a fate which seems almost entirely self-imposed' (Wood 1994: 4).

Nabokov himself describes the substitution of languages as an abrupt event amounting to a moment of shock. 'My complete switch from Russian prose to English prose was exceedingly painful', he says in an interview, 'like learning anew to handle things after losing seven or eight fingers in an explosion' (SO: 54). In reality, the linguistic shift was neither as sudden nor as terminal as suggested by Nabokov's metaphor of amputation. Not only did he learn to read and write English before he could read and write Russian as a child (SM: 24, 63), in his literary writing, he used French and English from early on, and he never completely abandoned Russian.[17] The abandonment of his 'natural idiom' is hardly the main reason for his 'private tragedy'. Rather, the linguistic exile appears to substitute for and cover up other, more traumatic losses, which are indeed beyond the control of the individual.

It may be part and parcel of Nabokov's 'private tragedy' that the poetic language of his writing cannot incorporate and articulate the actual impact of dislocation. Nabokov's emphasis on an extremely elaborate, entirely self-referential language creates a poetics which seeks to undo historicity and contingency and, in so doing, implies a certain gesture of violence. In fact, one could draw a parallel between the violence the first-person narrator inflicts on a real body and the violence the author does to his own exilic situation. In both cases, what becomes evident is the violence implicit in projects that seek to poetise the world. On the level of Humbert Humbert's language, the impact of violence is more palpable because there is always another narrative level serving as an instance of mediation and reflection. By contrast, the violence implicit in the exclusion of referentiality is more hidden and latent, but all the same present on the authorial level. As the novel cannot turn its implicit embrace of the narrator's language into an object of reflection, it refers us to a blind spot, an allegorical displacement or 'alien voicing' that inhabits Nabokov's overall aesthetic project.

It is in this sense that Nabokov's language is indeed related to loss – or even inflicts a double loss, namely by negating and thereby permanently 'losing' the referentiality of his actual losses. Part of the sadness which underlies the exclusion of referentiality, but is never articulated, is the aporia that, to speak with Fredric Jameson, historicity represents 'an absent cause' and as such is 'inaccessible to us except in textual form' (1981: 35). As a result, there is no possibility apart from the production of allegories which can never catch up with the 'absent cause' of their representational void and which thus confront representation as well the individual's claim to control with the opaqueness of their tropological displacement. Not directly available, and hence eluding any control, these representational limits may hurt all the more – exactly because the need

'Aesthetic Bliss' and Its Allegorical Displacement in Lolita 121

for self-referential aesthetics must remain obscure to the individual. While this allegorical displacement can be performed on yet another textual level, namely by the critic, it remains a blind zone in Nabokov's project.

The blindness to this allegorical gap emerging from the instability of language can be regarded as the exilic specificity and perhaps also the failure of Nabokov's aesthetic project. The dislocation of Nabokov's aesthetic language is, in other words, indicated by the fact that it forms the one area that he cannot put into question. His poetics celebrates a freeplay of signs and, at the same time, harbours the equally sad and secret knowledge that language is literally all the exile possesses. As he develops a self-referential language so as to mitigate and, in fact, exclude the painful referentiality of dislocation, the author, like the narrator, has 'only words to play with' (LO: 32). Language, therefore, plays a highly ambivalent role in Nabokov's aesthetics. Language forms the moment of its greatest resilience and triumph and, at the same time, points to its own limitation. It is hardly an accident that the project's point of fracture should be related to an ambivalent doubling of the narrator's involvement in aesthetic language. The exile Nabokov appears not to have ground enough to distance himself from the language of his narrator because language is his only frame of reference.

All of this can be summarised by the paradox that biography catches up with a highly aestheticised language. As Fredric Jameson writes in *The Political Unconscious*, 'the microscopic experience of words' cannot ward off history because they are grounded on the real:

> To imagine that, sheltered from the omnipresence of history . . . there already exists a realm of freedom – whether it be that of the microscopic experience of words in a text or the ecstasies and intensities of the various private religions – is only to strengthen the grip of Necessity over all such blind zones in which the individual seeks refuge . . . (Jameson 1981: 20)

As I have been arguing in this and the preceding chapter, it is precisely in turning to a supposedly autonomous realm that Nabokov's free-floating poetics comes to be re-inscribed by history as what it seeks to ward off because its irrevocable losses set painful limits to the individual and its imaginary possibilities.

Yet referentiality also returns in so far as Humbert Humbert's hybrid language implicitly reflects Nabokov's biography – not only as a writer but also as a reader and exile. The novel's rich network of allusions consists of the culturally polyglot coordinates of someone at home in literature, language and imagination, if nowhere else. The multiplicity of references corresponds to the free-floating self-fashioning of Nabokov's public persona – he emphasises that 'I see myself as an American writer raised in Russia, educated in England, imbued by the culture of Western

Europe . . .' (SO: 192), and also insists that 'the writer's art is his real passport' (SO: 63).[18] It is with *Lolita*, 'my little American muse' (SO: 37), that Nabokov makes his arrival in the United States and that almost two decades after his European emigration, he can transform the fate of exile into his own version of the American Dream. The novel's language underlines that Nabokov is an American writer in the sense that one always arrives in America as someone who necessarily comes from elsewhere and, more than anywhere else in the Western world, locates one's frame of reference in signs, texts, myths and fantasies, whether they derive from one's country of ancestral origin or the New World. One could therefore speculate that Nabokov's eventual move to Switzerland was meant to enhance the textuality of his America together with all his other cultural affiliations. Indeed, his late novels *Ada* (1969), *Transparent Things* (1972) and *Look at the Harlequins!* (1974) appear again much further removed from any cultural terrain than his American trilogy. In all cases, there is a discrepancy in his brilliant textual games. The poignancy remains that to poetise the world without catching up with exile is Nabokov's only option.

Notes

1. For a detailed discussion of the literary allusions, see Carl Proffer (1968) and Alfred Appel (1991).
2. The appropriation of the dead beloved as muse is foregrounded by Elisabeth Bronfen's reading of *Lolita* in her book *Over Her Dead Body* (1992: 371–81).
3. My discussion of irony refers to M. H. Abrams (1985) and Claire Colebrook (2004) for verbal, structural and romantic irony, and Stephen Greenblatt (1981) and Paul de Man (1983) for irony as allegory.
4. For a detailed discussion of Humbert Humbert and other unreliable narrators in Nabokov's oeuvre, see Renate Hof (1984).
5. Thomas Frosch makes a similar point. Discussing the shifts in tone that characterise the Annabel romance, he remarks that after 'the intrusion of the burlesque', the discourse of the romantic is reaffirmed by the analeptic love scene that concludes the episode (2003: 40–1).
6. As Leslie Fiedler (1997) and Michael Wood (1989) have shown, this trajectory appears to be vital to the American masculine subject. It is enacted by the soldier and the cowboy, who both embrace the front or frontier so as to avoid the home and preserve it instead as a wish and fantasy. Historio-culturally Humbert Humbert's extensive travelling can be read together with two phenomena paradigmatic for American postwar culture: the new tourism centred on the automobile, the highway and the motel (see Halberstam 1993: 173–9) as well as the masculine crisis and restlessness depicted in the 'road novels' of the time, notably Jack Kerouac's *On the*

'Aesthetic Bliss' and Its Allegorical Displacement in Lolita 123

Road (1957) and John Updike's *Rabbit, Run* (1960). I will return to this figuration of the masculine fugue in greater detail when I discuss the travelling of the protagonist in *North by Northwest*.

7. See, for example, the following passage with its alliterations and other forms of poetic repetition:

   > Our route began with a series of wiggles and whorls in New England, then meandered south, up and down, east and west; dipped deep into *ce qu'on appelle* Dixieland, avoided Florida because the Farlows were there, veered west, zigzagged through corn belts and cotton belts . . . crossed and recrossed the Rockies, straggled through southern deserts where we wintered; reached the Pacific, turned north through the pale lilac fluff of flowering shrubs along forest roads; almost reached the Canadian border; and proceeded east, across good lands and bad lands, back to agriculture on a grand scale, avoiding, despite little Lo's strident remonstrations, little Lo's birthplace, in a corn, coal and hog producing area; and finally returned to the fold of the East, petering out in the college town of Beardsley. (LO: 154)

8. My notion of hyperactivity is derived from Slavoj Žižek, who juxtaposes the Lacanian *passage à l'acte* with a flight into 'activity' and away from the real (1993: 45).
9. On the duplicitous gesture inherent in apostrophe, see Barbara Johnson (1987).
10. As Elisabeth Bronfen notes:

    > By having his infatuated poet explicitly designate her death as the condition for a reading of his text, her actual death completes his figural killing . . . The movement of signifiers is from literary death (Carmen's) to its parodic disruption, to a metaphor where the girl stands for his dead love, to its literalisation by virtue of a reference to an anticipated real death. (1992: 372)

11. Both the idea and formulation are taken from Barbara Freedman's psychoanalytic and deconstructive reading of *A Midsummer Night's Dream*, which focuses on the conditions of representation, notably the ways in which it points to its distortion and repression of the disturbing experiences made in the woods (1991: 172).
12. See, for example, Alfred Appel (1991: lxiv).
13. This is to say that even though there may be a 'change' (Bordo 2000: 307), I would not go as far as Ellen Pifer and attribute actual 'moral growth' to Humbert Humbert (2003: 104). In fact, rather than a means of mitigation, the recourse to aesthetic immortality aggravates the violence of his failure. I will return to the question of the ethical and the aesthetic in the next part of this chapter.
14. Other texts engaging with these and related issues include, for example, *The Real Life of Sebastian Knight* and *Pale Fire*.
15. Similarly, Véra Nabokov emphasised 'the pathos of Lolita's utter loneliness' (quoted in Bordo 2000: 305).
16. In the postscript, Nabokov refers to the 'constant, comforting presence' that the novel means to him (LO: 315).
17. *Speak, Memory*, *Strong Opinions* and Brian Boyd's biography make ample reference to Nabokov's multilingual education and the later linguistic shifts

in his literary writing. As a child, Nabokov was educated by a 'bewildering sequence of English nurses and governesses' before Russian tutors took over (SM: 68). Nabokov repeatedly emphasises his early polylingual fluency: 'I was bilingual as a baby (Russian and English) and added French at five years of age' (SO: 5); 'I was an English child' (SO: 81). As early as 1935, Boyd mentions, he wrote 'something quite unexpected: a small autobiographical sketch in English of his early associations with England in early childhood', which later became chapter four in *Speak, Memory* (Boyd 1993a: 420). In 1936, he wrote another three or four chapters, 'his longest effort yet in original English composition' (Boyd 1993a: 429). In his introduction to the final version of *Speak, Memory*, Nabokov makes mention of another cornerstone of his autobiography, namely 'Mademoiselle O' (SM: 7), a piece about his governess from the French-speaking part of Switzerland, which he originally wrote in French in early 1936 (Boyd 1993a: 422). In the same year, Nabokov translated his novel *Otchayanie* into the English version *Despair*. In 1938, prior to his emigration to the United States, he wrote his first English novel *The Real Life of Sebastian Knight*. As an 'American writer' (SO: 26, 131), he wrote all his novels in English, closely supervised the translation of his Russian texts into English, and translated *Speak, Memory* and *Lolita* into Russian. His poetry would always remain Russian. In fact, Nabokov regarded his Russian poems written in the United States as 'my best' and 'incomparably better than those of my European period' (SO: 89, 190). See Elizabeth Klosty Beaujour (1995) on Nabokov's bilingualism and Neil Cornwell (2005) on his transition to English.

18. 'I am an American writer', Nabokov states in *Strong Opinions*, 'born in Russia and educated in England where I studied French literature, before spending fifteen years in Germany. I came to America in 1940 and decided to become an American citizen, and make America my home' (SO: 26).

Part II
Hitchcock's Wanderings

Chapter 4

Inhabiting Feminine *Suspicion*

In *Rebecca* (1940), the first film Hitchcock made after moving from his British home to Hollywood, exile and memory take centre stage. Hitchcock's narrative revolves around an unnamed, orphaned heroine (Joan Fontaine) who longs for a home to overcome her dislocation and who finds out after her marriage that she cannot inhabit Manderley as its mistress. The film opens, however, with a retrospective frame underscoring the condition of exile in which the heroine finds herself after the house has burnt down. Her voice-over and the camera retrace how, in her dream, she approaches Manderley along the meandering drive, leading from the closed gate up to the mansion. The sequence underlines that she can return to the once magnificent country estate only by virtue of her imagination. While the continuing presence of Rebecca, her dead predecessor and the first Mrs de Winter, never allowed her to feel at home, the destruction of the house makes it possible for her to take possession of Manderley through the 'supernatural powers' of her dream work.

The heroine's revisitation of Manderley in her exile refers us back to the poetic re-creation of an 'imaginary homeland' in Nabokov's *Speak, Memory*. Indeed, similar to Nabokov's reconstruction of the family home, the fantasy work of Hitchcock's heroine enables her, at least momentarily, to reverse the state of things. When she reaches Manderley on her imaginary nocturnal journey, it seems to have returned to its former condition – 'time could not mar the perfect symmetry of these walls', her voice tells us. Just like Nabokov's 'stereoscopic dreamland', the scene is 'enthralled by the moon, fancy's rear-vision mirror' (SM: 78). 'Moonlight', she notes, 'can play odd tricks upon the fancy' and, indeed, for a brief moment, light seems to come from within the windows. A moment later, a cloud destroys the illusion, but despite its ruinous state, her dream temporarily restores the home to its past integrity. By undoing loss, her nocturnal visit invokes a retrospective wish fulfilment also at stake in Nabokov's autobiography. A similar parallel can also be seen in an early scene which underlines the power of nostalgic memory. In a particularly happy moment before her marriage, the heroine formulates an idea that is evocative of the way in which Nabokov and his mother proleptically commit their home to nostalgia. 'You know', she says during one of her outings with her future husband, Maxim de Winter (Laurence Olivier), who, haunted by his past, would rather forget than remember, 'I wish it could be an invention that bottled up memories like perfume that never faded, never got stale, that whenever I wanted I could uncork the bottle and live the memory all over again.' The 'bottled-up' memories of Hitchcock's heroine promise control over a past that has been safely stored. Immune to loss, they allow the individual to revisit the past at will, similar to Nabokov's nostalgic re-creation of his Russian childhood.

Hitchcock's narrative frame and Nabokov's autobiographical text both present classic narratives of exile, which seek to overcome homelessness through the powers of fantasy. Following the heroine's description of the ruined manor house as 'a desolate shell', we can also say that, as a preserved but inaccessible crypt, Manderley resembles Vyra, the family home, which Elena Nabokov and her son's text encrypt so as not to 'swallow' its irrevocable loss. As nostalgic sites, these lost homes invite the staging of an empowering game of '*fort-da*', but they simultaneously keep haunting their former inhabitants with the uncanny knowledge that a stable protective home is impossible. Not only does the nostalgic possession of the home hinge on the absence and relinquishment of the actual place. Hitchcock's *mise-en-scène* also invokes the stereoscopic spectrality of Nabokov's 'passportless spy' (SM: 78) by dissolving the heroine's position and suggesting that she may be possessed and revisited by a spirit of the past. It is not just that the film never offers any representations of her life in exile, but her disembodied voice may, in fact, have merged with Rebecca's spirit. Her phantasmatic possession of Manderley requires that contrary to the desire for a home she entertained as an orphan, she must give up any distinct location and identity. Even as her nostalgic dream enables her to 'go back' to Manderley, her revisitation suggests that her homelessness is greater than ever before.

The nostalgic scenarios of Hitchcock's *Rebecca* and Nabokov's *Speak, Memory* will serve as a foil for my reading of Hitchcock's *Suspicion* (1941). After his first Hollywood film, Hitchcock works in two other genres – the espionage thriller in *Foreign Correspondent* (1940) and romantic comedy in *Mr and Mrs. Smith* (1941) – before he returns to the mode of his first Gothic melodrama. Like *Rebecca*,

Suspicion is set in Britain, and Joan Fontaine plays the heroine again.[1] Even though she had never lived in Britain, Fontaine appears to have been cast because of her 'English' star image. Hitchcock was particularly intrigued by 'her potential for restrained acting' (Hitchcock in Truffaut 1985: 140). With their female lead and their settings, both *Rebecca* and *Suspicion* re-create England within the codes of Hollywood, and both films deal with a fundamental uncanniness of the home. In so doing, they resonate with Hitchcock's recent move to a new cultural context and a different mode of film production, in which he arrived as a stranger. My chief concern here is neither the analogy between the two film narratives nor Hitchcock's initial homelessness in the Hollywood studio system.[2] Rather, I want to argue that *Suspicion* departs from the nostalgia of *Speak, Memory* and the narrative frame in *Rebecca* so as to emphasise a scenario of deliberate self-dislocation, which presents itself as paradigmatic for Hitchcock's aesthetics. *Rebecca* circles around the desire to overcome homelessness even while this wishful fantasy is undermined by the uncanny spirit of the first Mrs de Winter. Ever after the heroine first sees Manderley on a picture postcard, the magnificent English home forms the pivot of her family romance, and it also remains the object of her nostalgic desire once it is lost. *Suspicion*, by contrast, takes a suffocating home as its point of departure. It is precisely to escape from her parental home that Lina McLaidlaw resorts to a fantasy scenario that both revolves around and brings about dislocation.

While the orphaned heroine in *Rebecca* lacks a home, a family and a name, the second Hitchcock heroine played by Fontaine is 'too much at home'. Not only is she clearly named, but her family name 'McLaidlaw' is reminiscent of the 'law laid down'. Furthermore, Lina appears to be firmly emplaced in the gentrified social symbolic network of her family and community. Coming from a 'good family', she is, according to another figure's description, 'a very carefully brought-up young lady'. As a docile daughter, she seems to subject herself to the symbolic order, represented primarily by her father. Decorated with a whole array of rank insignia, General McLaidlaw stands not just for the family's social prestige but also for the symbolic law. Yet, at the very beginning of the film, she accidentally encounters and almost immediately falls for John Aysgarth (Cary Grant), a stranger who appears to come from nowhere and thus emerges as a foreign body within her imaginary domain. At once charmed and menaced by his roguish energy, she follows a desire and fantasy which eventually separate her from the family home. In contrast to the classic family romance, which shields individuals from the fissures of the family home, Lina's romance exposes her to danger. After her hasty marriage to Aysgarth, which takes place secretly and against her father's will, she moves into her extravagant new house only to find out that she has married a potential murderer.

Although *Suspicion* is set 'among the rural gentry of pre-war England' (Miller 1983: 1157–8), its scenario does not convey any nostalgia for a safe and sheltered past, but instead maps a trajectory of radical dislocation. Made two years into the Second World War, Hitchcock's second 'English' Hollywood film runs counter to the classic narratives of exile traced by both *Rebecca* and Nabokov's *Speak, Memory*. Rather than re-creating an idealised home within the nostalgic framework of the family romance, Hitchcock has his mentally migrating heroine translate her discontent with the overly familiar into what I want to call a scenario of 'home paranoia'. As already argued in the introduction, this type of home narrative delineates a line of flight, an escape from a home plagued by psychic malaise. Imagination, in this case, is set in motion not by the loss and/or absence of the home, but by a domestic discontent which figures as a cipher for the impossibility of residing in a stable home. On the one hand, the subject's wandering – whether geographical or purely mental – offers a liberating escape, which can be read together with the necessary Oedipal separation from the parents. On the other hand, like any other home fantasy, scenarios of home paranoia signal that something is out of place, that the subject is dislodged first and foremost in his or her fantasy work.

Hitchcock's heroine can be seen to enact Freud's dictum that the subject is 'not even master in its own house' (1963: 285). To be more precise, her figuration of exile is related to the foreign body inherent in the subject's psychic apparatus, the alterity Freud posits as a result of the psychic split between consciousness and the unconscious. The paranoia by which she is 'flooded' is indicative of this split. Not only does she suspect that her husband may be a murderer, but the criminal violence at stake in her scenario appears to be her own wish-fulfilling fantasy. As a result, the uncanny not only comes to inhabit the concrete home, which Hitchcock almost invariably imagines as a site of crime and anxiety, but also a form of fantasy which is unsettling in its traumatic enactment. In contrast to the protective gesture of Nabokov's imaginary of the home, the fantasies of Hitchcock's heroine signal a fundamental homelessness, namely the idea that as a psychic stranger to herself, she can never fully be at home.

More specifically, Lina's psychic exilism registers as a traumatic confrontation with sexual difference. Aysgarth figures as a symptom of both. He is not only the sexual other, but his otherness, which is at once threatening and fascinating, refers to the real alterity at the core of her psychic apparatus. On the one hand, *Suspicion* configures sexual difference as a murder scenario, thus staging the subject's psychic split in terms of an extreme vulnerability, which potentially annihilates the self. On the other hand, the film provides a paradigmatic example of Hitchcock's appropriation of the Oedipal trajectory. By developing along the lines of the psychoanalytical process, the heroine's self-doubt and detection move towards an acknowledgement of her own psychic otherness – the prerequisite, according to Freud, of mature subjectivity.

Hitchcock's heroine, I shall argue in my reading, enacts a traumatic confrontation not only with sexual but also with cultural difference. She is not displaced in a geopolitical sense, nor is her fate directly related to any historical event of the time. Nevertheless the film reverberates with the historio-cultural situation of Hitchcock's chosen emigration, that is his self-willed confrontation with foreign cultural codes in a period of massive geopolitical displacement. Without pressing a strict analogy between cinematic scenario and historical referentiality, one could invoke Stephen Greenblatt's notion of 'social energies' (1988) to speak of a circulation of historio-cultural concerns and images which *Suspicion* taps into. In other words, Hitchcock develops his cinematic scenario of dislocation at a particularly telling moment, even though it may not be possible to determine the exact extent of this exchange.

By presenting three almost contemporaneous female-focalised narratives in which both the home and the self turn uncanny, *Rebecca*, *Suspicion* and *Shadow of a Doubt* signal an important moment in Hitchcock's development of the psychothriller. The genre became the hallmark of his aesthetics not only by building on the narrative control of the proverbial master of suspense but also by drawing on a psychic 'other scene'. As both Tania Modleski (1988) and Elisabeth Bronfen (2004a) point out, Hitchcock's making of *Rebecca* can be read as a paradoxical confrontation with otherness – because of the 'feminine' genre of Daphne du Maurier's novel and because of the codes of the Hollywood production system, which meant that Hitchcock was required by the producer David O. Selznick to tone down his puns and faithfully follow the 'feminine' spirit of the text. Otherness is thus not only negotiated by the various states and stages of the heroine's exilism, but it also comes to be incorporated into Hitchcock's aesthetic language.

Suspicion develops an aesthetics of dislocation in a similar way. In analogy to the narrative of Lina McLaidlaw's eventual assimilation of the other and her own otherness, the film plays through an ambivalent absorption of alterity in its aesthetic language. Notably in the ways in which he stages the heroine's fantasy scenario and her unsettling confrontation with cultural, sexual and psychic otherness, Hitchcock develops an aesthetics that is crucial to his psychothrillers. Similar to the heroine's absorption into the vortex of her troubling fantasy, the film's aesthetics collapses its distance from her focalisation. If Nabokov's exilism is propelled by the cryptophoric secret of the home's loss and absence, Hitchcock's aesthetics appears to fuse with a troubling overproximity.

So as to trace the figurations of exile in *Suspicion*, my reading will again focus on three areas, namely the psychic homelessness foregrounded by Lina's fantasy scenarios, the murderous secret of her family narrative and, finally, the dislocation enacted by the film's aesthetic language. In so doing, I want to highlight the stakes of Lina's mental wandering. What do her traumatic fantasies bring to the fore? What are the status and the consequences of the underlying fantasy work? And what does it mean for fantasy to veer towards vulnerability and mortality? Hitchcock once characterised his work by saying 'I deal in *fantasy*' (Hitchcock in Gottlieb 1997: 313) – a statement that could also be made about Nabokov's poetics. Yet in contrast to the nostalgic imagination inspiring Nabokov's re-creation of 'imaginary homelands', fantasy plays an altogether different role for Hitchcock and his psychothrillers, in which he aims at 'creating nightmares' for his audience (Hitchcock in Gottlieb 1997: 313). Indeed, while Hitchcock's and Nabokov's thematic and aesthetic concerns emerge in situations of cultural displacement, they are diametrically opposed in their exilic imaginary. In my readings of *Speak, Memory* and *Lolita*, I have emphasised the multiply ruptured ground from which Nabokov's texts are written as well as the protective gestures which they invoke so as to screen the real ruptures he has survived. Hitchcock was never violently displaced and traces figurations of exile which do not occlude the real as an 'absent cause', but actually seek out the radically unfamiliar in the supposedly familiar – be it the subject's psychic apparatus, the home or, as in *North by Northwest*, the nation. In this way, his oeuvre is not pitted against any violent rupture, but instead maps trajectories which wilfully embrace the unsettling effects of fantasy.

Traumatic Fantasy

Hitchcock opens *Suspicion* with a visual double joke: a black screen and a train in a tunnel. After the title card 'England – 1936', the screen goes completely dark, and only after we hear Cary Grant apologise for bumping into someone's leg as the train was 'going through a tunnel' does it light up to show how he settles into the train compartment occupied by the Fontaine figure. Hitchcock's beginning deftly points at his own cinematic medium. It emphasises that his films produce and project fantasies, but also that there is something in them that remains unknowable as they emerge against the backdrop of darkness and enter the light of day. The other part of Hitchcock's pun, the train going through a tunnel, also refers to his cinematic work. In retrospect, the scene in the train compartment reminds us of the numerous chance encounters, erotic affairs and derailments that either take place or begin on Hitchcock's trains. In *The Lady Vanishes* (1938), the train is the site of romance, dreaming and mysterious disappearing. In *Strangers on a Train* (1951), an accidental encounter leads to the proposal of a perfect 'crisscross' murder scenario. Yet, as the next chapter will demonstrate in greater detail, Hitchcock's trajectory of railway travel culminates in its most ironic treatment in the final scene of *North by Northwest* (1959), where he refigures the sexual intercourse of the romantic couple as a phallic train entering a 'love tunnel'.

Taking our cue from Hitchcock's double pun, we might say that it is the erotically resonant collision with the stranger that provokes Lina McLaidlaw's fantasy. Indeed, the 'accident' on the train works as a catalyst of her scenario of dislocation, which will prove to be traumatic in its enactment. At the same time, the film already introduces its heroine as an over-imaginative subject so as to suggest that something is 'out of place' from the very beginning. The scene on the train depicts her as a spinsterish figure of prim and rigid restraint. She is reading a child psychology book by a Henrietta Wright. Yet, while the author's name puns on 'right' and thus seems to encode her as an objective reader, the psychology book also indicates the inward mental direction of her reading. Moreover, her glasses suggest that her perception is all but reliable. Not only is she literally not able to see when she does not wear them, her impaired vision also implies that while watching, she may well see things as she wishes to see them.[3] In this particular scene, the optical aid functions as a dividing screen. As the reflection of the quickly passing landscape streams down her glasses (Miller 1983: 1144), they visually partition her off from the outside world, thus allowing her to withdraw to the imaginary inwardness of her psychic journey, in the course of which she will be radically derailed and dislodged. While the spectacles characterise her as a figure who embarks on a trajectory of reading, analysis and detection, they also underline the phantasmatic character of her mental activity.

Hitchcock's *mise-en-scène* of the first scene at her parental home further underscores Lina McLaidlaw's proclivity for daydreaming and links it to the centrality which the home occupies in her fantasy work. After an establishing shot of the ancient Tudor-style house, we are shown a grand interior, where opulent furnishings evoke the theatrical setting of a stage. Apparently again reading, or daydreaming, at the window, Lina occupies the very centre of the camera's frame, while the huge window and its grid structure not only serve as the backdrop of this interior tableau, but also as a screen which indicates that, severed from the exterior world, Lina is completely absorbed by her imagination. It appears as though the pattern of the window panes surrounding her figure are to signal that all the cinematic frames to follow are framed, focalised – or even projected – by her fantasy. By opening the film with the two scenes on the train and the home, Hitchcock emphasises that Lina's daydreaming circles around questions of the subject's (dis)location. To be more precise, her fantasy work plays through various facets of her being 'too much at home' as it reflects her imaginary investment in the family home, on the one hand, and the exilic effects of her mental migrations, on the other. While her psychic wandering opens a flight from the over-close presence of the actual home, it also points to a fundamental dislocation of the subject. It is this precarious knowledge of psychic homelessness which Lina's fantasy scenario sets against the overproximity of the family home.

By embedding Lina in the grid of the window panes, the scene in the sitting room not only places her at the very centre of the frame, and thus implicitly of her fantasy scenario, it also suggests that she is caught up in her parental home. In contrast to Manderley, which remains haunted by the spirit of Rebecca's 'maternal' overpresence, Lina's domestic space is dominated by the authority of the paternal law. Similar to the grid-structure of the window panes, the interior design of the McLaidlaw family home underscores that as a daughter, Lina is firmly embedded in a family genealogy in which, together with pedigree and property, the family law is handed down in the Name of the Father. Not only do the antique furnishings evoke associations of a long and stable family lineage (the two chairs which Lina will be given as marriage presents are 'museum pieces' to be passed along a line of descendants). Lina's favourite room, the library, is entirely dominated by the stern expression and authority of General McLaidlaw's portrait, which will come to 'haunt' her not only as the only material object she will inherit after her father's death but also as the representation of the symbolic law as such.

While her fondness for the library and the paternal portrait confirms her docile allegiance to the symbolic bond of the family, her fantasy work pursues a counter-trajectory. As if picking up on Freud's suggestion that the subject's daydreaming gives expression to a wish to correct a dissatisfactory situation (1959a: 146), her mental wandering takes its departure from a domestic discontent. She is plagued not by the absence

Inhabiting Feminine Suspicion 135

but the overpresence of the familiar. It is the overproximity of the home which in her case gives rise to a psychic malaise and a desire to liberate herself from her parents. Fantasy thus becomes the means of turning herself into a vagrant 'exilic' subject in spite or precisely because of her firm emplacement. In contrast to nostalgic imagination, which in *Speak, Memory* and in the frame of *Rebecca* allows a return home despite the loss of the actual place, the scenario of 'home paranoia' mapped in *Suspicion* opens a line of flight. But this is not all. In addition, her particular type of fantasy scenario also exposes the subject to a disturbing knowledge about the home which it inhabits both in a concrete and a psychic sense. The mental wandering of Hitchcock's heroine follows a twofold trajectory. It not only allows her to escape from the parental home but simultaneously enacts a fundamental psychic alienation.

Nourished by her romantic fantasies revolving around the stranger Aysgarth, Lina's mental migrations lead her to literally run away from the home of her parents. Yet, after getting married in a hasty, secret and 'illicit' ceremony, her home paranoia moves with her to her new home. After their honeymoon, which is telescoped into a quick succession of various destinations and tags glued to a suitcase, Hitchcock's heroine realises that while Aysgarth may have liberated her from the suffocating presence of her parental home, she does not know him at all; she has married a complete stranger. She is surprised to learn that, having 'been broke all my life', he does not have any money to pay for their elegant house. When she realises that he is a gambler and embezzler, she suspects that he may be withholding further secrets from her. More specifically, after the sudden death of her father, her core fantasy scenario comes to centre on the suspicion that Aysgarth may be plotting to kill his friend and business partner Beaky Thwaite. Beaky dies under suspicious circumstances, and she thinks that she herself might be the next victim. While she has been cut off from her inheritance, her husband might profit from her insurance money. If her new home thus turns uncanny, it is as a result of the intellectual uncertainty created not only by her doubt but also by her fantasy which continues to dislocate her.

Rather than introducing Aysgarth as an independent character, Hitchcock introduces him as the embodiment or symptom of Lina's fantasy and desire. His alleged criminalistic energy gives body to her own roguishness, which emerges in her Oedipal striving to separate herself from the authority of her parents and thus attain independence as a sovereign individual.[4] Already in the first scene on the train, she starts absorbing his transgressive mobility into her fantasy work. At first, Lina is irritated by the stranger's quasi-erotic intrusion and aggression which violate her propriety. Having accidentally bumped into her leg, he reaches – with no less erotic *double entendre* – into her purse and takes a stamp to pay for his first-class ticket. Yet, while initially the jokes and puns are on restrained and prim-looking Lina, the focalisation of the film quickly shifts. As the hung-over traveller begins to doze off, Hitchcock's heroine comes across a picture in a newspaper society column in which she recognises her fellow passenger standing next to an extravagantly dressed woman at a horse race. The ironical entry of the soundtrack at this very moment signals the onrush of her excitement and the fact that her daydreaming is now beginning to revolve around the rakish stranger. In a later scene, the image will be doubled by a glossy portrait photograph of Aysgarth she finds in a magazine. By structuring the heroine's fantasy scenario, the pictures have a function similar to the postcard of the Manderley estate in *Rebecca* – only here the photographic representations do not trigger a wishful fantasy to take up residence in an idealised absent home. Instead they nourish her desire for Aysgarth as a rebellious figure who will allow her to escape from the home she inhabits.

While the heroine in *Rebecca* is a homeless wanderer who lacks any clear position in the social order and fantasises that the aristocratic house she has seen on the postcard could provide her with a place of habitation and belonging, Lina is intrigued by the intruding stranger for opposite reasons. She falls in love with him precisely because, in contrast to herself, he appears to come from nowhere. He represents a 'foreign body', a subversive figure of mobility and transgression, whom she can play as a wild card in her own displacement from the symbolic domain of the parental home. In fact, it is to underline her desire as a disobedient daughter that Lina's daydreaming is visually linked with the two photographic representations. Her fantasy scenario feeds on the stranger's pictures as a visual counterpart to the paternal portrait in the library. In so doing, her fantasy work articulates an antagonism haunting the home – she would not be producing her fantasy scenario circling around the stranger if she were fully at home. In much the same way, her mental migrations follow a desire for the radically unfamiliar which, under the auspices of her new home, is configured as a scenario of both suspicion and murder.

With the suspicion harboured by its heroine that her husband may be plotting to kill her, *Suspicion* forms part of a group of films which Mary Ann Doane calls 'the paranoid woman's film' of the 1940s (1987: 123). The cinematic genre begins with *Rebecca* and includes, for example, George Cukor's *Gaslight* (1944) and Fritz Lang's *Secret Beyond the Door* (1948). Typical of the cycle of films is the quest of detection on which the heroine embarks after her wedding in order to unravel a threatening secret that troubles her new home. Her husband appears invariably mysterious, even sinister. Yet the enigma she seeks to solve is usually also linked to her own desire, which led to her hasty marriage to the stranger in the first place. Following this classic pattern, Lina's investigation, too, seems to focus on her husband's potential crime, but it is primarily her own fantasy scenario that comes to be highlighted in the process. Like *Rebecca*, where the heroine tries to solve the mystery of her husband's desire only to awake to a sober mature subjectivity, and like *Shadow of a Doubt* (1943), where young Charlie not only comes to suspect her uncle of murder but also increasingly doubts her close attachment to him, *Suspicion* foregrounds an interest in feminine subjectivity. Hitchcock's later psychothrillers tend to focus on a particular psychic disturbance of a male protagonist, for example, voyeurism in *Rear Window* (1954), necrophilia in *Vertigo* (1958), and matricide in *Psycho* (1960). The three domestic melodramas of his early American period, however, are all closely aligned with the focalisation of a female heroine, and even while she seeks to detect the secret of her male counterpart, Hitchcock's narrative interest focuses on her recognition and acknowledgement that subjectivity is subtended by a fundamental psychic homelessness.

In *Suspicion*, Hitchcock's emphasis on the female subject is particularly pronounced. In contrast to the psychological suspense novel *Before the Fact* by Francis Iles, alias Anthony Berkeley Cox, where the woman knowingly lets herself be poisoned, Hitchcock's cinematic refiguration never allows us to find out whether or not the husband plans to murder his wife. In the interviews with Truffaut, Hitchcock mentions that while he would have preferred Aysgarth to turn out a murderer as in the novel, he had to alter the ending because Hollywood conventions would not allow him to present Cary Grant as a murderer (Truffaut 1985: 142). By remaining ambiguous beyond the ending, *Suspicion* not only leaves open the question of Aysgarth's intentions, but also shifts its primary focus to Lina's fantasy life. As spectators, we inevitably ask ourselves why she should so readily fall for a stranger and put herself into harm's way and, even more to the point, why she should indulge in her fantasy that she may be his murder victim. At stake, in other words, are the implications of her psychic reality, and not so much the question whether her suspicion that her husband may plan to kill her is correct or wrong. Because the film is predominantly focalised by its heroine, the cinematic image, as Mary Ann Doane points out, comes to be permeated by her affects and speculations (1987: 149). As a result, it is virtually impossible to determine whether, in the end, Lina's paranoia is invalidated, as many critics assume.[5] In the final scene at the coast, just after he has either tried to push her out of the car or protected her from falling over the cliff, Aysgarth explains that unable to resolve his financial difficulties, he has been planning to commit suicide. Lina desperately wants to believe him and start all over again. However, the resolution remains ambiguous. Cinematically the couple's conversation and reunion in the car cannot entirely dispel the uncertainty that has been created and sustained by Lina's ambivalent focalisation of Aysgarth throughout the film. Back in the car, he puts his arm around her shoulder. Yet his embrace may also express a threat. Instead of moving towards a 'happy end', the couple may well drive directly back to an uncanny home.

What I want to foreground in my reading are the implications of Hitchcock's *mise-en-scène* which allows us to read the heroine's suspicion that she may have married a murderer as a wish-fulfilling fantasy. What is at stake in Lina's scenario, and what are the consequences of her fantasy work? Her suspicions may seem to circle around her husband, but her doubt and detection, I want to argue, develop along the lines of a 'self-analysis' which confronts her with her fundamental psychic dislocation as a subject. In *Strangers to Ourselves*, Julia Kristeva reads the stranger as a figure that confronts subjects with their own psychic strangeness. In *Suspicion*, Aysgarth does not only give body to Lina's fantasy, but he also objectifies a gap in knowledge that pertains to her own psychic apparatus. She desires not so much the man but the roguishness he stands in for. Or put differently, rather than simply being in pursuit of romance, her fantasy scenario circles around her own subjectivity and its transgressive relation towards symbolic authority. It is to this effect that her fantasy work increasingly absorbs his subversive and possibly criminal energy. While she is irritated by his intrusion on the train, she is later, at the Hunt Ball, delighted by his gatecrashing as an uninvited guest. Her suspicions after her marriage may initially work as a cover which shields her from the transgressive impulses of her fantasy work and instead projects them onto him. Yet, ultimately, her sceptical self-analysis confronts her with the self-annihilating forces of her fantasy.

Both in her murderous fantasy scenario and sceptical detection, Hitchcock's heroine of suspicions comes too close to a clandestine psychic knowledge, which in the interest of self-protection should remain hidden and secret. Her desire for a potential murderer implies both the possibility of self-annihilation and a covert enjoyment of this fantasy. In so doing, the fatal desire and violent self-expenditure at stake in her scenario point to a psychic otherness – and thus to a structure which can be described as both uncanny and 'extimate'. Picking up on

Freud's concept of the uncanny, Lacan coins the term 'extimacy' to further problematise the complex relation between the exterior and the intimate, and to highlight that the other appears as a strange element even as it is at the very core of the subject's psychic apparatus.[6] Indeed, the foreign body of knowledge that emerges in Lina's fantasy scenario is most intimate. Paradoxically enough, she engages in her psychic and mental migrations only to find herself in a situation in which she comes again too close to the 'home', though in a psychic sense. This is what I mean with my claim that Lina is a heroine marked by the overproximity of the home. She is not only too much at home in the genealogy of her family. In her attempt to separate herself from her parents, she finds herself in close proximity to a psychic secret, namely her desire to appropriate the criminal energy she attributes to Aysgarth. After their marriage, her desire to expose herself to his criminality and alleged otherness comes to flood the perception of her new home. While reading the hidden and latent so that all manifest surfaces and appearances acquire double meaning, her suspicion may initially focus on her husband and home. But in the traumatic enactment of her fantasy scenario, she confronts a troubling knowledge pertaining to her own desire.

The vanishing point of Lina's scenario is the gap marked by this psychic knowledge but also quite literally death. While in Nabokov's *Speak, Memory*, imagination is directed ambivalently towards and against the void of traumatic losses, *Suspicion* maps a form of fantasy which embraces mortality in a proleptic gesture. Not only do the fantasy scenarios scripted by Lina expose her to a radical vulnerability, but she can also be seen to literally enact their fatal implications over her own body. Unlike her friend, the crime fiction writer Isobel Sedbusk, who devises murder mysteries as a safe intellectual game, Lina maintains no distance from her scenario of potential danger and crime. At the beginning of the film, it seems as though she aspires to attain authority both over her fantasy work and Aysgarth. This is suggested by the centrality she occupies in Hitchcock's cinematic frame while daydreaming in the parental sitting room, or the claim she makes in one of her early conversations that she would be able to tame Aysgarth just like her horse. Yet any control she may have over her fantasy scenario is rendered ambivalent by her fantasised demise.

The self-shattering impact of her embodied fantasy work becomes particularly palpable when she exhausts herself with her mental migrations to such a degree as to lose consciousness. One of the scenes in question occurs after the dinner party at Isobel's, where Aysgarth starts a discussion of her latest novel and various murder methods. Having returned home, Lina stands in front of a bookcase, which evokes the murder trial described in the book Aysgarth has secretly borrowed from Isobel but which may also quite literally store the scenarios she has been 'feeding' to her husband by buying him crime fiction novels. Still standing next to the bookcase, she then faints as though overcome by an attack of jouissance, which could be read as a symptom either of her extreme fear or the intense and overpowering pleasure she takes in her murderous fantasies. After waking up, she finds her husband and her friend at her bedside. They tell her that she was given a sleeping pill by Isobel's brother, a forensic doctor who usually 'doesn't attend living people' but conducts autopsies (an occupation on which Hitchcock's camera already puns earlier by zooming in on the chicken the doctor is 'dissecting' on his dinner plate). For a brief moment in the film's *mise-en-scène*, Lina looks indeed as if she were laid out in a coffin. The two women continue their conversation about death by poison, and when Isobel assures Lina that this would provide a 'most pleasant death', a pendulum clock is superimposed onto Lina's body. Whether the condensation of these images refers to a fearful realisation that her time is indeed up, or whether it operates as a morbidly wishful anticipation of her death, in either case, it represents a powerful *memento mori* pointing to the vulnerability performed by Lina's imagination.

The paradoxical relation enacted between fantasy and vulnerability is crucial to Lina's scenario but also to Hitchcock's genre of the psychothriller. The emphasis of her imaginary on fragility reverses not only the apotropaic gesture of *Speak, Memory*, in which nostalgic imagination is pitted against a traumatic void. It also runs counter to the invincible feeling of invulnerability which subjects usually experience in the dangerous adventures conjured up in their daydreams. As Freud writes, the message of 'His Majesty the Ego, the hero . . . of every daydream' is 'nothing can happen to *me*!' (1959a: 149–50). In contrast, the fantasies produced by Hitchcock's heroine embrace a trajectory of self-expenditure. In so doing, they are radically opposed to any protective fiction and coincide instead with a type of fantasy that undermines all stability and may be described as the pivot of the Hitchcock psychothriller. On the one hand, Lina's proclivity to suspect everything and thus cultivate epistemological uncertainty and doubt could be read as a totalising narrative, namely as a trajectory that only her death will prove. The reading I want to privilege, however, is one of irresolvable uncertainty. Although her stakes are not money as in the case of her gambling husband but the question of life and death, Lina herself has turned into a gambler. By buying into contingency, she subscribes to an intellectual uncertainty and ambivalence which are to be sustained at all cost. While Nabokov's writing is haunted by the uncertainty of the subject's existence in exile, Hitchcock's heroine puts her own existence into question by producing radical doubt. Or put differently, her suspicion points to a fundamental instability of all symbolic bonds and all psychic knowledge as she exposes herself to her potential murder.[7]

In contrast to Nabokov's protagonists who narrate their own stories, Hitchcock's heroine does not have a narrative voice. Instead the cinematic narrative offers visual tropes which merge with her ambivalent focalisation and suggest that the home is inundated by her fears and affects in a transfer between the domestic and psychic uncanny. The most conspicuous instance of this cinematic imagery is the spider's web shadow that is projected by the skylight window onto the grand entrance hall as well as the winding staircase leading upstairs to the couple's bedroom. Refiguring the 'straight' window grid of the parental home with a difference, the curved shadow may also be seen to pick up on the dizzying circles of the waltz at the Hunt Ball, which immediately precedes the scene of the marriage proposal. As the dominant visual pattern, which returns time and again, the concentric circles of the web increasingly suggest that there is no escape from the uncanny domestic scenario Lina has moved into. On the one hand, she appears to be a prey caught in a death trap, while on the other, she also figures as the spider producing and/or organising the ensnaring web of her dangerous scenario. It remains uncertain who plays whom, who hunts whom and, finally, who preys on whom under the home's spider's web shadows as Hitchcock's visual narrative maintains the ambivalence of both her focalisation and position. In the best-known scene of the film, Aysgarth brings a glass of milk to Lina, who in turn suspects that it may be poisoned. The sequence is introduced by an anxious look of hers as she is waiting in the couple's first-floor bedroom, which is situated by the shadows at the very centre of the house. The high-angle shot that follows may look omniscient. Yet given Lina's framing look and her central position in both the web and the house, it is equally possible to see Hitchcock's camera in alignment with her perspective and fantasy space, although from her position in the bed she cannot actually see Aysgarth carrying the milk glass with its suspicious white glow through the nocturnal semi-darkness of the hallway and up the winding staircase overshadowed by the spider's web. The sequence not only plays on the question whether or not the milk is poisoned but also on the ambivalent centrality which Lina occupies as both the producer and victim of her scenario. Is she courting death, as perhaps suggested by the modulation of the sombre out-of tune waltz into a romantic melody once Aysgarth has said goodnight to her? Or is she afraid of the implications of her scenario as in the preceding scene, in which he locks the door of the house and, as if to further entrap a reluctant Lina in her dangerous snare, takes her hand so as to lead her up the staircase?

By maintaining ambivalence and uncertainty, Hitchcock refers to a moment in the fantasy of his heroine that remains fundamentally unknowable. In tracing her mental wandering, he suggests that her fantasy work is connected to an inaccessible 'other scene'. Significantly enough, her imagination does not protect her from but repeatedly propels her towards the knowledge of this scene. As if to gesture towards the specific organisation of her fatal fantasy, the film keeps returning to a number of visual patterns. Reminiscent of the unfathomable 'navel' which, according to Freud, haunts every dream and its interpretation as 'its point of contact with the unknown' (1958: 111), Lina's recurrent visual tropes point to a momentous void both in her psychic apparatus and in their medial representation. The visual patterns featured in close alignment with her perspective evoke vertigo. They include not only the spider's web shadow, dominating her new home, but also the whirlpool which she sees when she looks down from the cliff from which, she suspects, her husband may have pushed his friend Beaky; the rocky abyss next to the coastal road in the final scene when she expects him to kick her out of the speeding car; and the revolving sky as she is giving herself up to the self-expenditure of this fatal scenario.[8] These 'navels' do not carry any semantic meaning, but they point to the overpowering impact of her fantasy. Even though she visits the coastal cliff in order to prevent her husband from murdering his friend, her rescue scenario is overdetermined because she occupies several positions at once. On a manifest level, she may fashion herself as a rescuer (and thus unwittingly take the position of her husband, who indeed saved Beaky at this very site), but by approaching the abyss, she also positions herself as the potential murder victim. At the same time, her murderous scenario suggests that she may, in fact, desire to be witness to the crime, or even act as a murderer herself. It is to gesture towards this disturbing knowledge that the camera presents us with frames engulfed by the whirls of breaking waves.

The same ambivalent overdetermination is also invoked in what is the most complex layering of images in the film. The example illustrates that in her fantasy and doubt, Hitchcock's heroine propels herself towards a traumatic void. While Aysgarth and his friend Beaky are discussing whether they should have a final look at the coastal estate before calling off their plan for a joint development, Beaky and Lina combine scrabble blocks to form not only 'doubtful' but also 'murder', which Beaky suggests could be expanded to 'murderer'. While he makes his suggestion in naïve innocence, Lina associates her word formation both with a horrible suspicion and a compelling condensation of her overdetermined fantasy. With Lina as its focaliser, the camera cuts from a close-up of her recently formed 'murder' to her husband's profile before it then wanders to a photographic representation of the cliff he is holding in his hand. Then a close-up of her horror-stricken face is superimposed by the picture of the cliff, which turns a few degrees as if to absorb Lina into a vortex. Thus marked as her mind screen, the photographic image is all of a sudden animated by her mental theatre, in which a figure pushes another over the edge of the cliff. Lina's terrified face is superimposed by Beaky's vertical fall, but instead of his impact, Hitchcock presents us with a frame entirely flooded by breaking waves before cutting back to Lina at the very moment of her fainting. In so doing, he signals a break in the cinematic representation, which could be read in reference to Lina's overpowering fusion with a traumatic void. By pointing to this engulfing overproximity, the sequence underscores that in separating herself from the symbolic family bond and embracing Aysgarth as the 'foreign body' of her desire, the heroine comes too close to the jouissance that underpins her fantasy work.

Like *Rebecca* and *Shadow of a Doubt*, the two other female paranoia films Hitchcock made soon after his emigration from Britain to the United States, *Suspicion* foregrounds the psychic 'exile' of its heroine. The film's close alignment with its female protagonist underlines a form of fantasy work that is crucial to Hitchcock's development of the psychothriller. Talking about the 'nightmares' he creates in his suspense work, Hitchcock points out: 'I *play* with an audience. I make them gasp and surprise them and shock them' (Hitchcock in Gottlieb 1997: 313). In characterising his aesthetic project, Hitchcock alludes to the fact that his fame as the master of suspense is built on the deft and often ironic ways in which he orchestrates the advance and, above all, the delay of narrative information so as to involve the spectator in 'emotional disturbances which, for convenience, we call "thrills"' (Hitchcock in Gottlieb 1997: 109). His suspense is defined by the anxious ambivalence it triggers; in watching his scenarios, we both fear and desire to see their potentially disturbing outcome.[9] The female paranoia films of his early American career create radical ambivalence – and thus the crucial effect of his suspense – by condensing his narrative idiom with the way in which his heroines veer towards a knowledge of psychic dislocation.

As in *Rebecca* and *Shadow of a Doubt*, Hitchcock's visual narrative in *Suspicion* is closely aligned with the point of view of the heroine. Although the film begins by calling into question the reliability of her perception, Lina's doubt represents the primary motor of the suspense which we experience and enjoy as spectators. Even more importantly, by foregrounding her ambivalent focalisation, Hitchcock refers us both to the excess and the radical uncertainty marked by a psychic knowledge which cannot be resolved because it haunts the subject in a fundamental way. In Hitchcock's later psychothrillers, the subject's psychic dislocation tends to be translated into more specific psychic disturbances, some of which are even diagnosed as explicit 'case studies' within the diegesis, for example, in *Spellbound*, *Psycho* and *Marnie*, where psychoanalyst figures are shown to recite their interpretations of the 'cases' presented. Yet important psychic elements of Hitchcock's hallmark genre are introduced by *Rebecca*, *Suspicion* and *Shadow of a Doubt*, all of which emphasise a fundamental homelessness.[10] With Lina's suspicion, Hitchcock highlights a radical fragility in any sense of belonging, in symbolic bonds and subjectivity as such.[11] In so doing, the female paranoia film stages an anxiety, but also a knowledge about the vulnerable and tenuous status of existence. Likewise its generic anxiety functions as a means of pointing to the fissures that haunt the heroine's family bond and marriage relation. Both featuring and triggering affects of fear and anxiety as well as an overabundance of mental activity, the Hitchcock psychothriller unrelentingly propels itself towards a psychic 'other scene'. It gestures towards a knowledge that eludes consciousness but partly returns via fantasy. This dislocation is played through not only on the level of diegesis. By aligning itself with the heroine's perspective, Hitchcock's cinematic language, too, keeps emphasising that, at a fundamental level, subjects can never fully be at home – even if they seem to be as thoroughly embedded in the symbolic law of the family as Lina is when we encounter her at the beginning of her psychic journey.

Family Murder

As Hitchcock famously declared, television 'brought murder back into the home where it belongs' (Hitchcock in Gottlieb 1997: 58). With the legendary television mystery series he presented in the 1950s, Hitchcock himself literally broadcast murder to the family home. Yet even more significant are the consistent connections made in his cinematic work between murder, violence and the home. In *Shadow of a Doubt*, murder is not only brought to the domestic scene by the uncle who visits his niece and her family after having committed a series of murders. It always already inhabits the family home as the father and the neighbour, two figures who both seem overly timid and kind, constantly discuss and joke about how to commit the perfect murder. In Hitchcock's films, murder frequently occurs in the family, whether between different generations as in Norman Bates's matricide in *Psycho* or in the heterosexual couple as in Thorvald's killing and disposal of his wife in *Rear Window*. Clearly, both of these scenarios undermine the safety and protection promised by the classic family romance. At the same time, the family is threatened not by loss and contingency as in Nabokov's *Speak, Memory*, but by the danger and violence lurking within, which are literally 'home-made' and intrinsic to the Hitchcock home.

In this part of the chapter, I wish to explore the ways in which *Suspicion* casts both the home of the parents and the couple as sites of violent antagonism. The family may be introduced as a strong bond, but the home transforms into a scene of crime as the heroine separates herself from her parents and moves to her new house together with her husband. This shift from one place to the other is played out as a particularly violent version of the Oedipal drama and the subject's detachment from the parents. By emphasising the individual's separation from the parental home, Hitchcock's scenario of home paranoia radically differs from Nabokov's return to the happiness of his childhood, which recuperates ties, violently severed by history, in the form of the imaginary family reunion invoked by his text. While *Speak, Memory* revisits the plenitude and protection of the classic family romance in an attempt to undo concrete loss, the protective wholeness and integrity of the home are here radically called into question. Instead the family home is troubled by an inherent antagonism.

At the same time, the Oedipal separation from the family and the consequent confrontation with the sexual other can also be mapped onto the context of cultural emigration in which Hitchcock makes his female paranoia films. While the frame of *Rebecca* features a nostalgic re-creation of Manderley, *Suspicion* represents a liberation from the home as a site of origin and belonging. Hitchcock works again with his 'English' actress Joan Fontaine, but the *mise-en-scène* of the film can be seen to stage a separation from the British codes associated with the heroine's family origins. As I have been arguing, Lina's fantasy scenario revolves around Aysgarth as the symptom of her wish to liberate herself from her parental home. In this trajectory, her embrace of the foreign body of her 'alien' desire comes to be configured as a disturbing confrontation and fusion with the male, standing for both sexual and cultural difference. As a result, the home of the couple turns into a scene of antagonism, which intertwines sexual and cultural issues. The film sustains a fundamental uncertainty and alienation and yet, by following the Oedipal trajectory, it moves towards the acknowledgement that subjectivity is predicated on a fundamental homelessness and, in so doing, also performs an assimilation of psychic, sexual and cultural otherness. In what follows, I shall trace how Hitchcock's family narrative enacts both a violent version of Oedipal parturition and an ambivalent embrace of cultural and sexual difference.

The Oedipal pattern has often been regarded as the predominant trajectory of all Hollywood narrative.[12] It typically centres on the process in which a male individual separates himself from a maternal presence so as to identify himself with the paternal function and take up a symbolic position of his own. While following an Oedipal journey, both *Suspicion* and *Rebecca* trace the particular difficulties that trouble a feminine version of the pattern. In her seminal reading of *Rebecca*, Tania Modleski emphasises how the heroine needs to disengage herself from a figure of maternal overpresence in order to attach herself to a male love object (Modleski 1982a: 38–41). The 'spirit' of Rebecca, however, persists beyond the destruction of Manderley, not least of all by taking possession of the heroine's imagination in her nocturnal revisitation. The unnamed protagonist, therefore, faces the aporia that unlike the masculine individual, she cannot project the mother as sufficiently different to establish a stable identity of her own.

Like its predecessor, *Suspicion* also foregrounds a feminine trajectory, but configures the Oedipal passage in a different way. Lina separates herself from the parental home and takes up a position of her own – but she does so only to be haunted by the violent implications of this move. In order to disengage herself from the family home and its heritage, she violates the family bond, represented primarily by the father. She rejects his idea that the 'old maid' she will grow into is 'a respectful institution' and chooses instead to follow a trajectory of transgression. Or one might also say that instead of attaching herself to a father surrogate, she falls in love with a roguish figure who subverts paternal authority. Her embrace of Asygarth cuts her from her position within the family genealogy. Not only will her new alliance eventually deprive her of her inheritance. Already the proposal scene in the family library takes place literally opposite – and in opposition to – the representation of the paternal law, the forbidding portrait of General McLaidlaw. Knowing that she is contradicting her father's wishes, Lina accepts Aysgarth's proposal and laughs with him when the portrait almost comes down as her fiancé jokingly prods it to elicit a response from this stern representative of the law. The unlawfulness of their union is reinforced by the fact their wedding takes place as a secret and thus unauthorised act. The *mise-en-scène* further adds to the alleged illegality of the clandestine ceremony, by showing it only indirectly, framed by a window and obscured by pouring rain.

Significantly enough, pitted against the express wishes of the father figure, the marriage vows are imagined as a violent crime against the family. After Lina's wedding, the McLaidlaws vanish almost completely from the visual narrative, as if they had actually been annihilated by their daughter's rebellious disobedience. In her new home, the two antique chairs, which she is given as a wedding present, stand in as metonymical reminders of the parents but also as empty placeholders pointing to their disappearance. Moreover, the chairs and their destiny condense the 'criminal' core of her bond with Aysgarth, who sells the two heirlooms in an attempt to back up his dubious financial speculations and dealings. Lina buys them back, but the 'family crime' is reinforced when her separation from the family home comes to be re-encoded as an act of patricide. In the scene in which Aysgarth transmits the message of her father's death, the sombre focalisation permeating her new home turns particularly prominent. After detecting that he has embezzled money from his employer, Captain Melbeck, Lina writes a farewell note, but while she is writing, her upper body is partitioned by an ominous shadow line. Just after she has torn the letter, Aysgarth enters the twilit bedroom as an opaque presence dressed in a dark suit, and asks whether she already knows. The fact that she first misunderstands him and confuses her husband's crime with her father's demise suggests that in her imaginary, the paternal passing away is connected with and perhaps even caused by her marital alliance and its violation of her father's wishes. As Mark Crispin Miller points out (1983: 1171), Aysgarth appears with the death notice as if directly summoned by her tearing up of the farewell note that would have cancelled her bond as well as undone its violation of the paternal law. Cinematically this causality is reinforced by the connection established between the two figures and their huge matrimonial bed, which by filling the background space between them, stands in visual correspondence with the telegram and its fatal message.

After her father's death, Lina's only inheritance apart from her existing allowance, the paternal portrait, transforms into a palpable sign and persistent reminder that her marital bond is illicit. What may appear as an insignificant detail in the film's *mise-en-scène* actually suggests that the daughter keeps deviating from the father's law. In all the car journeys undertaken by Lina, the direction of motion, oddly enough, always remains the same. The narrative logic implies different routes. At one point, she drives from her new home to the cliff, where her husband and his friend planned a development. Later, after the reading of her father's will at the parental home, the couple are seen driving homeward. In the final scene, they find themselves on the way from their house to her parental home. Yet in all these different journeys, the car keeps moving in the same direction with the coast always on the right of the camera's frame. This negation of realistic space can be taken to point to Lina's trajectory of home paranoia. The destinations of her journeys tend to be elided – we hardly ever see the car arrive anywhere – so that a seemingly infinite itinerary is evoked as the car, unmoored in its movement, appears to drift on an axis of endless, and aimless, deferral. Moreover, her journeys emphasise that Lina seeks to escape from a father who, as Dolar puts it in his reading of the film, 'is not quite dead' (1992b: 147). Delineating her line of flight, the car literally moves away from the respective site at which the paternal portrait is stored. Ironically, this pattern sets in after the general's death, when presumably his symbolic representation becomes all the more powerful – and Lina's sense of guilt more haunting once she has realised the 'murderous' consequences of her Oedipal separation.

Like her detachment from her parents and its criminal configuration, her new home, too, comes to be flooded by a murderous imaginary. Only now murder is not associated with a gesture of separation, but refers to the violent ways in which the heroine imagines the cultural and sexual fusion implicit in her new home. What renders Aysgarth attractive for Lina – his radical roguishness – turns out to be threatening in its proximity. Drawing on Cary Grant's international star image, *Suspicion* suggests that Aysgarth represents a foreign, perhaps even an American element in a British setting. Even though General McLaidlaw once refers to him as someone's son who has turned out wild, he appears to come from 'nowhere' (his first name Johnny evokes the American slang expression 'Johnny-come-lately', meaning 'upstart', 'newcomer', '*nouveau riche*'). Reminiscent of Archie Leach, the working-class Englishman, who reinvented himself as the sophisticated Hollywood star Cary Grant, Aysgarth also believes in dreams of social mobility. 'I had always the notion', he explains to Lina when she finds out that he has no money of his own, 'that the secret of success is to start at the top . . . The way to make money is to think in a big way.' His mobile attitude clearly runs counter to the investment of Lina's family in pedigree and heritage. By introducing an economy of betting and speculating, of borrowing and misappropriating, Aysgarth subverts an order in which possessions are kept in the family and handed down from one generation to the next. While Lina is thrilled to receive 'father's most precious possessions', the two chairs which 'we had . . . in the family before I was born', and anticipates that 'these will be our first heirlooms to be handed down to our children and then their children', he sells them and, in so doing, expects to capitalise on more mobile forms of circulation and exchange.

This reading of cultural difference in *Suspicion* is further supported by the film's not entirely intended invocation of Hollywood codes in its *mise-en-scène*. In making his 'second English picture' in Hollywood, Hitchcock encountered 'the same problem we had in *Rebecca*, an English setting laid in America'. Yet while the director was 'displeased' with the glossy photography and grand settings (Hitchcock in Truffaut 1985: 141, 143), the cultural mixture of the film's production allows us to read Lina's move as a displacement to an American cultural frame, particularly with respect to the extravagant house Aysgarth sets up for her. Firmly embedded in the ancient English home of her parents, the heroine desires the alien as she falls in love with Aysgarth. The foreign connotations evoked by his intrusion enable her to displace herself from the stifling confines of her parental home. Yet, while his cultural difference is initially liberating, it reverts into a threat once his foreign mobility can no longer be absorbed. Early on in their relationship, Lina seeks to contain his difference, as if the child psychology book she is reading in the first scene on the train referred not only to her as a daughter having to separate herself from her parents but also to him as a figure who needs guidance.[13] However, she gradually comes to realise that his difference eludes her control, a knowledge that becomes irrefutable with the break signalled by her father's death. With the demise of her father, the family figure *par excellence*, the unfamiliar and foreign comes to be imagined as a murderous threat; Lina's romance turns into a traumatic fusion with Aysgarth's inassimilable difference. Her focalisation reconfigures the marital home as a site of potential murder, in which the self, cut off from its origin, is annihilated by its desire for the other.

Hitchcock's love scenes, Jean-François Truffaut once observed, are filmed like murder scenes, while his murder scenes look like love scenes (Truffaut 1985: 345). Indeed, the way in which *Suspicion* features the merging with the sexual other both as a desire and a threat is no exception in Hitchcock's oeuvre. On the contrary, Hitchcock frequently troubles the romantic couple – and thus the prominent preoccupation and purpose of a large part of Hollywood cinema. Not only do some of its formations require a dramatic amount of force – in the romantic suspense thriller *The 39 Steps*, for instance, the protagonist Richard Hannay (Robert Donat) and Pamela (Madeleine Carroll) are handcuffed and thus literally chained together before they can conceive of themselves as a couple. More often than not, the Oedipal trajectory and its creation of a heterosexual relationship are also accompanied by the fear of being annihilated by the sexual other. *Rear Window*, for example, introduces Lisa Freemont (Grace Kelly) through the dark shadow cast by the appearance of her figure over Jeff (James Stewart), who has been sleeping in his wheelchair. The next shot, focalised by him, shows her approaching face in extreme close-up towering above him before the camera cuts to a kiss which, due to its stretched-out slow motion, has a hallucinatory, disturbing effect. The position of Jeff, who is incapacitated by his broken leg, but above all Hitchcock's *mise-en-scène*, in which Lisa fills the cinematic frames and the space of the flat in a claustrophobic manner, suggest an underlying threat of engulfment and a loss of self.[14]

In keeping with this configuration, *Suspicion*, too, draws on sexual difference as a source of anxiety. Although it may be inspired by a proclivity for doubt and suspicion, Lina's murder scenario indeed articulates a real antagonism. Not only is there a decidedly aggressive edge to Aysgarth. Her scenario is nourished by actual violence. This becomes most conspicuous in the scene in which we see the two figures in windy weather on top of a hill. The extreme distance and the ambiguous *mise-en-scène* of this moment make it difficult to gauge what is actually happening. However, as the camera moves nearer, the two appear to be engaged in violent fighting. In medium close-up, the scene turns into an ambiguous erotic struggle – Aysgarth, still tightly holding her wrists, mocks her assumption that he was going to kiss her in their fight, while his later advance in the same scene is staved off by Lina as she demonstratively snaps her purse shut (which, of course, harks back to the earlier erotic pun on the train when he reaches into her purse). The scene's ambiguity is explicitly thematised when he connects sexuality to murder by provocatively asking her: 'What did you think I was trying to do – kill you? Nothing less than murder could justify such violent defence – look at you!'[15] Occurring early on in the film and their acquaintance, the scene prefigures an erotic relation charged by an ambivalent mixture of erotic attraction and sinister menace. Just after the scene on the hill, Lina overhears her father say that she is not the 'marrying sort' so as to immediately turn around and assertively kiss Aysgarth. However, her romantic desire for independence is inextricably linked with the idea that the self may be violently annihilated by the sexual other.

The suspicion that 'the institution of marriage is haunted by murder' (Doane 1987: 123), which is typically entertained by the heroine in the female paranoia film, can be read both historically and structurally. In contrast to other contemporaneous Hitchcock films which make explicit reference to the geopolitical conflicts of the time, *Suspicion* is usually taken to be completely removed from the historical situation.[16] But in an oblique way the film mobilises a resonant image repertoire: the antagonism of the heterosexual couple opens what could be called a 'home front' and prefigures the uncertainty of wartime gender relations. In so doing, it articulates concerns crucial to the Gothic romance and the female paranoia film as genres that held a particular appeal for female audiences in the war and postwar period. As noted by Diane Waldman, relationships during this time were characterised by marriages, separation and reunion as well as the temporary entrance of women into the workforce (1983: 30–1). In female Gothic and paranoia films, these conditions transform into the central question of the heroine's position in the context of shifting gender relations. While film noir typically focuses on the anxieties of a male protagonist, often a war veteran, who confronts urban America as a war zone of a lethal gender trouble, the genres of the female Gothic and paranoia film foreground the anxiety of the heroine that she will be punished for her empowerment. Like other Gothic and female paranoia films, *Suspicion* negotiates issues of (dis)empowerment in the field of vision. The perception of the heroine comes to be beset by paranoia and anxiety because, in investigating her home, she subverts the traditional gendering of vision as she seeks to become a subject, rather than an object, of the look.[17] At the same time, it is quite literally death that is anticipated by the heroine. Instead of being involved in the war, Aysgarth and Lina are implicated in their gender trouble at home, which, she fears, may turn into a fatal 'war' scene.

Over and beyond the historical shift of gender relations, Hitchcock points to a fundamental structural deadlock. Lina's scenario enacts the notion that the heterosexual relation is haunted by an antagonism reminiscent of Jacques Lacan's 'il ne va pas entre l'homme et la femme'.[18] On the one hand, her murderous scenario may offer a sense of coherence as it objectifies a domestic malaise inhabiting the couple's home. In other words, it may provide her with a minimal phantasmatic support needed to put up with everyday life as well as to remain in her home trouble. Yet, on the other hand, her scenario insists on the irresolvable antagonism highlighted by Lacan and typically haunting the Hitchcock couple. *Rear Window*, for instance, features several couples all of whom mirror each other in their antagonistic relation: the newly-weds spending almost all their time behind closed blinds until they begin to quarrel; the Thorvald couple, whose flat turns into a scene of murder; and not least of all the relation between Jeff and Lina, which is 'blocked' because he refuses to curtail his adventurous travelling by setting up home with her.

Elaborating on Lacan's dictum, Joan Copjec argues that sexual difference stands for real difference *par excellence* and as such resists complete integration into the symbolic. In contrast to ethnic and cultural differences, which are inscribed discursively, Copjec further suggests, sexual difference posits a real antagonism: 'a stumbling block of sense' which is 'produced by the internal limit, the failure of signification' (1994: 204). This means that the subject inhabits the symbolic 'as limit' – or put differently, it is as a result of sexual difference that the subject is partly unknowable, a stranger to itself (1994: 209). Drawing on this notion of the subject as split by sexual difference, one could therefore say that Lina moves via cultural difference into the register of sexual difference – or rather antagonism – where she comes up against her own psychic otherness. Her scenario of self-dislocation turns out to be disturbing indeed; its trajectory undercuts any stable subject position together with the certainty of any imaginary and symbolic bonds.

Performing not only a violent act of separation, Lina's Oedipal trajectory plays out the no less disturbing vicissitudes of assimilation. In contrast to nostalgic home narratives, her scenario of home paranoia is neither marked by a longing for a past home nor by the exile's stereoscopic perspective. Her move appears to be irrevocable, and so is her embrace of a traumatic fusion with the both sexual and cultural other. Hitchcock's narrative and *mise-en-scène* veer towards an antagonism that is irresolvable. This becomes particularly conspicuous at the end of the film, when Aysgarth insists on driving Lina to her mother's after she has exhausted herself with her murderous fantasy scenario. During the car ride, the camera cuts between the precipice of the cliff, her husband's profile and the car's speedometer, which registers a dramatic increase in speed. When Aysgarth all of a sudden decides to take a short-cut closer to the cliff, the door on her side opens and Aysgarth reaches over, either to close the door or push her over the fatal abyss. Her triple exclamation of his first name 'Johnny' culminates in a prolonged shriek and frenzied shaking of her head, underlined by her focalisation of the turning sky, as the car comes to a standstill. Following this dramatic moment of self-expenditure, Aysgarth offers his explanation, already mentioned above, that he had plans to commit suicide. Although his tight grip on her wrists, reminiscent of the scene of their violent encounter on the hill, may be more powerful cinematically than his verbal assertion, Lina desperately wants to believe and persuade him of a romantic renewal of their relationship. Back in the car, the couple take an unprepared U-turn in the direction of their home, which may return them directly to a scene of antagonistic struggle.

This is precisely the point: Hitchcock's heroine may indeed return to a site of home and gender trouble. Yet she appears to do so after having acknowledged that the antagonisms haunting the subject and the heterosexual couple cannot be resolved. As Stanley Cavell argues in his cross-mapping of Shakespearean tragedy and the philosophical tradition of scepticism (1987), the subject and the other both posit a limit to knowledge. Shakespeare's protagonists, notably Hamlet and Othello, cover up this epistemological problem as they resort to scenarios of sceptical doubt for which they seek to find certainty. By contrast, the trajectory of Hitchcock's heroine plays out the impossibility of resolving uncertainty and ambivalence. Having enacted this knowledge over her own body, Lina may now also embrace it as the turning point of the couple's disturbing fusion. By driving home with Aysgarth, we may surmise, she no longer imagines him as a necessarily dangerous threat, nor does she reduce him to a reflection of her own psychic otherness. As Cavell might put it, she has come to acknowledge him in his separateness. Assimilation in this case means not to completely absorb the other but to sustain the ambivalence of its irreducible difference even though its defies secure knowledge.

Aesthetics of Overproximity

Hitchcock's treatment of dislocation and assimilation in *Suspicion* marks a critical moment. He not only makes *Suspicion* and *Rebecca*, his two films about displaced British heroines, shortly after his transatlantic move, but as in *Shadow of a Doubt* – his film about a typical all-American family home, in which young Charlie grows up to discover the fissures haunting the seemingly idyllic town community, her family, and her own desire – he explores psychic homelessness in a pronounced attunement with feminine subjectivity. In his British career, Hitchcock already widely worked in the genre of the domestic melodrama and the spy thriller. Yet it is after arriving in Hollywood that he shapes important elements of the psychothriller, the genre which has secured his permanent place in the cinematic archive. In this final part of the chapter, I argue that Hitchcock creates his language of dislocation in analogy with the figuration of exile played through by his heroine. Dislocation and assimilation also permeate the aesthetics of the film, which thus re-enacts issues negotiated at the diegetic level. While Nabokov's writing encrypts a traumatic gap or void, Hitchcock's cinematic language veers towards real otherness as an 'absent cause' and, in so doing, stages a split in the film's enactment of dislocation and assimilation. Similar to the heroine and her fantasy scenario, Hitchcock's aesthetic position oscillates between control and self-expenditure. In its alignment with the heroine's perspective, the film's aesthetics does not simply posit the feminine as the other but actually 'inhabits' its otherness. So as to prepare the ground for my argument, I want to propose another textual reference, namely the 'feminine aesthetics' that underpins Gustave Flaubert's writing of his romantic novel *Madame Bovary*.

Though perhaps unconventional and eclectic, the comparison, I believe, is pertinent because Flaubert's comments on his aesthetic project highlight a dialectic of empowerment and expenditure that resembles Hitchcock's cinematic language. Significantly enough, this shared ambivalence draws on the close relation of the texts to their respective heroines, Lina McLaidlaw and Emma Bovary. Flaubert's well-known desire was to write 'a book about nothing, a book with no external attachment, which would hold together by the internal strength of its style' (letter to Louise Colet, 16 January 1852; Flaubert 1997: 170).[19] Yet while he was obsessed with style and his proverbial quest for *le mot juste* in writing his novel, Flaubert also appears to have taken great pains to engender in himself dreams and fantasies supposedly common among romantically inclined young women such as his heroine Emma Bovary. In his correspondence with his beloved, the author Louise Colet, he writes: 'Over the last two days I have been trying to enter into the world of *young girls' dreams* and for this purpose I am sailing across the milky ocean of the literature that deals in castles and troubadours with little white-plumed velvet hats' (3 March 1852; Flaubert 1997: 175). A few days later he has indeed immersed himself in 'young girls' dreams up to his ears' (20 March 1852; Flaubert 1980: 56). Instead of simply foregrounding authorial control, Flaubert appears to actually live or stage his text by embodying the fantasies of young women. Later he emphasises the great psychological effort he has invested in his text, which he wishes to be of anatomical precision. However, the pains involved in the composition of the text are to be effaced by formal perfection so as to go unnoticed by the reader.[20] To this effect, the perfect aesthetic control of the writing paradoxically requires that its author dissolve himself and become indiscernible: 'like God in the universe, present everywhere and visible nowhere' (9 December 1852; Flaubert 1980: 204). It is through 'la Bovary' that Flaubert constitutes himself as a novelist of great renown, while paradoxically enough the novel's style of writing seeks to efface almost any authorial trace.[21]

What is at stake in Flaubert's comments on the writing process is a paradoxical ambivalence between embodiment and disembodiment, empowerment and disempowerment. On the one hand, Flaubert enacts 'young girls' dreams' in order to fashion his text, and indeed his incorporation of supposedly feminine fantasies results in his empowering textual mastery. On the other hand, his 'feminine' role-play implies not only a depersonalised form of control but also signals a disintegration of the self. 'Why is it', Flaubert asks himself, 'that while crying I have often looked at myself in the mirror so as to see myself? – This disposition to rise above myself is perhaps the source of all virtue. It leads you away from your personality, far from keeping you there' (8 May 1852; Flaubert 1980: 84–5). Flaubert dissolves – into tears – but while doing so, he observes himself in a manner which reminds us of the self-consciously controlled performance of an actress, or of his protagonist Emma and the mirror image in which she (mis)recognises herself as the heroine of a romantic love story (Flaubert 1992: 131). Indeed, there are remarkable analogies between Flaubert's self-fashioning and Emma Bovary's wandering of the mind. Caught up in the boredom with her socially undistinguished position (Emma belongs neither to the sophisticated society she encounters at the ball nor to the peasants who are relegated to a spectator position outside the windows), she fashions her desire to be elsewhere as a desire to imitate and, in fact, author the kind of romances she knows as a result of her prolific reading. Already as a young man, Flaubert oscillates in a comparable manner between 'immense, insatiable desires' and 'an atrocious boredom and incessant yawns' (14 November 1840; quoted in Heath 1992: 92). Like the heroine he will create several years later, he feels displaced and romantically yearns for a different existence: 'I think . . . I was born elsewhere, for I've always had what seemed like memories or intuitions of perfumed shores and blue seas'(14 November 1840; quoted in Heath 1992: 92).

One could go as far as to say that in a fashion similar to his heroine, who appears to be at home nowhere because she dislocates herself as a reader and 'author' of romantic texts, Flaubert displaces himself by privileging the writing of letters (in the sense of both *billets doux* and fictional literature) over direct intercourse with his lover Louise Colet. Rather than travelling to Paris and meeting Colet in the stirring metropolis, he prefers to wander in his imaginary realm, as if his textual production had to be protected from her physical presence. Instead of their relationship, it is his work and imagination that he experiences as overtly erotic.[22] The intellectual 'ejaculation' of sentences in his writing allows him to distance himself from Colet's feminine otherness.[23] Consuming erotic energy, writing is encoded as both exhausting and purifying. Close to their final break-up, he declares in a triumphant tone: 'I am no longer a sexed being, thank God!' (letter to Louise Colet, 12 April 1854; Flaubert 1980: 548). Later he describes writing as a potent sexual act in his advice to his friend, the novelist Ernest Feydeau, to 'save your eternally erect penis for style, fuck your inkwell' (undated letter written at the beginning of 1859; quoted in Kaplan 1991: 203). However, what sounds like a self-assured macho statement is undermined by the duplicity of writing. On the one hand, Flaubert describes the material medium of writing, as 'my natural element', while on the other hand this 'beautiful liquid' is also dangerously attractive and, in fact, threatens to engulf him: 'This sombre and dangerous fluid! How you can drown in it! How it attracts you!' (14 August 1853; Flaubert 1980: 395). Although writing and fantasy enable the author to distance himself from Colet, they are dialectically counteracted and flooded by an excessive self-expenditure arising from his somatic over-identification with a textual body.

Flaubert is so immersed in his writing that the boundaries between the fiction and the world become fluid to the point of being completely blurred. It is not the physical quality of Flaubert's self-expenditure alone that is remarkable, but also the fact that it duplicates the excessive textual performances which Emma Bovary literally enacts over her body as she seeks to imitate the romantic texts she has been reading. In a particularly palpable way, the corporeality of Flaubert's writing exceeds the textual boundary of his fiction when, composing the scene of Emma's protracted and painful agony, he actually somatises the symptoms of his dying heroine.

> When I was writing Madame Bovary's poisoning scene I had such a taste of arsenic in my mouth, I was so poisoned myself, that I had two bouts of indigestion one after the other, and they were quite real because I vomited up all of my dinner. (20 November 1866; Flaubert 1997: 316)

What interests me in the case of Flaubert, and what, I shall argue, suggests an analogy to Hitchcock's aesthetics is the ambivalent assimilation of a foreign body. Not surprisingly this body is semanticised as feminine, in line with the cultural codes according to which the feminine figures as the other *par excellence*. Posited by cultural discourses as inaccessible, 'femininity' eludes full assimilation; even if incorporated, it will retain an alien element which resists complete absorption. One could go as far as to say that, culturally, femininity occupies a position of extimacy in structural analogy to the inaccessibility of the unconscious.[24] At the same time, as suggested by a figure such as Emma Bovary, femininity tends to be culturally aligned with a representational overinvolvement, that is with an excessive proximity to images and texts.[25] Both these cultural strands are knotted together in Flaubert's migrations of the imaginary. His incorporation of a textual body of supposedly feminine fantasies is excessive – precisely in its 'feminine' overidentification – and, at the same time, it also remains highly ambivalent. On the one hand, Flaubert was 'most impressed when a local doctor suggested to him that he was a hysterical old woman' (Wall in Flaubert 1992: xvi).

On the other hand, he claims to have overcome the despised 'whitish fat' of femininity in himself and wishes to transform Louise Colet into 'a sublime hermaphrodite'.[26] In one of his letters to her, he articulates the sense that literature and culture have been feminised:

> Everything is now dissolving through a slackening, a humid element, through tears, chatter, through milk. Contemporary literature is steeped in menstruation. We all need to take iron to overcome the Gothic anaemia that Rousseau, Chateaubriand and Lamartine have transmitted to us. (15 January 1854; Flaubert 1980: 508–9)

Nevertheless he believes his enactment of feminine psychic sufferings to be so authentic that his novel 'will gently excite many a feminine wound. More than one woman will smile as she recognises herself in it. I will have known your pains . . . damp with pent-up melancholy' (1 September 1852; quoted in Heath 1992: 91). Writing *Madame Bovary*, Flaubert thus vacillates between an avowal of identification – famously claiming 'Madame Bovary – c'est moi!' – and the insistence on the novel's impersonality, that is its lack of communication with its author. What ultimately makes Flaubert's incorporation of a feminine foreign body so intriguing is the fact that while he desires a position of distancing control, he also immerses himself in its otherness, which results in authorial empowerment but also implies a loss of self.

I have taken this detour through Flaubert's aesthetic performances because a similar double gesture also appears to underpin Hitchcock's cinematic position. On the one hand, *Suspicion* picks up on aspects also at stake in *Rebecca*, notably the 'feminine' genre elements of Gothic melodrama, the focus on the heroine's fantasy life and her home, which Hitchcock felt compelled to mark as alien to his project: 'It's not a Hitchcock picture', he said about *Rebecca*, 'it's a novelette, really. The story is old-fashioned; there was a whole school of feminine literature at the period . . .' (Hitchcock in Truffaut 1985: 127).[27] On the other hand, *Suspicion* features a female protagonist who somatises her fantasy work over her body in a gesture that is reminiscent of Flaubert and his heroine Emma. Even more importantly, the film's cinematic language enacts an overproximity to Lina in an aesthetically analogous way. Going perhaps even further than the oscillation between sympathy and irony in Flaubert's novel and its use of free indirect discourse, the film indicates its aesthetic proximity by rendering Lina the main focaliser and thus immersing itself in her paranoia. Lina's ambivalent focalisation is so predominant that it 'floods' the film including its ending. If the opening scene on the train makes fun of her spinsterish and restrained appearance, there is less and less ironical distance as the film increasingly adopts her point of view.

As Mary Ann Doane notes, cinema does not have the same possibilities as the novel of distinguishing between various levels of narration and focalisation. Because the image is dominant, cinematic narration has a tendency to blur the boundary between subjectivity and objectivity. There is no clear dichotomy between subjective and objective shots. Point-of-view shots are hardly ever fully subjective and depend on the third-person mode of the unmarked image. At the same time, subjectivity can bleed into a seemingly objective narration (Doane 1987: 147–8). In her reading of *Suspicion*, Doane points to the consequences that this medial condition of cinematic representation has in the particular ways in which the film collapses 'the opposition between subjectivity and objectivity' (1987: 149). She emphasises not only that Aysgarth's verbal explanations at the end fail to reinstall an objective norm since they cannot counterbalance the image that has been supporting Lina's suspicion. She also underlines that Lina's paranoia exceeds the strictly subjective shots to infuse and permeate the *mise-en-scène* (1987: 149). While Doane's critique concerns the difficulty of localising feminine subjectivity in the visual modes of this and other female paranoia films, I should like to read this coalescence as an important aesthetic gesture.

Hitchcock's fusion with the heroine's perspective introduces a dialectic which, similar to Flaubert's writing, oscillates between aesthetic empowerment and overidentification. On the one hand, the appropriation of feminine focalisation functions as a lever of control, that is as proof of the film's power to incorporate and absorb a position of otherness. On the other hand, it also implies a collapse of distance. Since the development of the *auteur* theory by the French *Cahiers du Cinéma* group in the 1950s, Hitchcock's cinema has usually been viewed in terms of his aesthetic signatures which mark and distinguish his authorship despite the collaborative production mode of film.[28] Tania Modleski adds another angle to this when, in her book on Hitchcock and feminist theory, she points to a pivotal ambivalence and suggests that 'time and again in Hitchcock films, the strong fascination and identification with femininity revealed in them subverts the claims to mastery and authority . . . of the director himself' (1988: 3). By calling into question his authorial control, she locates moments allowing her to insert and affirm a feminine position in 'those parts which "know" more than their author' (1988: 119). This project is possible and, at the same time, important to her because Hitchcock's aesthetics is characterised by an ambivalence; it is, as she puts it, neither 'utterly misogynistic' nor 'largely sympathetic to women and their plight in patriarchy' (1988: 3). While following Modleski's ground-breaking work, I want to turn the argument in a somewhat different direction.

Suspicion, I claim, follows a feminine focalisation precisely to posit an incalculable overproximity. Modleski compellingly argues in her analysis of *Rebecca* that in his initial attempt to ironise and thus subvert the feminine spirit of Daphne du Maurier's novel, Hitchcock attempted to almost literally regurgitate its femininity by inserting into the original screenplay two scenes of vomiting on boats (1988: 43). Similar to the feminine elements of *Rebecca*, the paranoid focalisation in *Suspicion* suggests an incorporation of the feminine as a foreign body, which parallels Lina's assimilation of cultural and sexual difference at the diegetic level. At stake is thus a rhetorical ambivalence similar to the one staged by Flaubert, who tastes the arsenic taken by Emma and who has to vomit as if to suggest that his identification with the poisoned heroine might be toxic. As Modleski argues in connection with *Rebecca*, 'femininity . . . remains alien and disturbing, neither expelled nor "digested"' (1988: 43). While femininity marks an extimate position, Hitchcock's aesthetics, like Flaubert's, opts for assimilation, however ambivalent.

The flooding of the image with Lina's paranoia functions as an important rhetorical gesture. In the course of her mental migrations, Lina is engulfed by a psychic secret which, in the interest of protection, should be kept at bay. Similarly, the film comes too close to her perspective. This proximity underlines that in moving towards a dislocating otherness, Hitchcock's aesthetics in *Rebecca* and *Suspicion* is based on a figure of ambivalent assimilation, regardless of whether the material at stake involves the psychic and/or cultural other. Similar to Nabokov, who in his writing pays homage to the power of poetic imagination, Hitchcock can be said to place his focus on issues of fantasy. Yet, while Nabokov invokes a protective gesture, Hitchcock's scenarios of home paranoia map a type of imagination which is far from reassuring. As suggested by my reading of *Speak, Memory*, Nabokov celebrates an imaginary return to the family despite the loss and absence of the actual home. Put differently, his re-creation of an 'imaginary homeland' is nourished by the protective fiction that there is, in fact, a home one could inhabit if only displacement had never occurred. In contrast, Hitchcock's aesthetics stages an irrevocable dislocation, not only by virtue of a home which is almost invariably imagined as a source of anxiety and horror but also by a form of fantasy split in its enactment of wish fulfilment and anxiety. By zooming in on the troubling effects of fantasy and horror, Hitchcock foregrounds an alienation that troubles individuals not only in their concrete homes but also in their imagination. If Nabokov re-creates 'imaginary homelands' and, in so doing, preserves the possibility of belonging, Hitchcock is interested in 'creating nightmares' for his audiences. His film scenarios time and again dissolve the distance occupied especially, but not only, by the spectators. In so doing, his aesthetics insists that at a fundamental level, subjects cannot fully be at home precisely because of their fantasy work – even though their scenarios may revolve around the question of their home and belonging.

Although Hitchcock's visual narrative largely adopts and, in fact, privileges Lina's point of view, it remains haunted by an alien element. Something remains opaque, thus rendering its assimilation ambivalent. Yet, in contrast to Modleski, who would emphasise that femininity resiliently resists full integration and thus undermines the aesthetic control of the male director, I read this alienating moment as the crux of Hitchcock's aesthetics. In showing itself unable to fully absorb Lina's fantasy work and desire, the film points to an unknowable moment, which following Freud's vocabulary, I have been calling the 'navel' of fantasy. It is not only that in *Suspicion*, the subject's core fantasy circles around violence, crime and murder. At stake is also an inaccessible 'other scene'. What the heroine's fantasy work points to is a fundamental dislocation of subjectivity. It is precisely in immersing itself in her scenario of radical homelessness that the aesthetics of the film is exilic. Like the mental wandering of the heroine, Hitchcock's cinematic language keeps pointing to a moment in fantasy which is unfathomable and, at the same time, ineluctable because it poses an engulfing overproximity.

Notes

1. Although *Foreign Correspondent* culminates in a dramatic final scene on top of Westminster Cathedral, which Hitchcock had shot by a second unit in London during the Blitz, he considered *Suspicion* to be his second English Hollywood film: 'You might say *Suspicion* was the second English picture I made in Hollywood: the actors, the atmosphere, and the novel on which it's based were all British' (Hitchcock in Truffaut 1985: 141).
2. This analogy is explored by Elisabeth Bronfen's reading of *Rebecca* (2004a: 31–63).
3. In his reading of the film, Mladen Dolar puts emphasis on what he calls 'the drama of the gaze'. Similarly, I shall also suggest that the heroine functions as the predominant focaliser: 'we see only through Lina's eyes and we see nothing outside her horizon.' At the same time, Dolar underlines the phantasmatic character of her vision: 'Watching is her principal activity: she is there, inert and passive, marking every scene with her gaze full of worries, suspicions and fears. She is watching, but she does not see' (1992b: 143).
4. A comprehensive discussion of the rogue can be found in Jacques Derrida's book *Rogues* (2005). Rather than discussing individual roguishness in the context of the family, Derrida focuses on the roguish kernel that becomes apparent in the inseparability of and contradiction between modern democracy and sovereignty.

5. Diane Waldman, for example, argues that the film predominantly adopts Lina's point of view only to render it false by Aysgarth's explanation in the final scene:

> As in *Rebecca*, the unusual emphasis on the point of view of the heroine has been put to the service of the invalidation of feminine perception and interpretation, equating feminine subjectivity with some kind of false consciousness, as the male character 'corrects' the heroine's false impressions. (1983: 33)

Within Hitchcock criticism, *Suspicion* is often discussed with respect to its altered ending. Critics tend to find the change unsatisfactory because it shifts the weight from Aysgarth's criminality to Lina's paranoia, which is then often discredited as mere fantasy. However, not only do such readings have difficulty in situating the locus of supposed objectivity within a film characterised by its subjective focalisation, but they also presuppose a notion of fantasy which stands in opposition to 'reality'. Mark Crispin Miller, for example, goes as far as to argue that Lina stands in as a substitute for a cinema audience indulging in what he describes as escapist fantasies proffered by the so-called woman's film (1983: 1150–1). Instead I propose shifting attention to the psychic reality of Lina's scenario of home paranoia.

6. See Dylan Evans (1996: 58–9) for a short definition and Jacques-Alain Miller for an extensive elaboration of Lacan's concept of *extimité* (1988: 121–9).

7. I am referring here to Stanley Cavell's reading of the sceptical trajectory followed by the male protagonists in Shakespearean tragedy (1987). Using the feminine other as the stake of (impossible) knowledge, the sceptical scenarios of Hamlet and Othello are both totalising and fatal. By contrast, the doubt of Hitchcock's heroine not only pertains to herself but also sustains ambivalence.

8. *Vertigo* uses a similar pattern in an even more conspicuous way. The whirlpool harks back to the early scene in *Rebecca* in which Maxim de Winter contemplates suicide while standing on a cliff – and thus to a cinematic moment which Laurence Olivier was to quote several years later in his adaptation of *Hamlet* (1948), the drama of doubt and scepticism *par excellence*.

9. See Richard Allen's persuasive discussion of Hitchcockian suspense in *Hitchcock's Romantic Irony* (2007: 38–71).

10. In her reading of *Rebecca*, Elisabeth Bronfen emphasises Hitchcock's concession in the Truffaut interviews that

> making this film inspired him to enrich many of his later films with the psychological elements he found in Daphne du Maurier's novel. In retrospect one can surmise that it was exactly this encounter with a decidedly feminine novel that marked the turning point in his handling of the psychothriller genre . . . (2004a: 52)

11. In her study on hysteria, Elisabeth Bronfen argues that at the core of the message broadcast by the hysteric and her symptoms is the fragility of the symbolic and, 'perhaps above all, the vulnerability of the body, given its mutability and mortality' (1998: xiii).

12. See in particular Raymond Bellour (2001).
13. Asked by Aysgarth what she thinks of him in comparison to her horse, she assertively responds: 'If I ever got the bit between your teeth, I'd have no trouble handling you at all.' Later, when she discovers that he cannot pay for their home because he has no money of his own, she explains in a both endearing and patronising way: 'Johnny, I'm beginning to understand you. You're a baby!'
14. In *Phoenix Tapes #5 Bedroom* (1999), the video artists Christoph Girardet and Matthias Müller montage a sequence of kisses and embraces which highlights the underlying aggression of the couple in Hitchcock's oeuvre. For a selection of stills, see the catalogue *Notorious: Alfred Hitchcock and Contemporary Art*, edited by Kerry Brougher et al., accompanying the exhibition of artwork recycling Hitchcock's visual language at the Museum of Modern Art Oxford in 1999. Developing a typology of Hitchcock kisses, Sidney Gottlieb makes a similar argument (2002).
15. Mary Ann Doane also refers to the 'conjunction of sexuality and murder' in this scene (1987: 124).
16. Contemporaneous Hitchcock films that are explicitly political include *Foreign Correspondent* (1940), *Saboteur* (1942), *Lifeboat* (1944) as well as the propaganda films commissioned by the British Ministry of Information *Bon Voyage* and *Aventure Malgache* (both 1944). According to Joel W. Finler, *Suspicion* and *Mr and Mrs Smith*, a comedy which also circles around the home trouble of a couple, though in a much lighter tone, were 'totally removed from the current world situation' (1992: 50).
17. In her chapter 'Paranoia and the Specular', Mary Ann Doane suggests that the female paranoia film turns around a crisis in vision and feminine subjectivity, that is 'a dialectic between the heroine's active assumption of the position of the subject of the gaze and her intense fear of being subjected to the gaze' (Doane 1987: 123–54, 127). On the punishment of the woman who looks, see Linda Williams (1984). In her analysis of 'feminine perception' in Gothic films of the 1940s, Diane Waldman (1983) observes an interesting shift towards a validation of the heroine's vision in the later films. In *Suspicion*, the struggle on the hill turns not least of all around looks and visual control. Claiming that 'your hair is all wrong', Aysgarth manipulates Lina's hairstyle so as to then subject her to his critical look when she looks at herself in the mirror to reverse the change: 'You don't look very good like this. You look more like a monkey with a bit of mirror. What does your family call you – monkey-face?'
18. In *Encore*, his Seminar XX, Jacques Lacan discusses the notion 'that no relationship gets constituted between the sexes . . .' (1998: 66).
19. Whenever possible I quote from the selection of Flaubert's letters included in the English edition of his correspondence (Flaubert 1997). The translations from the far more comprehensive French edition are my own (Flaubert 1980).
20. 'This is first and foremost a work of criticism, or rather of anatomy. The reader (I hope) will not notice all the psychological work hidden beneath the form, but he will feel its effect' (2 January 1854; Flaubert 1980: 497).
21. 'As disorderly as I am in my other books, in this one, I try to be as buttoned-up and to follow a straight geometrical line. There will be no lyricism, no

reflections, the personality of the author will be absent' (31 January 1852; Flaubert 1980: 40).
22. 'I am *exhausted*. My head is pounding. Since two in the afternoon (apart from about 25 minutes when I was having supper) I have been writing *Bovary*. I've reached the Big Fuck, I'm right in the middle of it. We are in a sweat, and our heart is nearly in our mouth . . . I am like a man who has just come too much (if you will forgive the expression). I mean a sort of lassitude which is full of exhilaration' (letter to Louise Colet, 23 December 1853; Flaubert 1997: 232–3).
23. At one point Flaubert equates the process of writing with 'masturbating (my head) without interruption so as to ejaculate sentences' (28 October 1853; Flaubert 1980: 459).
24. A prime example of these cultural discourses is of course Freudian psychoanalysis, which centrally deals with feminine desire as enigma ('What does woman want?') and famously refers to femininity as a 'dark continent'. Joan Copjec points to the pivotal role which the inaccessibility of femininity plays within psychoanalysis when she points out that 'psychoanalysis can claim to found itself on the unconscious and on the desire of the woman, precisely because it so rigorously registers their inaccessibility' (1994: 123). For an in-depth analysis and discussion of the extimate position which femininity occupies within the psychoanalytical discourse, see Elisabeth Bronfen (2001).
25. This notion becomes particularly palpable in the discourses on and of hysteria, which, having no organic cause, somatises or embodies cultural images and is, therefore, often described as a malady of representation (see Bronfen 1998). With respect to cultural notions of cinematic spectatorship, Mary Ann Doane points out:

> There is a certain naiveté assigned to women in relation to systems of signification – a tendency to deny the processes of representation, to collapse the opposition between the sign (the image) and the real. To 'misplace' desire by attaching it too securely to a representation . . . The idea that the cinematic image functions as a lure . . . seems to apply even more insistently in the case of the female spectator who, in the popular imagination, repeatedly 'gives in' to its fascination.

As a result, 'femininity' positions itself *vis-à-vis* representation in 'proximity rather than distance', in 'passivity, overinvolvement and overidentification' (Doane 1987: 1–2).
26. Flaubert believes himself to have overcome the 'softness' of femininity contradicting virile force when he writes: 'At bottom, I am the man of fogs, and it is with patience and study that I have rid myself of all the whitish fat that engulfed my muscles' (26 July 1852; Flaubert 1980: 140). The ambivalence towards femininity is also evident in the following passage addressed to Colet shortly before their final separation:

> I have always tried (but it seems to me that I have failed) to transform you into a sublime hermaphrodite. I want you to be a man down to the belly (and below). You suffocate me and disturb me and damage yourself with the feminine element. – There are two principles in you (and often visible in one and the same action) . . . Re-examine your life, your inner adventures and the external events.

Even reread your works, and you will perceive that you have an enemy in you, one I do not recognise, who in spite of the most excellent qualities, the best perception and the most perfect conception, has rendered you or makes you appear as the very opposite of what is requisite. (12 April 1854; Flaubert 1980: 548–9)

27. Tania Modleski (1988) and Elisabeth Bronfen (2004b) both discuss how in the making of *Rebecca*, the 'feminine' material comes to stand in for an encounter with the other. Bronfen goes on to suggest that this constellation can be mapped onto the encounter the British director himself makes with the foreign Hollywood codes.
28. Particularly important contributions to this area have been made by William Rothman (1982), Slavoj Žižek (1992) and Tom Cohen (1994, 2005a, 2005b).

Chapter 5

Wandering and Assimilation in *North by Northwest*

At an early stage in the preparation of the screenplay for *North by Northwest* (1959), the screenwriter Ernest Lehman summarised his ambition in the following laconic statement: 'All I want to do', he said, 'is write the Hitchcock picture to end all Hitchcock pictures.' Asked by the director what such a film would entail, he replied: 'Something with wit, glamor, sophistication, suspense, many different colorful locals, a real movie movie' (Lehman 1999: vii). As if following Lehman's wish for a film that would sum up Hitchcock's previous work in a retrospective homage, the voyage undertaken by *North by Northwest* revisits many of the recurrent elements composing his universe. His self-citations include, among others, the mistaken identity of the protagonist, a series of iconic sites and national monuments as well as the *rite de passage* of the romantic couple in conjunction with an espionage plot.[1] Typical of Hitchcock's romantic spy thrillers is also the chase after a red herring or, in Hitchcock's coinage, a 'MacGuffin', which serves as a pretext structuring the quest narrative and leading to the formation of the couple.[2] Drawing on the idea of the MacGuffin as an empty decoy, the film never discloses the content of the government secret which the foreign spies are about to transport beyond the American border. Instead, when the cryptic statuette is broken in the climactic scene on Mount Rushmore, Hitchcock has it reveal a roll of microfilm. His self-referential gesture thus underlines that what we have been watching is indeed 'a real movie movie' revolving around the medium of film.[3]

As argued by Stanley Cavell, *North by Northwest* plays 'a summary role' in Hitchcock's oeuvre (1986: 253).[4] In his long conversations with the director, François Truffaut suggests that the earlier romantic spy thriller *The 39 Steps* (1935) can be regarded as the 'compendium' of his work in Britain, while its American remake, as he suggests to Hitchcock, 'epitomizes the whole of your work in America' (1985: 249). The notion that *North by Northwest* occupies a defining place in Hitchcock's oeuvre also informs my reading. More specifically, I argue that while the enactment of a dislocating form of fantasy in *Suspicion* (1941) correlates with Hitchcock's exilic departure from his British home, *North by Northwest* (1959) signals his relation to American culture in general and a specific cinematic code in particular. As pointed out by Stanley Cavell, *North by Northwest* offers numerous cinematic references, not only to the three previous films Hitchcock made with Cary Grant, namely *Suspicion* (1941), *Notorious* (1946) and *To Catch a Thief* (1955), but also to Grant's roles in the romantic scenarios of the sophisticated Hollywood comedy in the 1930s and 1940s, through which he established his star image (Cavell 1986: 250–1).[5] The romantic thriller represents Hitchcock's most explicit Hollywood film precisely because of its engagement with the codes of romance. In fact, my wager is that – to pick up on Nabokov's description of *Lolita* – *North by Northwest* can be regarded as the record of Hitchcock's love affair with Hollywood cinema. Preceded by *Vertigo* (1958) and followed by *Psycho* (1960), the film not only coincides with the peak of the director's career in America, it also comments on the position of Hitchcock's aesthetic language within the Hollywood system.

By comparing *North by Northwest* to Nabokov's American novel *Lolita*, I will use parts of my discussion as a summary to tease out the implications of the cross-mapping I am proposing in this book. The two texts, I argue, are paradigmatic for the different ways in which their authors inhabit their respective languages as well as for the different conditions under which literature and cinema migrate to a foreign culture. What are the specific means and options offered by the two media systems? To what extent are the texts shaped by the different exilic departures of their authors? How can we relate Nabokov's investment in poetic language to the fact that he was twice violently forced into exile, whereas Hitchcock chose to emigrate so as to be able to work within the codes of Hollywood mainstream cinema? Without being biographical in the strict sense, my discussion proposes that the two texts can be read back to the referentiality of exile in so far as it inspires diverging narratives and different aesthetic positions.

With its medial self-referentiality and ironical playfulness, *North by Northwest* shows close aesthetic affinities with *Lolita*. The novel and the film both foreground their sign-character by invoking other texts and images – a vast literary archive in the case of Nabokov and a number of emblematic sites and sights in the case of Hitchcock. At first glance, the film also resembles the novel in its narrative trajectory. Hitchcock's protagonist Roger O. Thornhill presents himself as a self-assured and fast-talking Madison Avenue advertising executive and, like Humbert

Humbert, he is a deft manipulator of words and images. Reminiscent of the novel's protagonist and his travels, first with Lolita and then in search of the playwright Clare Quilty, Thornhill finds himself involved in a 'cryptogrammic paper chase' (LO: 250). Similar to Humbert Humbert, who is first pursued by Quilty and then seeks to reconstruct the other's itinerary, Thornhill traces the hotel records of George Kaplan, a fictional decoy, who has been devised by the American counter-intelligence office and for whom he is accidentally mistaken by a spy racket. As he is framed for a murder committed by one of the spies, he embarks on an American odyssey, taking him in both picaresque and picturesque ways from New York and Grand Central Station to Chicago, an out-of-the-way bus stop on a vast plain of mostly bare fields, to Rapid City in South Dakota and the national monument on Mount Rushmore.

As in *Lolita*, the protagonist's hyperactive travelling can be regarded as an extension of his logorrhea as well as an imaginary flight from symbolic and sexual difference. In fact, one could say that resembling Humbert Humbert's escape from the 'stale flesh' of his first wife Valeria and then from the suburban home of Charlotte Haze (LO: 26), Thornhill embarks on his journey in order to avoid a troubling femininity embodied by his dominant mother as well as by his two ex-wives. Although his home paranoia exposes him to considerable danger, the idea that the world is conspiring against him represents a self-aggrandising and hence narcissistically satisfying scenario similar to Humbert Humbert's fantasy of aesthetic omnipotence. At the same time, the film narrative diverges from the novel in significant ways. While *Lolita*, as argued in my reading, maps a textual closure that effaces the world outside Humbert Humbert's image repertoire, *North by Northwest* channels the journey of its protagonist into a symbolic *rite de passage*.

The film performs an Oedipal passage leading from free-floating imagination to the subjection of the individual under the symbolic law as a register of lack, difference and curtailment. According to Raymond Bellour's well-known contention, the Oedipal pattern forms the blueprint of Hollywood cinema *par excellence*. Its narratives, he claims, invariably dramatise the entry of the male subject into the social symbolic (2001). The exclusively masculine orientation of the pattern appears hardly justifiable. As Tania Modleski (1988) and Elisabeth Bronfen (2004a) have shown, *Rebecca*, the first film Hitchcock made in Hollywood, traces the problematics entailed by a specifically feminine Oedipal trajectory, notably the female protagonist's difficulty in separating herself from her dominant maternal predecessor. The reason why I nevertheless refer to Bellour's classic psychoanalytical reading of *North by Northwest* is to emphasise the ambivalence which Hitchcock highlights in the troubled route of his protagonist.[6] His voyage appears far more straightforward than the two female trajectories developed in *Rebecca* and *Suspicion* as well as the vicissitudes of the subject and its socialisation foregrounded by a large portion of Hitchcock's oeuvre. The romantic thriller not only formulates Thornhill's symbolic re-insertion as an acceptance of sexual difference in the figure of Eve Kendall (Eva Maria Saint) but goes so far as to put the formation of the couple under the aegis of the national symbolic law. Referring to his own work on the romantic Hollywood comedy in *Pursuits of Happiness* (1981), Stanley Cavell argues that marriage in *North by Northwest* is of national importance (1986: 260). At the same time, the ending reverberates with anxieties which are already at stake in the heroine's traumatic enactment in *Suspicion* and from which Thornhill has been literally running away for much of the film. Given the eventual emphasis on symbolic integration, this chapter traces the ambivalence that underpins Hitchcock's gesture of symbolic assimilation in *North by Northwest*. What is at stake in Hitchcock's ultimate affirmation of symbolic codes? What are the costs and gains of this gesture, and how are they treated cinematically?

Thornhill's imaginary economy and its rupture are not merely played out on the plot level, but also find a correspondence in the *mise-en-scène*. As if to underline the film's medial production and projection of images in analogy to its protagonist, an advertising man dealing in signs, the opening titles feature a flat surface screen with 'rectangular outlines, resembling film frames' (Keane 1980: 49). After a while the two-dimensional grid transforms into the window frames of a Manhattan high-rise block. On its mirror façade, we see the bustle of the off-screen traffic on the street below mediated by its distorted reflection. The grid structure will be reproduced as a formal device throughout the film, for example in the interior design (the floor and windows) of the Mount Rushmore cafeteria or the arrangement of the vast deserted fields in the famous cropdusting scene. Together with the many rear projections featured later, the opening sequence emphasises the artificiality of the film's cinematic language. As Marian Keane notes, 'the world conjured announces itself as . . . the reflection of a world projected on the flat and receptive screen' (1980: 49). While the film opens by referring to its own mediality, it is also marked by a disturbance which prominently erupts into the deceptive surface of fields in the cropdusting scene and which can be read together with the eventual rupture of Thornhill's narcissistic economy. Before the lone figure of the protagonist is attacked by the aerial sniper on the vast plain of fields, the man waiting for the bus remarks that the cropdusting plane is superfluous in a landscape 'where there ain't no crops'. In fact, as pointed out by Truffaut, the scene as a whole is 'totally gratuitous' (1985: 256), a moment of pure cinema turning around space and movement in an almost abstract way.[7]

It is in this highly formalised sequence that Hitchcock incorporates what Slavoj Žižek calls the 'Hitchcockian blot': 'a small supplementary feature, a detail that "does not belong," that sticks out, is "out of place," does not make any sense within the frame of the idyllic scene' (1991: 88). The airplane emerges as a disturbing blot and, in so doing, parallels the rupture of Thornhill's narcissistic economy in the course of his trajectory. The sudden appearance of the airplane not only signals the literal vulnerability of the subject exposed on a seemingly infinite landscape devoid of any shelter and protection. It also figures as an anamorphotic stain pointing to a real surplus that has to be excluded from symbolic reality even as it also keeps insisting as a foreign body. If *Lolita* develops an aesthetic language that elides and excludes referentiality, the cinematic language of *North by Northwest* can be seen to rupture the screen of the imaginary and the symbolic. In so doing, it highlights an antagonism which harks back to Lina's fantasy and its flooding of the cinematic screen in *Suspicion*. Similarly, the narrative of the film not only equates the traversal of the imaginary with a renunciation of the individual's fantasy of omnipotence, but also points to the antagonisms that trouble the subject and its symbolic relations.

My reading of the film highlights three areas, namely Thornhill's challenge of the symbolic law in his 'mad travelling', the Oedipal voyage towards sexual difference and, finally, the national allegory traced by the film, which I map onto the different medial migrations of Hitchcock and Nabokov. In the previous chapter, I argued that *Suspicion* transforms the heroine's traumatic enactment of fantasy into an aesthetic motor which is typical of the psychothriller. My key argument here is that *North by Northwest* underscores the degree to which Hitchcock works in highly symbolic codes. His romantic thriller traces the ambivalences that underpin the Oedipal voyage and the formation of the couple on the plot level and, by appropriating and modulating these narrative patterns, simultaneously reflects on his own position in Hollywood cinema as a highly codified system. This is precisely what constitutes the pivotal gesture underlying Hitchcock's chosen emigration: his access to and assimilation of symbolic structures together with their underlying contradictions.

As we shall see in the course of this chapter, it is by acknowledging the fundamental void on which the subject's position is grounded that Thornhill attains symbolic agency. At the same time, his voyage into the symbolic leads him into a literal as well as a figurative darkness. Observing the Hollywood code according to which sexual intercourse must not be represented on screen, Hitchcock's final shot shows a phallic train forcefully entering a vaginal tunnel. While in *Suspicion*, it is the collision with the stranger on a train in a tunnel that gets the heroine's fantasy going, the barely veiled sexual image of the tunnel's entrance at the end of the film ironically underlines that Thornhill has gained a symbolic mandate, but simultaneously has to incur a curtailment of his imaginary wandering. The visual pun suggests that as the luxurious sleeping-car compartment travels into the darkness of the night and the tunnel, the fusion of the couple entails not only pleasure but also anxiety. Hitchcock's irony points to this disturbing knowledge by moving through tenebrous terrain in both literal and figurative ways.

In analogy to the symbolic integration of his protagonist, Hitchcock himself gains access to American mainstream film by appropriating and interrogating the codes of Hollywood cinema. It is not by accident that the iconic presidential faces on Mount Rushmore provide the setting of the penultimate scene, in which the couple re-establishes itself and the nation against the foreign spies. *North by Northwest* represents a commentary on Hitchcock's appropriation of Hollywood together with the contradictions underpinning any symbolic identification. One could go as far as to argue that the film represents a self-ironical comment on the iconic status Hitchcock's work had gained in the late 1950s when, as a result of his cinematic cameo appearances and the weekly murder mystery series he presented on television, he – or rather his carefully crafted public persona of the imperturbable Englishman – came to enjoy the celebrity of 'a national figure' (Spoto 1983: 440).

Mad Traveller

In its cross-country chase, *North by Northwest* performs a 'mad travelling' that is reminiscent of the mental wandering in *Suspicion*. Roger O. Thornhill and Lina McLaidlaw are both plagued by a domestic malaise which gives rise to their respective flights from the parental home. While Hitchcock's previous film develops in close attunement with his heroine and her traumatic fusion with the male sexual other, the romantic spy thriller follows a masculine version of home paranoia. The film begins with a flight from home that initially resembles Humbert Humbert's imaginary escapism. Similar to his trajectory, which is pitted against motherhood as a trope of mutability and mortality, and hence against what posits a limit to the individual and its imagination,

Thornhill flees the curtailment of his two failed marriages as well as his overpresent mother with whom he finds himself caught up instead. However, the itineraries of *Lolita* and *North by Northwest* also diverge from each other in significant ways. In contrast to Humbert Humbert's attempt to find permanent refuge in the aesthetic realm of his imaginary, Thornhill's voyage represents a renegotiation of his relation to the symbolic. Like Lina's mental wandering, his travelling can be read as a symptom articulating a discontent with the symbolic law, and similar to her acknowledgement of a fundamental otherness, his vagrancy culminates in an ambivalent symbolic re-insertion.

To be more precise, Thornhill's wandering can be read as a 'hysterical' gesture following Elisabeth Bronfen's analysis of hysteria as a language of personal and cultural discontent (1998). As Bronfen shows in her readings covering a vast archive of medical discourses and cultural performances, hysteria articulates a critique of symbolic systems. Rather than going back to any organic lesions, its symptoms point to a fundamental vulnerability of identity and the symbolic at large. Importantly enough, it is by using and resiliently imitating cultural discourses that hysterics broadcast their complaint to paternal figures and other symbolic representatives. Their protest is both lodged in a language which forms part of their critique and addressed to the very representatives of the system they interrogate. Thornhill's wandering functions precisely along these lines. His fugue broadcasts a discontent that is, from the beginning, couched in the codes which are the object of his protest. His voyage traverses several sites that are prominently placed in the national symbolic order, including among others Grand Central Station in New York, a quintessential Midwestern plain of fields and the presidential monument on Mount Rushmore. At the same time, his trajectory hinges on a confrontation with several paternal figures, notably Philip Vandamm (James Mason), the head of the spies who mistake him for the non-existent government agent George Kaplan, and the unnamed CIA 'Professor' (Leo G. Caroll), who has invented Kaplan as a decoy.[8]

As Thornhill's appearance at the beginning of the film suggests, he moves in the social symbolic but, in so doing, does not hold a position and is unable to assume one. Instead he engages in what one might call a narcissistic economy, a play of signs which is nourished by the language of his profession. The very first scene of the film aligns him with the world of advertisement and consumerist culture in which the public image is everything. His talk and dictation in the presence of his secretary Maggie highlight that as an advertising man he deals both in and with mythical signs. The present he has Maggie send to his lover suggests a wholesale commodification of all relations; the box of candies individually wrapped in gold paper, he thinks, will make her think 'she's eating money'. A moment later, after tricking a man out of his cab with the claim that 'I have a very sick woman here', he points to his smart manipulation of words and appearances when he explains to his secretary that 'in the world of advertisement, there is no such thing as a lie . . . There is only expedient exaggeration.' Although he treats the advertising slogans he produces as interchangeable, he is immersed in the myths of his profession. The opening of the film characterises him as successful with respect to his manipulation of signs. In the course of the narrative, however, it becomes clear that there is one area in which he does not operate as an interpellated subject, namely the register of symbolic difference.

Thornhill's trouble with the symbolic law is primarily played out by his inability to enter into a mature sexual relation. Not only has he already been married and divorced twice. The beginning of the film foregrounds the blockage of the Oedipal route by his infantile dependence on his dominant mother (Jessie Royce). One of his tasks for his secretary, in the first scene, is to call his mother as soon as she is back at the office, and when he is in trouble at the police station after the spies have made him drunk and set him out in a stolen car, he calls 'Mother' instead of the lawyer he would actually need. The dominant role of the mother is already implied by the message he asks his secretary to deliver to her, namely that when they meet for dinner, he will have had two drinks 'so she needn't bother to sniff my breath' like 'a bloodhound'. Similarly, when after his abduction detectives check up on his statement, Mrs Thornhill mocks and exposes her son as a preposterous storyteller.

The disturbance of the Oedipal route through a strong maternal attachment is far from unique in Hitchcock's oeuvre. *Psycho* (1960) and *The Birds* (1963), the two psychothrillers that immediately follow *North by Northwest*, never dissolve the mother-son dyad in favour of another object choice: Norman Bates kills and literally embodies the maternal figure and her prohibition of his access to women, while the birds and their freak attacks on Bodega Bay appear mysteriously linked to Mitch Brenner's possessive mother and her disapproval of the woman he invites to their home. However, rather than linking maternal overpresence to an eruption of real violence as the two psychothrillers do, *North by Northwest* stresses a temporary blockage in the voyage to eventual romance. As Slavoj Žižek points out in his reading of the film's Oedipal trajectory, the passage to a mature sexual relationship is disturbed, because the maternal super-ego displaces the paternal metaphor, by which symbolic relations must necessarily be mediated (1991: 99). Avoiding a proper symbolic identification, Žižek argues further,

Hitchcock's protagonist represents the paradigmatic example of the 'narcissistic subject': he 'knows only the "rules of the (social) game" enabling him to manipulate others; social relations constitute for him a playing field in which he assumes "roles," not proper symbolic mandates ...' (1991: 102). Not able and/or willing to assume a symbolic identity, he engages instead in a seemingly boundless play of signs and roles.

One of the pivotal signifiers of the film is Roger O. Thornhill's trademark ROT. On the one hand, it refers to the vacuity of his performance. As he points out himself, the oversized middle initial O stands for 'nothing'. His first and last name are, therefore, held together by a gratuitous detail which, in keeping with his advertising job, invokes an imaginary surplus. On the other hand, the 'nothing' of his middle initial can also be taken to refer to the symbolic lack inherent in subjectivity. According to the Oedipal pattern, access to the symbolic law is regulated by a repression and curtailment of pleasure. The individual has to incur a lack in order to become a subject of symbolic desire. At the same time, the subject is confronted by the real antagonism that underpins sexual difference and subjectivity and as such cannot be fully integrated into the symbolic register.[9] The Oedipal trajectory grants the subject access to a symbolic position and, at the same time, entails a fundamental limitation of the individual's sense of omnipotence. Implicitly, the empty signifier of Thornhill's middle name already signals the constitutive lack on which the subject's position is predicated. It is precisely this knowledge that Hitchcock's protagonist defies in his social game.

While Thornhill's trademark harbours a nothingness he cannot yet acknowledge, his travelling is precipitated by the other crucial signifier of the film: the name of the non-existent government agent George Kaplan, who has been invented by the counter-intelligence office and for whom he is accidentally mistaken by the spies. Like *The 39 Steps* and *Saboteur*, *North by Northwest* follows the classic formula of Hitchcock's 'wrong man' narrative. Thornhill is confused with an agent whom the spies believe to know too much. Framed for a crime he has not committed, he runs to clear his name and – just like the protagonists in the two other romantic spy thrillers – finds his love object in the course of his quest.

The first encounter with the spies at the hotel bar marks the particularly complex departure of Thornhill's home paranoia and his 'mad travelling'. Significantly enough, the spies have George Kaplan paged at the precise moment at which Thornhill turns around to send a telegram to his mother, after realising that his secretary cannot reach her on the phone. As it turns out later in the film, his accidental response to the name Kaplan triggers a liberating flight from home as it literally ruptures the maternal relation – his message to the mother never gets through. At the same time, the coincidental attachment of the name carries a disturbing potential in its derailment of Thornhill's narcissistic economy. The empty signifier can be seen to refer to the symbolic register and the notion that names cannot be chosen by individuals but are imposed on them. Resembling the empty O in his trademark but made up by a paternal representative, the 'Professor', 'Kaplan' represents a trope of symbolic curtailment. Neither the spies, who believe that Kaplan exists, nor Thornhill, who rejects the alien name, are aware of its symbolic significance. In fact, the scene at the hotel bar suggests a curious interpellation. In trying and failing to contact the mother, Thornhill implicitly answers to the call of the spies. Not only does his abduction enable him to embark on his wandering and elude the curtailment of symbolic difference he would have to confront in a relation with the feminine. While rejecting the name and identity the spies seek to impose on him, he simultaneously performs a temporary flight from his social roles as son and advertising executive together with the mature mandate as husband he cannot yet assume.

In its literal escape from any position, Thornhill's spatial and imaginary migration recalls the phenomenon of the classic male fugue. While focusing on a particular travel epidemic, Ian Hacking, in his book on *Mad Travelers* (1998), discusses the symbolic escapism of the male fugueur that also underpins Hitchcock's film. In late nineteenth-century Bordeaux, Hacking observes, Dr Albert Pitres, a neurologist trained by Jean-Martin Charcot, and his student Philippe Tissié witnessed a stupendous spread of excessive wandering among lower- and middle-class men. Developing in a niche between criminal vagrancy and emergent romantic tourism, the symptoms of the fugueurs or 'mad travellers' involved a compulsion to set out for the road and walk for weeks on end. During their protracted travelling which took some of them to such faraway places as Moscow or Constantinople, the mad travellers did not only typically lose their identity papers. When stopped, arrested and checked by the authorities, they could neither remember who they were nor where they came from. In their 'pathological' tourism, they thus enacted an escape from symbolically controlled space in general and the social norms and identities imposed on them in particular.

Thornhill's line of escapism resonates with the fugueurs' amnesia in resilient ways. Like the mad travellers' fugue, which 'relieves them of responsibility' (Hacking 1998: 50), his wandering allows him to take flight from any symbolic identity. His mad travelling avoids symbolic difference similar to the negation of referentiality through Humbert

Humbert's textual imaginary. Or one could also say that his scenario covers up what he cannot do yet, namely assume a mature identity in the symbolic. However, in contrast to both Humbert Humbert's escape and the fugueur's line of flight, Thornhill's wandering does not seek to elude the symbolic, but instead performs a hysterical complaint. In fact, his migrations can be seen to hyperbolically transpose the traditional image of feminine hysteria disseminated by old medical discourses. Evocative of the somatic symptoms of hysteria, which were often explained by the theory of the vagrant uterus wandering in its discontent through the patient's organism, the masculine hysteric Thornhill transforms into a literally vagrant body. Similar to the mental migrations of the heroine in *Suspicion*, which gesture towards a foreign body in the subject's psyche, his wandering across a national landscape brings to the fore a symbolic malaise.

His sense that 'all is not well' is underlined not least of all by his initials mentioned above. 'Thornhill's identifying "rot" as his trademark', Stanley Cavell writes, 'irresistibly suggests to me Hamlet's sense of something rotten' (1986: 253). Alluding to Hamlet's line 'I am but mad north-north-west' (Act II.2.374), the film also harks back to the symbolic crisis played out in Shakespeare's tragedy and, above all, to the inability of the son to assume symbolic agency in his suspicion that there is something rotten in the paternal law. In so doing, Hitchcock's scenario of home paranoia also invokes what Eric Santner, in his book on Schreber and modernity, calls a 'crisis in symbolic investiture' (1996). As Santner emphasises, Daniel Paul Schreber developed his psychosis shortly after being appointed presiding judge of the Saxon Supreme Court, which meant that he could never take up his position. It was precisely when he was commissioned with his new legal and social status of ultimate authority that he came to be troubled by what he perceived as a 'rottenness' in the symbolic law. According to Santner's reading, Schreber's breakdown refers to a disturbance in the subject's relation to social and institutional authority – that is, the idea that symbolic investiture fails as a result of the subject's sense that something is wrong in the symbolic order. His crisis highlights how the fallibility of the symbolic law and thus a paternal vacuum may give rise to a malfunction in the processes which regulate the transfer and assumption of symbolic positions.

Experiencing symbolic authority as 'an obscene overproximity' (Santner 1996: 32), Schreber felt that the borders of his persona were violated by paternal agencies. Santner situates this delusional persecution in the context of a symbolic crisis emerging in nineteenth-century *fin-de-siècle* Germany and soon after amalgamating into fascist ideologies. At first sight, it might be tempting to read *North by Northwest* along the lines of Schreber's hallucinations. After all there appears to be an obscene transgression in the way in which both agents and counter-espionage agents conspire against Thornhill in their attempt to subsume him under their plots. Vandamm and his unscrupulous spy racket continue to mistake him for the non-existent government agent Kaplan, and the 'Professor' decides to protect his actual agent by doing nothing to dispel the error, although he is aware of the fact that this will expose Thornhill to fatal danger. The spy thriller resonates with fears and anxiety related to Cold War paranoia and conspiracy culture. But the type of crisis highlighted by Hitchcock's film departs from the classic scenario of paranoid psychosis. Thornhill's trajectory neither implies a foreclosure of the law nor a 'consequent "imprisonment" of the psychotic subject in the imaginary' (Evans 1996: 156).[10] Instead his hysterical wandering enacts the sense that there is something 'rotten' in his access to the symbolic law.

By embarking on his flight from both the home of his mother and the marriages he cannot yet sustain, Thornhill is propelled by the paternal function, which is mediated by Vandamm and the 'Professor'. After his abduction, the spies get him drunk and set him out in a stolen car. Having escaped the spies' first attempt on his life, he goes to see Lester Townsend, the United Nations diplomat into whose mansion he had been abducted and whose name Vandamm had appropriated. At the very moment at which he produces a picture of Vandamm found in Kaplan's alleged hotel room, Townsend gasps and collapses in his arms. Thornhill, mechanically grasping the knife plunged by one of the spies into Townsend's back, is framed for a murder which he both has and has not committed. As pointed out by Bellour, the murder is linked to a complex substitution. Townsend is killed by order of Vandamm, who has usurped his name and house and commits the murder of the 'father' in the place of Thornhill (Bellour 2001: 85–90). The confusion of Thornhill with the 'United Nations murderer' literally sets him on his Oedipal itinerary. Immediately before boarding the train from New York to Chicago, he calls his mother and tells her that he cannot go to the police and thus turn to the symbolic law – 'at least not yet'. As a fugitive from the law, he continues to wander in a symbolic limbo. At the same time, the phone call marks his final maternal contact. As if to underline his subsequent separation, the figure of the mother disappears forever, while the narrative focus shifts to the paternal function against which he protests in his attempt to clear his name.

Immediately after getting onto the train, Thornhill runs into the woman ('Eve') who will eventually come to represent symbolic difference to him. However, before he can assume a symbolic mandate, his wandering performs a self-aggrandising scenario. Being photographed with the incriminating knife in his hand and 'wanted for murder on every front page in America', he all of a sudden finds himself at the centre of everyone's attention.[11] Moreover, he appears to magically protect himself with his literal and figurative agility against the danger to which he is exposed on his American odyssey. The averted danger displaces the acknowledgement of the symbolic lack that a mature position would entail. In fact, the film's *mise-en-scène* suggests that Thornhill continues to play the social game which is highlighted by Žižek's reading. This is most palpable in his histrionics at the auction, where he turns, as it were, to his professional image-making technique and transforms the perilous situation into a veritable publicity stunt. Menaced by Vandamm's henchman in a public space without the public being aware of his predicament, he starts to make ludicrous bids, pretending that he does not understand the rules of the game, until his unruly behaviour becomes the focus of attention and cause to notify the police.

At first glance, Thornhill's narcissistic vagrancy resembles Humbert Humbert's imaginary flight. Both protagonists engage in a play with words and signs so as to avoid the curtailment of their imaginary. However, while the novel traces the withdrawal of its protagonist into his solipsistic image repertoire, the hysterical wandering and symbolic critique in the film delineate a reverse trajectory. In fact, there is a significant difference in Thornhill's and Humbert Humbert's appropriation of cultural signs and images from the very start. By depicting him as an advertising man in a uniform grey flannel suit, Hitchcock affiliates his leading man with the cultural hegemony of corporate business and consumerism in postwar America. By contrast, Nabokov's protagonist not only rejects the commonplaces of popular culture, but shortly after arriving in New York, he also resigns from his job in the 'pseudoliterary' business of advertisement, which consists 'mainly of thinking up and editing perfume ads' (LO: 32). Instead he chooses to 'complete my comparative history of French literature for English-speaking students' (LO: 32) before he eventually writes his memoir, paying homage to his creation of Lolita in particular and to literature in general. Like the sign systems of consumerism and advertisement invoked by *North by Northwest*, literature obviously also represents a collective discourse. Yet Nabokov and his (less successful) protagonist embrace literary language as the aesthetic means of a uniquely individual mode of expression. While I will return to Nabokov's investment in literary language towards the end of this chapter, it will suffice to recall here the notion of the individual artist which the *auteur manqué* Humbert Humbert invokes together with other romantic tropes of creativity. Although his confession addresses a jury, his emphasis on the singularity of his obsession means that his textual romance plays itself out in a radically individual realm. In his journeys through the literary archive, Nabokov's protagonist revels in his seemingly boundless textual imaginary as his play with words and texts actually retreats into solipsistic closure.

In contrast, Thornhill's hysterical wandering always remains embedded in a collective frame of reference. Hitchcock's protagonist 'absents' himself from his workplace so as to broadcast a complaint which pertains precisely to the cultural symbolic and his inability as a narcissistic individual to assume a proper subject position. His narcissistic economy may be read as the symptom of a crisis of masculinity having to do with consumerist culture. His profession is paradigmatic of the shift of the typical postwar workplace from production to the corporate identity of white-collar work. As an advertising executive, he belongs to a class of professionals who shape signs and images, but who are potentially haunted by their own semiotic influence. In order to promote his aims, Thornhill turns himself into a manipulator of words and appearances as well as a product of polished performances.[12] However, his wandering not only plays out an erosion of masculine identity into a series of social roles. Significantly enough, Hitchcock's protagonist enacts his symbolic discontent by traversing a number of iconic national sites. In fact, *North by Northwest* presents its itinerary as a tongue-in-cheek treatment of various settings, notably the out-of-the-blue attack on the Midwestern plain of fields and the chase over the presidential faces on Mount Rushmore. If the film thus locates his wandering in a far more collective domain than the novel, it does so both to articulate a sense of cultural alienation and to tell a narrative of eventual assimilation. While Nabokov has his protagonist cite literary tropes in order to express his singular obsession, Thornhill's travel not only follows a dominant pattern of mainstream cinema but simultaneously proposes a national allegory.

Oedipal Voyage

The 'mad travelling' of *North by Northwest* resonates with a typically American myth revolving around a masculine escape from a feminine home and community.[13] As Michael Wood suggests, cinematic genres such as the western, the war and adventure film replace the home with 'corporate masculine adventures' (1989: 43). The figure of the cowboy, the soldier and adventurer go to war or return to the wilderness not only to preserve and advance the collective interests of the community. By embracing an all-masculine front or frontier, they simultaneously substitute the repercussions of an irresolvable gender trouble with a homogeneous male bond.[14] Hitchcock begins his film with a reference to the antagonism of the sexes – as the elevator operator Eddie remarks at the beginning of the very first scene, he and his 'missus' are 'not talking'. Yet, rather than offering an escape route from sexual difference, the manic cross-country chase of Hitchcock's protagonist highlights his difficulty in entering into a mature sexual relation in both hyperbolic and comic ways. Eventually the romantic thriller insists on the necessity of halting the seemingly boundless wandering of its protagonist. In channelling his masculine home paranoia into an Oedipal voyage, Hitchcock has him face what the classic fugueur seeks to avoid, namely the symbolic law and the real antagonism of sexual difference together with the lack and curtailment they entail for the subject.

Compared with *Suspicion*, where both the heroine's mental wandering and the couple's final return home remain deeply ambivalent, the voyage and resolution of the later film seems to be of a palpably happier cast. The masculine Oedipal trajectory appears to allow Hitchcock to stage the eventual symbolic integration of his protagonist in a far more unequivocal way. While *Suspicion* is characterised by what I have been calling an overproximity between the focalisation of the heroine's disturbing fantasy work and the film's *mise-en-scène*, *North by Northwest* can be seen to shape its highly codified language in such a way as to aesthetically underscore the eventual symbolic integration of its protagonist. Moreover, the film's treatment of Oedipal and romantic patterns can be read back to Hitchcock's career. If in *Suspicion*, the heroine's dislocation through her fantasy work resonates with Hitchcock's development of the psychothriller in the context of his emigration, *North by Northwest* comments on his position in Hollywood and his appropriation of mainstream cinema. At the same time, I argue that in his emphasis on symbolic systems, Hitchcock points to something that remains inassimilable. Both his aesthetic language and narratives suggest that symbolic integration harbours an irresolvable antagonism. While shifting from the dark ambiguity of the female paranoia film to cheerful exhilaration, the romantic thriller both affirms the symbolic integration of its protagonist and ironically underlines the cross-currents at stake in this process. In the following, I want to trace the ways in which Thornhill's imaginary wandering is directed into the formation of the couple. What are the gains and costs of this trajectory? How is the antagonism of symbolic assimilation staged by Hitchcock's cinematic language?

Reminiscent of Lina McLaidlaw's first encounter with Aysgarth, Thornhill first meets Eve Kendall on the train. However, in contrast to the heroine in *Suspicion*, Thornhill chances upon 'Eve' as the imaginary woman who initially supports his narcissistic economy. He has just said goodbye to his dominant mother on the phone, when all of a sudden he finds himself in the hands of a benign maternal figure, who first protects him from the police in the corridor and then hides him in the womb-like container of the upper berth in her sleeping compartment. In allusion to the many accidental encounters in Hitchcock's cinematic railway travels, Eve remarks that 'we're just strangers on a train'. Yet for Thornhill she does not represent the other. Rather, he mistakes her as a narcissistic support. By seducing him in a forward way, Kendall notes that over and above having taste in clothes and food, he is 'clever with words': 'You can probably make them do anything for you. Sell people things they don't need. Make women who don't know you fall in love with you.' Flattered by her remarks on his professional use of language, he replies: 'I'm beginning to think I'm underpaid.' It is no coincidence that the *mise-en-scène* of their erotic encounter – their suggestive conversation in the dining car and then the amorous *tête-à-tête* in her compartment against the backdrop of a romantic sunset – could come straight out of one of his commercials. 'Beats flying', he actually says at one point during their amorous exchange as if to advertise the advantage of train travel, 'doesn't it?'

Moreover, Eve fits his narcissistic scenario because, rather than representing a disturbance, she initially seems to represent a mere diversion in his wandering. If he is, in a sense, 'on the loose', her erotic overtures on the train make her something of a 'loose' woman. In analogy to the boundless character of his wandering, her adventurous seduction seems to promise that their fast-developing romance will stay free from any binding commitment. However, Thornhill seems so absorbed in his narcissistic scenario that in contrast to us, the spectators, he remains unaware of Kendall's sideward glance in the close-up of her face that ends the love scene on the train. The direction of her look not only refers us to her complicitous involvement with Vandamm, whom we see receive a secret message from her in another train compartment. Her looking also crosses Thornhill's narcissistic scene and indicates that she has interests of her own.

For Thornhill, their imaginary rapport is disturbed for the first time the next day. On the morning after their night together, Eve arranges a meeting with Kaplan which turns out to be a fatal trap. Significantly enough, the scene in the train station, in which she pretends that the police are approaching and sends him to the fatal rendezvous, ends again with a medium close-up of Kendall. As in the previous close-up, her face and her look refer to a space beyond his imaginary. At the same time, Hitchcock's superimposition of her figure onto the vast and empty plain of fields aligns her with the land and the insidious danger to which it will expose him. The perfidious plane attack is dispatched by Vandamm, but the fatality flooding the landscape implicitly comes from the woman. The mortal danger suddenly confronting Thornhill may already point to the loss of imaginary omnipotence he will eventually have to endure. Yet this knowledge is deflected by the reversal of his idealised image of Eve into the opposite, no less phantasmatic trope, namely a fatal femininity luring its victim to death. If initially she stands in as a protective maternal 'womb', she now menaces the male hero on an open stretch of land which is perverted by her incalculable femininity into a potential 'tomb'.

This is all the more significant if we consider that the vast expanse of earth, which is liminally positioned between culture and nature, evokes the traditional territory of the American male fugueur. Together with a Midwestern prairie, the flat landscape evokes the genre of the western and its westward shifting of the frontier. More specifically, it reminds us of how in the name of civilising both a native population and nature, the cowboy keeps returning to the wilderness and, in so doing, repeatedly leaves behind a feminine home. In a similar vein, the barrenness of the mostly harvested fields is reminiscent of a combat zone, the waste and no-man's land of a field of conflict. As already argued above, the soldier and the cowboy can be said to embrace the homogeneous male bond of the front and the frontier so as to escape from gender trouble. In contrast, Thornhill not only looks oddly displaced as an isolated tiny figure wearing his urban grey flannel suit in the vast plain of fields. The scene also underlines that the genre of Hitchcock's romantic thriller allows his protagonist no cover from sexual antagonism. On the contrary, the plain of fields is transformed into a zone literally flooded by a war of the sexes. Thornhill's imaginary fugue is double-crossed by Eve even though he makes a miraculous escape from the plane attack. When he returns to Chicago and follows her to the auction, he finds her in cahoots with Vandamm. The knowledge of real sexual antagonism is again deflected as she becomes a figure of treacherous conspiracy and betrayal by turning from the previously idealised seductress into a duplicitous femme fatale.

Eve Kendall's translation into an imaginary cliché – the woman who seduces him first in a seemingly benign way and who then seems to annihilate him in a fatal fashion – is reminiscent of Humbert Humbert's fashioning of the nymphet as well as his transformation of Dolores Haze into a textual trope based on previous literary texts. Within Hitchcock's oeuvre, one might also think of the way in which *Vertigo* reflects on the transformation of the woman into an image. In the film immediately preceding *North by Northwest*, Scottie (James Stewart) falls for Gavin Elstner's staging of his wife Madeleine (Kim Novak) as suicidally haunted both by her dead relative Carlotta Valdez and by her portrait because the scenario of the woman's proximity to death corresponds with his own melancholia and, above all, his necrophiliac desire. Representing a far more sober position, Scottie's friend Midge (Barbara Bel Geddes) points to his phantasmatic obsession by painting a far less idealised image, which combines her down-to-earth self-portrait with a disturbing caricature of the idealised femininity he has fallen for (Allen 2007: 139–40). However, Scottie holds on to the image that mirrors his fantasy and desire. After failing to save Madeleine from her alleged death, he seeks to re-create her in Judy Barton, the woman who had, in fact, embodied Madeleine all along. The complex commentary of *Vertigo* on the transformation of the other into an idealised sign of one's fantasy and desire culminates in catastrophe when, in the final frame, Scottie looks down from the church bell tower from which Judy has just fallen to her death. In contrast to the fatal rhetoric implied by both *Vertigo* and *Lolita*, *North by Northwest* follows a far more optimistic route precisely because Thornhill is shown in the course of his voyage to traverse his narcissistic scenario and phantasmatic images of 'Eve'. Rather than holding on to a misrecognition as Humbert Humbert and Scottie do, he moves towards a recognition of the other's separateness, although to relinquish his narcissism means to face his own lack and limitation. It is in this acknowledgement that the film situates the possibility of romantic renewal.

Hitchcock's film, Stanley Cavell argues, can be read together with what he defines as the genre of the so-called 'comedy of remarriage'. In *Pursuits of Happiness* (1981), Cavell suggests that this group of romantic Hollywood comedies made in the 1930s and 1940s is characterised by a development from a failed first to a successful second marriage. His readings emphasise the importance attributed by the films in question to the creation of a new woman for the remarriage and thus for the romantic renewal of the couple to be successful.[15] While Cavell suggests that Hitchcock's film 'derives from the genre of remarriage' (1981: 250), he also notes a significant departure from the classic pattern. Like the classic remarriage couple, Kendall and Thornhill have a prehistory in the form of the night they shared on the train, and their adventures can be seen to test their romantic suitability as a remarriage couple. Yet, rather than a redemption of the woman,

North by Northwest requires a rebirth of the male subject in the course of their joint quest.

Picking up on Cavell, I want to argue that Hitchcock stages a traversal of Thornhill's fantasies of 'Eve' as well as a symbolic initiation and integration of the male subject that occurs under the auspices of her sexual difference. Returning to Cavell's central thesis about the remarriage comedy, Slavoj Žižek points out in his reading of the film that 'the only proper marriage is the second one. First we marry the other *qua* our narcissistic complement; it is only when his/her delusive charm fades that we can engage in marriage as an attachment to the other beyond his/her imaginary properties' (Žižek 1991: 178). This trajectory of recognition pertains to Hitchcock's male protagonist more than to the woman. While Thornhill's imaginary fugue encapsulates Eve in his narcissistic fantasy, she already has a different attitude towards the law as a secret agent working for the government. Already early on, she points out that she is 'a big girl', a notion which he turns into a *double entendre* by saying that she is big 'in all the right places'. Similarly, in a later scene, in which he remarks that he would not even let his mother undress him as 'a little boy', she replies: 'You're a big boy now.'

When Thornhill eventually relinquishes his narcissistic appropriation of Eve, he discovers what he has been covering up all along, namely the ultimate void in being which is related to the symbolic as a register of difference. By following an Oedipal pattern, the film suggests that the individual's symbolic subjection requires giving up both the freedom and omnipotence of one's imaginary wanderings. The crucial turning point in Thornhill's voyage occurs when he agrees to stand in for the empty signifier Kaplan after protesting that he is not 'a red herring'. Faced with the dangerous situation at the auction, he turns himself in to the police and learns from the 'Professor' that 'Kaplan' has been invented as a decoy in order to protect the actual government agent. He realises not only the fatal danger their affair has put Eve into, but also his previous misrecognition of her as the idealised and then the treacherous woman. When he consents to impersonate Kaplan, he assumes a concrete mandate as a government agent. This mission is not synonymous with the figurative mandate which the allegorical language of psychoanalysis foregrounds in the subject's assumption of a symbolic mandate once the separation from the mother has been successfully completed and the identification with the father's position accepted. Nevertheless one might say that the film invokes the Oedipal pattern as an allegorical layer. By temporarily adopting an alias, Thornhill puts an end to his 'mad travelling' as fugueur. What he gains instead is a symbolic position and agency. If he has, so far, only been reacting to the plots of others, he is now in a position to act on his own. Once the 'Professor' breaks his earlier promise to save Kendall and instead intends to send her off with Vandamm, Thornhill will be able to wrest her from both the 'Professor' and Vandamm.[16]

North by Northwest underlines that Thornhill's emergence as a mature subject is closely connected to the antagonism of sexual difference. As in *Suspicion*, Hitchcock reconfigures sexual difference as murder, though in a lighter, more codified fashion than in Lina's fantasy of a sexual fusion that is potentially fatal. During the first erotic encounter on the train, the two protagonists flirtatiously play with the idea that Thornhill is going to murder Eve that night, thus alluding to the *petite mort* trope of sexual orgasm. In the subsequent scenes, however, it is Eve who metaphorically 'kills' him, first in the cropdusting scene and then in the Rushmore cafeteria, where she shoots him with fake bullets. Similar to *Suspicion*, the sexual other emerges as the source of a potentially fatal danger. At the same time, her 'killings' can be read as highly codified moments, giving rise to Thornhill's rebirth as subject or, as Cavell calls it, his 'death and revival' (1986: 262). Her 'wounding' bullets can be taken to underscore that his illusion of omnipotent selfhood has effectively been ruptured. While Kendall's fake shooting of Thornhill is designed to mislead the spies, it figuratively stages his assumption of a symbolic mandate from which any imaginary surplus has been subtracted. Using Žižek's vocabulary, one could, therefore, say that the film foregrounds a symbolic transfer creating a new symbolic reality and inter-subjective relation (1991: 103). It is precisely because Thornhill acknowledges his radical split as subject that he is able to meet Kendall on terms beyond his imaginary misrecognition.

The scene in the pine forest immediately after Kendall's fake shooting of Thornhill invokes the 'meet and happy conversation' that is crucial to Cavell's definition of the comedy of remarriage (Cavell 1981: 146).[17] In order to underscore the equal terms of their encounter, the scene is choreographed with symmetrical precision. Initially positioned next to two cars at the very left and the very right of the frame respectively, Roger and Eve slowly move towards each other until they arrive at the centre of the frame, at which moment the camera cuts from a long to a medium shot, thus focusing on their intimate 'togetherness'. In the course of their conversation, Eve talks about the trouble caused by men like Thornhill and their unwillingness to marry, to which Thornhill jokingly responds that 'hating' her in his fantasy was 'more fun'. Their conversation about how they have hurt each other indicates how far they have moved beyond any narcissistic delusion and towards an acknowledgement of each other's separateness. The mediation of their relationship by the symbolic law is underscored not merely by the presence of the 'Professor' and his attempt to separate them 'all in the line of duty'. Hitchcock goes as far as to connect their relationship to a national framework by having the presidential faces of Mount Rushmore – and thus the monument on which they will forge their bond of marriage in the final scene – tower and preside over the scene of the couple's conversation.[18]

North by Northwest comes full circle when, as Cavell puts it, Thornhill succeeds in 'finally getting a message through to a woman' (1986: 262). As already mentioned above, the film begins with the remark of the elevator operator that he and his 'missus' are not on speaking terms, as if to refer to Thornhill's initial difficulty in entering into communication with the other sex. At the end of his voyage, which is literally put into motion by his failure to maintain maternal contact, he has not only replaced the mother with another love object. The scene in which he transmits a note to Kendall, warning her about Vandamm's plan to kill her, also underlines that his relation to her is based on an acknowledgement of his split subjectivity. As if by miraculous means, Thornhill has emerged from all his dangerous ordeals unscathed. He physically hurts himself for the first time as he is climbing up to Kendall's room in Vandamm's house, where she faces imminent danger. While wiping the blood off his hand, he perceives his initials on his handkerchief and then decides to scribble his vital message to her into the matchbook also carrying his trademark. At this point, we may surmise, his middle initial O no longer refers to an imaginary surplus but to the 'nothing' he has come to accept together with his symbolic position. Or one might also say that approaching the end of the Oedipal voyage, his relationship to the woman is informed by his acknowledgement of symbolic lack and alienation. It is this knowledge that he literally communicates to her.

Within Hitchcock's oeuvre, *North by Northwest* proposes a trajectory that is without any doubt unusually optimistic. Not only is the film characterised by a particularly light and witty tone, but its optimism appears to be connected to its emphatic alignment with symbolic codes. Hitchcock quotes the romantic Hollywood comedy so as to draw on the genre's promise of romantic renewal. While many of his films veer towards a romantic formation of the couple, *North by Northwest* is his only romantic thriller that shows the pair to have actually married (Cavell 1986: 250). Likewise the Oedipal trajectory can be said to underpin a large part of his work, but its enactment in *North by Northwest* emphasises the symbolic identification of his protagonist more than any of his other films, many of which focus on a derailment of the pattern. At the same time, I want to argue that what renders *North by Northwest* a romance of such auspicious integration – namely the gain of a symbolic position and the recognition of the other's difference – also entails a disturbing knowledge. The happy end of Thornhill's voyage cannot be separated from the curtailment and real antagonism against which he has tried to protect himself in his mad travelling. While affirming the gains of symbolic identification, the film also points to anxieties that subtend the subject's insertion into symbolic difference. The reason why *North by Northwest* nevertheless maintains its optimism lies in the ways in which it sustains the ambivalence of symbolic assimilation and ironically codifies its cross-currents.

The film's ambivalence is most palpable in its treatment of the romantic resolution. In his establishment of the couple, Hitchcock follows the paradigmatic pattern of mainstream cinema highlighted by Bellour and his claim that the male Oedipal trajectory forms the Hollywood blueprint *par excellence* (2001). At the same time, Hitchcock also ironically undermines the codes of the happy ending he is proposing. In their final love scene on the upper berth of their sleeping compartment, Eve remarks that what they are doing is 'silly', to which Thornhill answers 'I know, but I'm sentimental'. It is tempting to read these very last lines as a meta-textual commentary on Hitchcock's self-conscious play with codified convention. Similar to the romantic exchange between Eve and Roger, the film's conversation with the language of Hollywood cinema follows a double gesture by both affirming and subverting the 'sentimental' codes it appropriates. What is at stake is not just a formal exercise in the playful subversion of formulaic conventions, but also a reflection on what it means to identify with symbolic codes and norms.

By having his protagonist complete the Oedipal trajectory, Hitchcock simultaneously underscores the costs, the resistances and antagonisms subtending the norms of this formula. As in the previous romantic thrillers *The 39 Steps* and *Saboteur*, the odyssey through dangerous ordeals represents a romantic quest that tests the viability of the couple. At the same time, Hitchcock's ambivalent appropriation of the Oedipal pattern is conspicuously played out by the enormous lengths to which his cinematic plot goes in order to culminate in the final union of the couple. By having his protagonist chase across half of America, the film underlines the difficulty his protagonist has in curtailing his imaginary wandering and subjecting himself to the antagonism subtending sexual difference. In *The 39 Steps*, Hannay and Pamela find themselves literally handcuffed together by the spies before they become a couple. Even in the final image, where they hold hands, the pair of handcuffs can still be seen to dangle from his wrist. The coercive force by which they had been bound together thus appears to linger in their voluntary bond. In much the same way, the sexual relation in *North by Northwest* becomes conceivable as a binding commitment when Roger and Eve find themselves inescapably tied together by imminent danger. It is when they are precariously suspended between the grotesquely distorted faces on Mount Rushmore that Thornhill proposes to Kendall. In a hyperbolic manner, Hitchcock's setting thus suggests that Thornhill's acceptance of his position *vis-à-vis* the woman both requires and coincides with his subjection to the law of these enormously enlarged father figures.

In the final shot, the move towards the happy union of the couple is further refracted by the overdetermined image of the train penetrating a tunnel in mountainous terrain. Hitchcock's visual pun represents both an invocation of and a joke about the codes that prohibit the direct depiction of sexual intercourse in Hollywood cinema. The image harks back to an earlier sexual metaphor. During their first encounter on the train from New York to Chicago, just after Thornhill has lighted Eve's cigarette, she pulls his hand to her face and suggestively blows out the match. As a pleasurable foreplay, the earlier scene prefigures the sex they are about to have in her sleeping compartment. By contrast, the forceful entry of the train into the tunnel in the final scene is not just more drastic but also deeply ambiguous.

For a brief moment, Hitchcock's *mise-en-scène* suggests that the couple may actually be travelling towards the erotic bliss promised by the happy conclusion of the romance genre. The resolution of the literal cliffhanger on Mount Rushmore hinges on a phantasmatic dissolve, which means that, unlike the love object in *Vertigo*, Eve does not fall to her death. Roger is still struggling and holding her hand as she is precariously hanging over the precipice of Mount Rushmore. Then, all of a sudden, the two agonised faces miraculously dissolve into honeymoon relaxation. He addresses her as 'Mrs Thornhill' and lifts her to the upper berth of their sleeping compartment. By preventing catastrophe, Hitchcock's self-conscious editing both affirms and simultaneously undercuts the happy end of romantic initiation. Indeed, the consummation implied by the final image of the tunnel is far from unequivocal. The superimposition of the word 'The End' onto the train entering the tunnel points to a sense of irrevocable closure in the subject's voyage into the symbolic. The sombre cross-current highlighted by Hitchcock's irony suggests that to gain a symbolic identity means to curtail the wandering of one's free-floating fantasy. Moreover, the overt sexual symbol also harks back to the anxiety underpinning the very first scene in *Suspicion*, where Aysgarth intrudes into Lina's compartment in the blackout during which the train is going through a tunnel. While Lina's fantasy scenario appears to be triggered by a figurative instance of rape, the voyage here concludes with the return of a no less disturbing image of sexual fusion. The disappearance of the train into the tunnel may be taken to refer to the anxiety of being devoured and annihilated by an overpowering femininity.

Hitchcock's romantic narrative and visual puns both appropriate and refract cinematic conventions. They emphatically embrace codes and simultaneously point to the paradoxes of such an embrace. His irony suggests that one cannot be part of the symbolic without also being troubled by the anxieties and antagonisms that underlie its fictions. In his conversation with Truffaut, Hitchcock remarks that he 'made *North by Northwest* with tongue in cheek; to me it was one big joke' (Truffaut 1985: 102). It is important to note that in contrast to Nabokov's apotropaic poetics, Hitchcock's irony is not pitted against a traumatic knowledge. Rather, it highlights contradictions which pertain not only to the voyage of his protagonist but also, as we shall see in the final part of this chapter, to his own position in his media system. By invoking patterns of mainstream cinema, Hitchcock thus ironically underscores the discrepancies which trouble any symbolic integration, including his own assimilation in Hollywood.

Language of Exile and Assimilation

In what ways can *North by Northwest* be read back to the specific aesthetic possibilities that are available to Hitchcock and Nabokov in their exilic situations and their respective literary and cinematic languages? What are the implications of Hitchcock's decision to move to Hollywood and participate in its particular media system? To what extent is Nabokov's dislocation reinforced by the particular poetics of his literary writing? My interest concerns not just Hitchcock's and Nabokov's different biographical departures but also the specific ways in which their aesthetic media migrate to another culture. The reason why I focus again on *Lolita* and *North by Northwest* as my two examples is because the two American texts can be seen to form records of Hitchcock's and Nabokov's love affairs with the specific aesthetic languages which they absorb and develop in the context of their cultural exile, namely the English language in the case of Nabokov and the language of Hollywood cinema in the case of Hitchcock.

While *North by Northwest* and *Lolita* both trace the wandering of their protagonists, they are inflected by diverging narrative and aesthetic interests. Hitchcock's film eventually puts an end to Thornhill's pronounced mobility so as to emphasise a curtailment of imaginary vagrancy, both in his voyage into the symbolic and in his romance, which is intimately bound up with the re-establishment of the national symbolic law. In contrast, Humbert Humbert writes his memoir in the solitary confinement of a prison cell, where he awaits his trial for the murder of Clare Quilty. It is not just that *Lolita* has Humbert Humbert end up on the wrong side of the law. By inscribing its protagonist into the canon of literary love confessions, the flight into an individual imaginary realm remains predominant. Most important of all, Nabokov's language keeps moving in the direction of 'aesthetic bliss' as the one area where his ironical distance from his problematic protagonist breaks down. If the novel thus keeps following the imaginary wandering implicit in Humbert Humbert's aesthetic refuge, the film's narrative and aesthetics suggest a symbolic integration that is both troubling and enabling. The divergence of the two texts, I want to propose, is by no means accidental. Rather, it can be taken to signal the different rhetorical gestures that Hitchcock and Nabokov perform with respect to their own cultural exile.

In order to elucidate the differences in their exilic and aesthetic trajectories, it will be useful to recall the critical narrative developed in my readings. Nabokov's aesthetic language, I have argued, attempts to poetise the world in the face of traumatic losses and geopolitical displacement. It is against the backdrop of violent rupture that *Speak, Memory* re-creates an 'imaginary homeland' in and through poetic language. *Lolita*, in turn, forms Nabokov's romance with the language of his American host country. However, its poetics is haunted by the impossibility of addressing the underlying void of loss and displacement. Both the autobiography and the novel embrace language but are dislocated precisely because of their aesthetic refuge. Paradoxically, therefore, Nabokov's writing protects itself against the traumatic void which it refigures without end.

It is crucial to reiterate that in contrast to Nabokov, Hitchcock never faced violent displacement. Instead he invokes figurations of exile in his deliberate emigration and the orchestration of his cinematic scenarios. In *Suspicion*, he foregrounds a fantasy that becomes traumatic in its enactment and, in so doing, breaks with nostalgic and protective forms of imagination; rather than with the familiar, the scenario of the film is coupled with a desire for the other. Similar to the female psychothriller, *North by Northwest* explores the mental wandering of its protagonist. But instead of a traumatic fantasy, the romantic thriller stages Thornhill's resistances in his move towards symbolic assimilation. Thus, while Nabokov's poetic language reverberates with a refiguration of his traumatic losses that is perpetual and, on some level, impossible, Hitchcock takes the dialectics of alienation and its acknowledgement as the theme and the aesthetic force of his cinematic language.

Hitchcock and Nabokov meet in their prolific play with pre-existing signs and images, but their appropriations refer again to differences in their exilic, aesthetic and medial trajectories. *Lolita* pays homage to literary language and imagination through a multiplicity of intertextual allusions. In so doing, the novelistic text puts emphasis on the power of individual imagination so as to elude a painful referentiality in very much the same way as Nabokov's autobiography does. Hitchcock, on the other hand, because he participates in the mass medium of film, invokes references that are far more collective. *North by Northwest* is arguably the most explicit example of his appropriation of Hollywood cinema. The spy thriller not only summarises many of his aesthetic interests, but the film also forms a national allegory by citing tropes that tap into cultural concerns. In contrast to Nabokov's attempt to undo the contingency of his geopolitical loss and displacement in and through his highly individualised language, Hitchcock absorbs common metaphors into his cinematic idiom so as to explore anxieties that circulate in US culture at large.

As a spy thriller, *North by Northwest* pursues a preoccupation with espionage that has a long prehistory in Hitchcock's work. Following the British version of *The Man Who Knew Too Much* in 1934, spy narratives came to form a crucial component of his aesthetic universe.[19] Similar to Nabokov's texts, which frequently feature figures who spy on themselves and/or others so as to refer to the individual's uncertain existence in exile and/or states of individual delusion, his films often turn on sight and perception as a trope of psychic alienation. However, Hitchcock also makes explicit use of the spy narratives to intertwine individual quests with national concerns. His spies typically function as narrative triggers. They mistake the identity of unsuspecting protagonists who all of a sudden find themselves between two sides and run to clear their names, or put future couples through ordeals which test their romantic viability. Together with the MacGuffin, the exact nature of the spies' threat is never identified. Instead the national collective is, as it were, saved by the re-establishment of the protagonist's identity, the formation of the couple or – in the two versions of *The Man Who Knew Too Much* – the reunion of the family. Hitchcock's spy thrillers thus propose a treatment of quests that connects individual desires with collective politics.

North by Northwest enacts the mutual implication of the individual and the collective in a particularly palpable manner. By drawing on popular discourses of the time, Hitchcock treats not only the Oedipal pattern and Hollywood conventions but also Cold War metaphors as parallel levels of the same allegorical trajectory. More specifically, the film traces several homologies by referring to anxieties having to do with the mother and the home. The dominance of Thornhill's mother not only fits the psychic and cinematic dimensions of the Oedipal narrative, but it also plays on the fear of so-called 'momism' as a typical Cold War scenario. A classic example of cinematic momism is John Frankenheimer's later political thriller *The Manchurian Candidate* (1962), in which a soldier is brainwashed in Korea and made into an assassin serving the un-American interests of his dominant mother. At stake is the notion of a strong maternal attachment that prevents sons from growing into responsible citizens and, as a result, makes them susceptible to foreign – speak Communist and hence un-American – influences and activities.[20] As a result, the fear of the maternal comes to be connected with a fantasy of alien invasion and contamination, in which the mother and foreign agents alike threaten both individual and collective boundaries. By quoting this contemporary trope with its anxieties cast along national lines, Hitchcock's film relates the mother to the foreign spies as an 'enemy within'. Rather than preserving the family home and the geocultural homeland as a nostalgic recollection as in Nabokov's autobiography, the mother threatens a psychic, and by implication a national, integrity. In analogy to the maternal threat, the exposure to fatal danger in iconic settings, both on the vast Midwestern plain of fields and on Mount Rushmore, plays on the idea that the foreign spies are not only out to attack us, but they are going to do so on our national monuments. By thus evoking an allegorical interplay between the home and the nation, the mother and the spies can be regarded as Hitchcock's 'secret agents' who allow him to 'spy' on our fears and fantasies.

As an allegory of symbolic integration, *North by Northwest* works towards a correspondence between the subject's desire and a national framework. Significantly enough, it does so by treating the family and nation as parallel tropes. Not only does Thornhill flee from the mother and the spies at the same time. The mutual implication of metaphors pertains above all to the formation of the couple under the aegis of the national symbolic law. The romantic union offers an Oedipal resolution of Thornhill's maternal trouble, and it simultaneously re-establishes the social symbolic. The scene on Mount Rushmore underlines in a hyperbolic way how the individual and collective narrative levels run parallel to and mutually reinforce each other. It is while they are suspended between the oversized presidential faces that Thornhill proposes to Kendall. The threat posed by the spies to the national order is, in turn, averted immediately after he has made his proposal and thus declared his symbolic commitment. Attacked by the spies, Thornhill manages to push one of them into the abyss. Then, as he holds Eve by one hand over the precipice, his other hand gets crushed by the other spy who is shot just in time by the sergeant accompanying the 'Professor'. The timing of the scene seems to imply that Mr and Mrs Thornhill are rescued by the representative of the national symbolic law. Yet the film actually suggests that the problematic plotting by the 'Professor', who, in the name of national security, exposes American citizens to fatal danger, is miraculously halted by the formation of the couple. It is the couple who redeem him as a symbolic representative and protect the interests of the nation.

Hitchcock's climactic scene on Mount Rushmore hyperbolically performs and ironically refracts the mutual implications between the couple, the family and the nation as they are suggested by the cultural tropes and contemporary discourses he appropriates. Yet his film also draws on Hollywood's imaginary. The narratives typically produced by Hollywood transcode the individual in terms of the collective and vice versa. As a result, Hollywood represents a site particularly resonant in the ways in which it maps and negotiates the relations between individual desires and cultural concerns. As Hitchcock's most explicit Hollywood film, *North by Northwest* highlights his own affiliation with mainstream film and culture. It is, in other words, possible to add yet another allegorical layer to the narrative of symbolic assimilation traced by the romantic thriller. As implied by the film's national allegory, Hitchcock's cinematic language stands in close exchange with the 'social energies' that circulate in the culture and the media system he came to inhabit after his transatlantic move. The irony with which the filmmaker treats the cultural tropes, the national sites but also the cinematic conventions of his host country may suggest that he occupies the perspective and distance of a foreigner. Indeed, Hitchcock never quite seems to lose his sense of alienation. During his Hollywood career, he keeps cultivating his stereotypically English persona. His position in Hollywood, however, resembles his cameo appearances, in which he presents himself as a detached observer and a personally involved participant at one and the same time. His films clearly work with and within the mass medium of Hollywood film, not only by appropriating but also by interrogating its codes and conventions. Hollywood allows him not just to refine the iconic stature of his public persona and, above all, the cinematic idiom of his filmmaking. It also provides a framework which enables him to explore cultural anxieties and to formalise them through the language of a highly codified media system.

The divergence between Hitchcock's citation of collective tropes and Nabokov's emphasis on individual imagination resonates with the particular conditions of their cultural exile. In contrast to Nabokov's move into 'aesthetic bliss', which occurs against the backdrop of multiple displacements and bereavements, Hitchcock's cultural exile is not just a voluntary one. But his emigration is directly connected to the cinematic language in which he wants to work – and which is available in Hollywood more than anywhere else. This means that he inscribes himself into American culture in and through a media system that is not only located at the very heart of mainstream culture but also regulated by a specific set of codes. Indeed, it is important to note that Hitchcock's and Nabokov's exilic situations and the ways in which they migrate to America correlate with their specific media. Their medial affiliations are a crucial factor in their different figurations of language, cultural exile and assimilation.

In contrast to the far more individualised discourse of literature, film relies on a highly specialised division of labour and hence the collaboration of various levels of production. Classic Hollywood was defined to a large extent by individual studios, which worked with their own stars, directors and screenwriters and which also defined distinct styles, often by cultivating specific genres.[21] Moreover, Hollywood as a whole established a grammar which followed normative patterns such as linearity, coherence and unity and which was regulated by continuity editing and censorship techniques. These cinematic codes became so defining – not just in Hollywood but also elsewhere – that they turned into the blueprint of all narrative film.

On the one hand, film forms the American art *par excellence*, while on the other hand, it offers a visual grammar that is far more global than the language of literature. Hollywood not only occupies a hegemonic position worldwide, but from the very beginning, European immigrants made important contributions to its intercultural transfers and translations. This cultural exchange was intensified at the time of Hitchcock's move to Hollywood, when in the context of the Second World War, many European directors, including Fritz Lang, Douglas Sirk, Billy Wilder and Jean Renoir, were forced into exile.[22] Unlike other immigrants, Hitchcock did not seek refuge, but like many of them he found a cultural and medial context in Hollywood in which he could 'arrive'. Hollywood was the reason why he chose to emigrate, and it also provided a malleable matrix for his cultural arrival in his host country.

After moving to Hollywood, Hitchcock was initially confronted by the restrictions and interventions on the part of his producer David O. Selznick. Having brought him to America to direct *Rebecca*, Selznick made him realise that in the studio system he, not the director, was in the position of the master.[23] The collaborative conditions of the film industry do not allow the type of authorial control that is available to the author in literature. However, Hitchcock not only wrested control from the studios by meticulously planning every aspect of his films,[24] he also came to stake out his distinctive mark through the highly codified context to which he chose to relocate. Hollywood sponsored a set of conventions and techniques which nourished his work and which he was, at the same time, able to refract tongue-in-cheek. It was precisely the modulation of Hollywood codes that enabled him to further shape and refine his signature as an *auteur*. In *Rope*, for instance, the extremely long takes form both a comment on and a departure from the usual reliance of continuity editing on the shot-reverse-shot pattern, while *Psycho* violates narrative norms and expectations by having its female protagonist killed even before the first half of the film has elapsed. In a similar vein, the Oedipal romance in *North by Northwest* closely correlates with Hitchcock's cinematic medium. The film's quotation of the narrative pattern together with contemporary Cold War tropes is both a precondition and a logical consequence of his cinematic work in general and his interest in Hollywood in particular. By highlighting the costs and gains of the film's voyage, Hitchcock both affirms and troubles the resolution which, more often than not, in classic Hollywood cinema, is embraced in the formation of a heterosexual couple.

In contrast to Nabokov's violent uprooting, Hitchcock appears to have made his choice to cross the Atlantic in order to participate even more fully in the predominant mode of his cinematic medium. During his American career, he worked in England only on very few occasions. He returned for his war effort, namely the two propaganda films *Bon Voyage* and *Aventure Malgache* (both 1944), which he made for the British Ministry of Information, and then for the two feature films *Under Capricorn* (1949) and *Stage Fright* (1950). Only after the classic studio system broke down in the early 1960s did he once again return to England to make his penultimate film *Frenzy* (1972). In fact, if his work ever becomes truly dislocated, it is when his language loses its basis together with the collapse of classical Hollywood, which goes to show the great degree to which he was integrated in its cinematic apparatus.

While Hitchcock emigrates in order to gain access to the predominant system of his aesthetic medium, Nabokov's language is inflected by his dislocation in a different way. Similar to Hitchcock's work, his texts also prominently play with pre-existing cultural tropes, but his sign systems are never aligned with a comparable collective framework or media system. In fact, Nabokov emphatically asserts a mode of radically individual expression in an attempt to undo traumatic facticity. To speak with Fredric Jameson (1981), his poetics seeks to ward off the pain of historicity as well as the limits they set to the self. However, in asserting the autonomy of both text and author, Nabokov's writing simultaneously points to the impact of dislocation it seeks to occlude. His language keeps circling around his particular fate, his 'private tragedy' (LO: 316), which he does not and cannot directly address but which haunts his seemingly autonomous aesthetics. His texts ironically invoke a myriad of cultural texts and tropes but, in so doing, they appear to be haunted by the secret knowledge that the particularity of his individual dislocation cannot be matched by the means of poetic language.

Moreover, it is important to bear in mind the specificity of literary exile. By moving to Hollywood, Hitchcock relocates to the very centre and capital of filmmaking. In contrast to film, literary language represents not just a far more individual mode of aesthetic production and reception, but it is also more specific in its cultural and linguistic affiliations so that loss and displacement may register all the more acutely if language is all that is left to the individual. As Joseph Brodsky suggests, the exiled writer resembles someone in a capsule of language gravitating into outer space (1994: 10). The image of the individual writer isolated in and through his or her language both does and does not fit Nabokov. His decision to adopt English as the exclusive language of his literary prose may seem to radicalise the situation of linguistic exile in a manner that is indeed evocative of Brodsky's metaphor. At the same time, his abandonment of the Russian mother tongue, which was 'already a language of exile, a language in shadow' (Wood 1994: 4), not only led him to 'invent' America, as he writes in his postscript to *Lolita*, but also to reinvent himself as an American writer. As a feat that is extraordinary in exile literature, his shift to another language performs an empowering refiguration of exilic rupture by creating 'a new world to rule' (Said 1984: 167). In the same gesture, the self-imposed linguistic loss displaces other more traumatic losses which are indeed beyond the control of the individual. The triumphant gesture of Nabokov's American novel thus goes hand in hand with a discrepancy that his language cannot reflect. His bereavements and displacements are the reason why he needs to assert aesthetic control but also why, on some level, control remains out of reach.

While the poetics of *Lolita* remains haunted by exilic referentiality which Nabokov's language cannot catch up with, *North by Northwest* offers a very different commentary on symbolic assimilation. By working in the mainstream medium of film, Hitchcock participates in a powerful apparatus. His alliance with Hollywood means that his narrative is oriented towards hegemonic norms and resolutions.[25] But it also provides the immigrant with a viable frame of reference. By putting an end to the wandering of his protagonist, *North by Northwest* underscores the anxiety of losing imaginary omnipotence. Yet, by emphasising the arrival in the symbolic, the film also offers a commentary on what Hitchcock gains through the constraints of his medium.

It is thanks to his medial affiliation that Hitchcock has enough 'ground' and distance to ironically reflect on symbolic contradictions and his own position in mainstream culture. His public persona of the stereotypical Englishman may suggest that he works in Hollywood as a stranger. However, when he audaciously appropriates and interrogates cinematic conventions, he always does so from within the very system to which he chose to relocate. It is because he embeds himself in the predominant context of his medium that he can both affirm and refract its conventional metaphors tongue-in-cheek. His romantic thriller is paradigmatic for this gesture as it both embraces and ironises the symbolic alliance proposed by the romance genre. As I have been arguing in my reading, Thornhill's wandering stages the enormous resistances against which he is inserted into the symbolic. Furthermore, it is with ironical ambiguity that the couple is rescued and recuperated on Mount Rushmore. While its union is validated by the gigantic faces of the national fathers, Hitchcock simultaneously pokes fun at the grotesquely distorted faces of the presidential monument. By founding the couple in a literally precarious way, namely as they are suspended over the abyss of Mount Rushmore, Hitchcock points to his ambivalent appropriation of romantic conventions and of the way in which Hollywood tends to allegorically align the couple and the family with a collective frame of reference.

Nowhere else in the film is Hitchcock's ironic appropriation of signs more palpable than in the final visual pun. In an interview, Hitchcock himself commented on the film's ambiguous resolution by wittily remarking that 'there are no symbols in *North by Northwest*. O yes! One. The last shot, the train entering the tunnel after the love scene between Grant and Eva Maria Saint. It's a phallic symbol. But don't tell anyone' (Hitchcock in Naremore 1993: 182). Hitchcock's statement is typically overdetermined. On the one hand, he flippantly pretends not to use any symbols. On the other hand, he points at his hyperbolic image in a gesture that is both clandestine and emphatic – 'It's a phallic symbol. But don't tell anyone.' His statement points to his ironic refraction that underpins this particular pun but also his invocation of cultural and cinematic signs at large.

Hitchcock and Nabokov not only refigure different conditions of exile, but they also inhabit their aesthetic languages in different ways. As argued in my readings, Nabokov's aesthetic patterns seek to undo traumatic losses and, in so doing, point to an existential appropriation of art. His writing re-creates a home in and through language but remains dislocated by the losses his poetisation cannot address. By contrast, Hitchcock's film scenarios refer to an exilic logic which underpins the fantasy work of subjects as well as the symbolic formations they find themselves in. Rather than being propelled by the rupture of geopolitical displacement as Nabokov's prose is, Hitchcock's films take as their aesthetic energy the antagonisms troubling the subject, the family and the home as well as the nation. If Hitchcock has so much ground in his cinematic language, this is because he turns the contradictions that haunt symbolic identifications, including his own adoption of Hollywood mainstream codes, into the object of self-conscious reflection.

While Hitchcock and Nabokov both have recourse to irony so as to continually remind us of the mediated character of the textual worlds they both create and manipulate as authors, the question of irony also foregrounds the differences in their trajectories. As an instance of figurative language, irony both creates and presupposes distance. Yet ironical distance does not inform their aesthetics in the same way. *North by Northwest*, I have argued, revolves around the disturbing antagonisms that underpin symbolic positions. The film invokes irony precisely to point to these contradictions. It is by articulating their anxieties in a highly codified language that Hitchcock finds an exhilarating distance. Nabokov's textual irony and relentless playfulness, on the other hand, seek to ward off what cannot ever be distanced in spite of its denial. In *Lolita*, the unconditional embrace of 'aesthetic bliss' not only collapses the distance from Humbert Humbert's 'refuge of art'. It also eclipses the referentiality of exile and, in so doing, comes to be inscribed by an allegorical irony, which we can perform as critics but which remains beyond the reach and control of the author. While Hitchcock explores the anxieties that underpin the tropes nourishing his cinematic language, Nabokov's writing remains haunted by the inaccessible void of traumatic losses.

Both Nabokov's textual surplus and Hitchcock's domestic paranoia signal that something is out of place. Their exilic figurations, however, differ in the ways in which dislocation can or cannot be self-consciously articulated as part of their language. While Nabokov's poetic embrace in the face of traumatic loss is as desperate as it is empowering, Hitchcock's cinematic idiom relocates to the medial context of his choice. His ambivalent assimilation allows his films to ironically traverse tenebrous terrain. It is because his thrillers stage the exilism haunting subjects that his cinematic language came to inhabit the Hollywood archive.

Notes

1. A particularly important intertextual reference is the romantic thriller *The 39 Steps*, which can be described as the British precursor of *North by Northwest*. Further examples featuring a wrongly accused protagonist include *Saboteur* (1942) and *The Wrong Man* (1956). Particularly spectacular are the monumental finales of *Foreign Correspondent* (1940) and *Saboteur*, which take place on top of Westminster Cathedral and the Statue of Liberty respectively.
2. 'The theft of secret documents was the original MacGuffin', Hitchcock says in his definition of the purely functional device he developed in his interest for spy stories:

   > So the 'MacGuffin' is the term we use to cover that sort of thing: to steal plans or documents, or discover a secret . . . The only thing that really matters is that in the picture the plans, documents, or secrets must seem to be of vital importance to the characters. To me, the narrator, they're of no importance whatever. (Hitchcock in Truffaut 1985: 138)

3. Also see James Naremore's reference to this self-reflexive moment: 'The MacGuffin becomes a self-reflexive joke: a statuette containing government secrets breaks open to reveal what looks like a roll of 35mm motion picture film' (1993: 10).
4. The 'summary role' of the film is also emphasised by Mirian Keane (1980: 44), Willam Rothman (1988) and James Naremore (1993: 3).
5. See, for example, Cary Grant's roles in Howard Hawks's *Bringing up Baby* (1938), Garson Kanin's *My Favorite Wife* (1940) or George Cukor's *The Philadelphia Story* (1940).
6. Bellour's analysis of *North by Northwest*, 'Symbolic Blockage' (2001: 77–192), first appeared in French in 1975. Also see Robert Corber, who reads the film's use of the Oedipal pattern together with Cold War ideologies (1993: 193–202).
7. Bellour offers a detailed analysis of this particular scene (2001: 107–78).
8. James Mason, of course, is also the actor playing Humbert Humbert in Stanley Kubrick's cinematic adaptation of *Lolita* (1962).
9. On the real antagonism of sexual difference, see Joan Copjec (1994: 204–9) and my discussion of *Suspicion* in the previous chapter.
10. For an in-depth discussion of psychosis and the foreclosure of the Name-of-the-Father, see Bruce Fink (1997: 79–111).
11. Hitchcock points out that the extreme high-angle shot showing Thornhill run across the United Nations park creates 'the impression that the whole world is conspiring against his small silhouette' (Hitchcock in Naremore 1993: 184).
12. Steven Cohan reads *North by Northwest* 'as a representation of what the culture perceived during this period as a "masculinity crisis"' (1995: 45).

In his analysis, Cohan discusses the absorption of masculinity into consumerist culture at the time and argues that the film enacts a notion of masculinity as masquerade. As a result, hegemonic norms are deconstructed even while they may be affirmed in the end (1995, 1997).

13. See Leslie Fiedler's classic study *Love and Death in the American Novel*, particularly the chapter 'The Failure of Sentiment and the Evasion of Love' (1997: 337–90). The idyllic site where the American male feels at home, Fiedler writes, 'cannot be . . . city or village, hearth or home; for isolation is the key, the non-presence of the customary – in the words of Henry James, "the absence of what he didn't want." And what "he" especially does not want is *women*!' (1997: 355).

14. As Michael Wood further argues, the protagonists need to escape the home even though it is at the heart of the American dream:

> Home is what we know we ought to want but can't really take. America is not so much a home for anyone as a universal dream of home, a wish whose attraction depends upon its remaining at the level of a wish. The movies bring the boys back but stop as soon as they get them back; for home, that vaunted all-American ideal, is a sort of death, and an oblique justification for all the wandering that kept you away from it for so long. (Wood 1989: 40–1)

15. In his reading of *The Philadelphia Story*, Cavell emphasises the question posed by the film 'whether the heroine is a goddess made of stone or of bronze, or whether a woman of flesh and blood . . .' (1981: 140).

16. While criticising the psychoanalytic reading proposed by Bellour (2001) and followed by myself for robbing the film of its aura, Richard Millington (1999) also emphasises the gain of agency, though in a different sense. The film, he argues, not only offers a diagnosis of American middle-class culture, it goes further to enact a shift, in the trajectory of Thornhill and Eve Kendall, from emptiness to a fully embodied selfhood, from scripted roles to strategies of improvisation.

17. In *Pursuits of Happiness*, Stanley Cavell returns to Milton's notion of 'a meet and happy conversation' to suggest that the genre of the remarriage comedy turns around 'an entire mode of association, a form of life', which can be summed up by a 'thirst for conversation': 'Talking together is for us the pair's essential way of being together, a pair for whom . . . being together is more important than whatever it is they do together' (1981: 146).

18. In his reading of *The Philadelphia Story*, Cavell traces an analogy between the bond of the couple and the bond between citizens and the state (1981: 150–9). Picking up on a repeated phrase of Cukor's remarriage comedy, he suggests that Hitchcock's couple, too, is of 'national importance' as they derive from the remarriage comedy and its emphasis on a pursuit of happiness (1986: 260). I will return to the film's alignment of individual desire with a national framework in the last part of this chapter.

19. His work in the genre begins with his 'series of six consecutive thrillers made between 1934 and 1938 . . . known as his "classic thriller sextet"' (Kapsis 1992: 22), namely *The Man Who Knew Too Much* (1934), *The 39 Steps* (1935), *Secret Agent* (1936), *Sabotage* (1936), *Young and Innocent* (1937) and *The Lady Vanishes* (1938). He keeps returning to the genre in

the course of his career, for example in *Foreign Correspondent* (1940), *Saboteur* (1942) and *Notorious* (1946), or in his American remake of *The Man Who Knew too Much* (1956).
20. For an in-depth analysis of political demonology and motherhood in Cold War cinema, see Michael Rogin's text 'Kiss Me Deadly: Communism, Motherhood, and Cold War Movies' (1988: 236–73). Robert Corber also reads *North by Northwest* in reference to the threat of 'momism' (1993: 191–218), while Steven Cohan briefly refers to the same issue (1995: 47–8).
21. On the classic Hollywood studio system, see Susan Hayward (1996: 354–67).
22. James Morrison's study (1998) traces the influence of European directors on Hollywood as well as the question of Bakhtinian 'other-voicedness'. Elisabeth Bronfen (2004a) offers analyses of the both literal and figurative ways in which exile and nostalgia inscribe themselves into Hollywood cinema. Focusing on German filmmakers in Hollywood, Thomas Elsaesser (1999) discusses the tropes and images which accompanied their literal move to Hollywood.
23. See Elisabeth Bronfen's reading of *Rebecca* (2004a: 31–63) as well as Leonard Leff's monograph on the collaboration of Selznick and Hitchcock (1987).
24. Dan Auiler's *Hitchcock's Notebooks* (1999) provides insights into the various stages of Hitchcock's planning and the tight control he wished to have over all the aspects of his films. As Debra Fried points out, Hitchcock's minute planning allowed him to shoot only the necessary footage and thus to extend his control over the editing process and the final product. Emphasising that he worked 'with and within' the Hollywood codes (1999: 23), Fried also shows how Hitchcock reworked standard conventions into signature features. One of her examples is the mutual implication I have also been highlighting between the importance of the couple and the political concerns of the nation.
25. Robert Corber (1993), for instance, argues that the films Hitchcock makes in the 1950s support a Cold War consensus which links issues of national security to the hegemonic norms of heterosexual middle-class identity.

Chapter 6

Epilogue: Psychoanalytic Dislocation

What does it mean to map psychoanalysis, its critical narratives and tropes, onto aesthetic refigurations of exile as I have done in my readings of Hitchcock's and Nabokov's literary and cinematic texts? Does a psychoanalytical perspective miss the specificity of individual exile because it emphasises the subject's psychic dislocation as a universal human condition? Fredric Jameson, reflecting on interpretation, criticises the tendency of interpretative allegory to rewrite a specific event – or its figuration in an aesthetic text – in terms of a master narrative and thus to reduce it to the latent meaning of a privileged key. History, he argues, does not constitute a meaningful narrative. Rather, it happens in a random and contingent fashion. Following his notion of history which like the Lacanian real 'resists symbolization absolutely' (1981: 35), exile, too, refers us to a rupture that is unrepresentable and articulates itself only through the effects of what Jameson would call an 'absent cause'. Yet is it possible to entirely repudiate allegory in our reading? What are the gains and the limits of a critical language that reads exilic texts in accordance with the allegorical tropes developed by psychoanalysis? And how, finally, can we evaluate the recurrent references Hitchcock and Nabokov make to Freud?

My readings in this book have made two allegorical claims. As I have been arguing, exile can be read as the 'absent cause' of Hitchcock's and Nabokov's respective narratives and languages, while Freud's metaphors revolving around the subject and its family relations lend themselves particularly well to an analysis of aesthetic figurations of exile. In this final part, I will focus on psychoanalysis as a cultural archive of tropes frequently invoked – and debunked – by Hitchcock and Nabokov in their texts, but also as the critical framework which underpins my own readings. I have decided to turn to Freud and his tropes so as to isolate and retell the home narratives that inflect Hitchcock's and Nabokov's aesthetics. The repetitive gesture performed by my critical narrative is intended. My readings have time and again returned to the same patterns, namely to family romances in the case of Nabokov and scenarios of home paranoia in the case of Hitchcock. The transcoding of their texts into these interpretative paradigms has entailed a continual rewriting of their characteristic narrative trajectories on my part.

What my repetitions demonstrate as a critical gesture is the notion that something resists symbolisation and can thus only be circumscribed in continuous approximations. As Jameson points out, the real of history is '*not* a text, not a narrative, master or otherwise', but 'as an absent cause, it is inaccessible to us except in textual form . . .' (1981: 35). Whether in the aesthetic or the critical domain, the process of textualisation is not only impossible to avoid, but it also constitutes the only approach to what must, strictly speaking, remain unrepresentable. As we look at the extreme textuality of Nabokov's aesthetic and narrative patterns, we cannot help but notice the void that is not represented – because it cannot be brought into the realm of representation. Yet language is all that is available to Nabokov and his readers. In fact, all we may be able to do as critics is to rewrite and, to some degree, imitate the surfeit of his writing. Only in this way can we circumscribe how history persists in his poetics, namely in the ways in which his aesthetic formalisations seek to create coherence in the face of contingency. Or put differently, it is by positing loss and bereavement as the ground and vanishing point of his writing that we can isolate the political implications of his aesthetics.

Psychoanalytic vocabulary represents such a pertinent 'key' because of the allegorical interests that underpin my reading of Hitchcock's and Nabokov's home narratives against the backdrop of exile and dislocation. In analogy to aesthetic figurations, which transform exile into a powerful trope of textual creation, Freud's psychoanalysis oscillates between concrete cultural alienation and an allegorical language which describes the subject's fundamental homelessness. Having become what might be called the modern discourse of dislocation *par excellence,* Freud's critical tropes and narratives partly developed in response to the social marginalisation he experienced as the founder of a contested discipline and as a Jew living and working in the anti-Semitic culture of Austria. His last substantial piece, *Moses and Monotheism,* which he wrote in a lengthy process of composition, foregrounds issues of exile in several ways. The highly speculative study, which he himself called 'a kind of historical novel' (Freud quoted in Gay 1998: 605), not only rewrites the Jewish exodus from Egypt to posit the traumatic murder of an Egyptian Moses, the founder of monotheism, and the re-emergence of his belief after a long period of latency. The text also performs a mode of writing that might be called 'exilic' as Freud keeps repeating and circling around his theses in the three closely connected essays that make up his book. As Peter Gay suggests, the curious structure attests to 'the political pressures acting on Freud during these years' (1998: 605). The concrete exile experienced by Freud features in the two prefaces, both of which were composed in the first half of 1938, and introduce the third and final essay completed in England. Indeed, it is Austria's *Anschluss* to Nazi Germany and the subsequent outburst of anti-Semitic mob violence across the country that both separate and connect the two prefaces. While the first preface refers to Freud's Austrian exile under the increasingly precarious circumstances in Vienna, where he felt that he could rewrite the material of the previous two essays into a third one but not publish the book, the second preface describes how he found refuge in England. It was after his flight to London, where he spent the last eighteen months of his life, that he could finally complete and publish his study. In a broader sense, Freud's move to England meant that his psychoanalysis was to find a home and wide cultural circulation through the English translation of his work by the Hogarth Press.

While Freud's theories developed and disseminated in reverberation with his experience of cultural alienation and displacement, psychoanalysis has, of course, gained currency as a highly allegorical discourse. Freud's discovery of the unconscious forms the fundamental premise of his hermeneutics. As 'another scene', the unconscious remains inaccessible, not unlike Jameson's 'absent cause'. At the same time, the notion of the unconscious feeds the proclivity of reading psychic representations and symptoms not only in terms of underlying desires and wishes but also in reference to a circumscribed set of formulae, including Oedipal patterns or the family romance. By rewriting dreams and fantasies according to his analytical master narratives, Freud's language transposes the individual and intimate into the universal. The circumstances under which subjects are exiled or cannot otherwise inhabit their homes are always specific. But as Freud would argue, they give rise to narratives that can be read according to formulae transcending the particular. Most important of all, our fantasy work signals that something is out of place – regardless of whether or not an actual home has been lost. As a result, our imagination refers us to a knowledge of 'exile' that is psychic and pertains to all subjects.

What brings the allegorical language of psychoanalysis into productive dialogue with exile narratives is their shared gesture of textualisation. Freud's discourse resonates with the aesthetic refiguration of exile and its real rupture as it theorises the relation between an inaccessible other scene, on the one hand, and the world of symbolic signs and representations, on the other hand. At the same time, it also performs the notion that both authors and critics continually rewrite prior texts and tropes. Many of Freud's concepts draw on mythical and literary texts and have, in turn, come to represent an important reference point for aesthetic practices. In their prolific allusions to cultural sign systems, Hitchcock and Nabokov make particularly frequent reference to Freud. Yet they respond to the cultural influence of his allegorical language and its popularisations in different ways. The divergence in their attitudes to psychoanalysis, I want to argue, offers yet another perspective from which we can evaluate the differences of their aesthetics, notably the ways in which their language and imagination point to an 'exilic' knowledge underpinning Freud's hermeneutics. What is at stake in Nabokov's vehement rejection of psychoanalysis? Why does Hitchcock's cinematic idiom align itself more readily with Freud's allegorical language even though it often does so tongue-in-cheek? What can a psychoanalytical reading of their literary and cinematic texts yield if we consider the self-conscious references made by the two *auteurs*?

Whenever Nabokov invokes psychoanalysis in his letters, interviews, prefaces and novels, it is to rule out any affinities with the ideas of its founder. Not only does he describe Freud as 'the Viennese Quack' (SL: 400) or the 'Viennese witch-doctor' (IB: 9), but he also keeps emphasising that 'all my books should be stamped Freudians, Keep Out' (BS: 11).[1] In the case of Freud, he appears to have followed his own motto whereby 'a creative writer must study carefully the works of his rivals . . .' (SO: 32).[2] As, for example, in the 'fake "primal scenes"' which Humbert Humbert makes up to mislead his psychiatrists in *Lolita* (LO: 34), his texts time and again anticipate and debunk psychoanalytic patterns and readings. Paradoxically enough, this strategy implies an almost obsessive return to Freud, which suggests that the rival discourse cannot be distanced and dismissed easily. The struggle, Jenefer Shute argues, is a 'territorial' one. Nabokov appears 'acutely aware' that his aesthetic concerns – notably the central roles played in his texts by imagination, memory, desire, madness and verbal puns and jokes – not only touch on the psychoanalytical discourse but, in fact, coincide with 'a region already colonized by Vienna' (1984: 640). It is thus to reclaim what is at the very core of his poetics that he wages his war against Freud.[3]

In his rejection of psychoanalysis, Nabokov appears to distance himself from a discourse which draws heavily on literature, precedes his own writing and may have the last word as an interpretative system. At issue appears to be the individual autonomy of imagination at large and of his own imaginative work in particular. According to Nabokov,

Epilogue: Psychoanalytic Dislocation 205

imagination cannot and must not be reduced to an archive of collectively shared patterns and structures as they are postulated by psychoanalysis.⁴ In *Pnin*, for example, the 'artistic genius' of the boy Victor is said to express itself in his 'non-conformity'. Contrary to the expectations of his parents, both of whom work as psychotherapists, he responds neither to the Oedipal scenario of 'Freudian romance' they wish him to enact nor the uniform tests they have him undergo (P: 72–6). 'To the Winds, Victor was a problem child insofar as he refused to be one' (P: 75). Elsewhere, too, Nabokov juxtaposes individual uniqueness with all normative regimes. More specifically, he reduces psychoanalysis – especially its popular versions in postwar American culture – to symbols which are indeed reductive and which thus allow him to ridicule them as part of what he calls the 'topical trash' of general ideas or, in Russian, *poshlost* (LO: 315).

While Nabokov invokes Freud only to ban his cultural influence and hermeneutics from his writing, Hitchcock appropriates and incorporates his allegorical language into his own cinematic idiom. *Spellbound* (1945), Hitchcock's most explicit engagement with psychoanalysis, clearly contributed to the transformation of Freudian concepts into household knowledge as well as the optimistic belief in therapeutic treatment that became popular in the postwar American cultural mainstream. The film opens with a text which was added by Hitchcock's producer David O. Selznick and which describes psychoanalysis as a method of straightforward catharsis: 'The analyst seeks only to induce the patient to talk about his hidden problems, to open the locked doors of his mind. Once the complexes that have been disturbing the patient are uncovered and interpreted, the illness and confusion disappear . . .' The film's 'uncovering' of psychic trauma also runs parallel to the solution of the crime mystery as if suggesting that the 'hidden problems' can be unravelled like a detective plot. Hitchcock's return to Freud is, however, far more complex.⁵ His films repeatedly poke fun at simplistic solutions. In *Marnie*, for instance, the recollection of a childhood trauma does not cure the protagonist but forces her into a child-like dependence on her amateur analyst; in *Psycho*, the voice of 'mother' ventriloquising Norman Bates proves to be far more fascinating than the explanatory comments presented by the psychiatrist. In fact, it is precisely in ironically undermining explanations of this type that Hitchcock performs psychoanalytic premises and structures, notably the notion that at a fundamental level, psychic conflicts cannot be resolved. At the same time, his films stage their scenarios of psychic dislocation by drawing on Freud's family and home narratives. In so doing, they rewrite the personal in terms of the collective and vice versa; they enact a transcoding which goes hand in hand with his work in the mass medium of Hollywood film, which typically creates narratives connecting individual desires to cultural concerns.

So as to summarise and modulate my critical narrative in yet another variation of the key my readings have been invoking, I want to introduce two final examples. Nabokov's first English novel, *The Real Life of Sebastian Knight* (1941), and Hitchcock's first all-America film, *Shadow of a Doubt* (1943), not only refer us to characteristic figurations of exile – the former traces shifts between languages and cultures that are both disorienting and empowering, while the latter zooms in on the criminal secret that comes to disturb a prototypical small-town family.[6] They also signal the distinct ways in which Hitchcock's and Nabokov's aesthetic languages intersect with psychoanalytic discourse. Both texts invoke family narratives that hinge on a *doppelgänger* figure. Following Freud's classic concept of the double, Hitchcock's protagonist, the young woman Charlie (Teresa Wright), moves from a narcissistic fantasy of wholeness to the sobering recognition that any sense of belonging is troubled by fissures built into the very notion of home. Nabokov's novel suggests a trajectory that is opposed to Hitchcock's. The doubling of Sebastian Knight and his surviving half-brother foregrounds a situation of cultural displacement and, at the same time, inspires an imaginary repossession of the lost family home. While Hitchcock's narrative patterns and visual tropes draw on Freud in a self-conscious manner, Nabokov's writing can be seen to overlap with psychoanalytical concerns despite his denial of any influence by this school of thought.

Like *Suspicion* and *North by Northwest*, *Shadow of a Doubt* begins with a situation of a domestic malaise. In her daydream reveries, Charlie observes that while the family ought to be 'the most wonderful thing in the world', her family 'has just gone to pieces'. Indeed, something appears to be amiss in the seemingly idyllic small-town world of the Newton family living in Santa Rosa, California. Otherwise Charlie would not suffer from boredom, her little sister Anne would not always obsessively read, her father Joe and his neighbour Herb would not constantly talk about plots of perfect murder, while her mother Emma would perhaps not feel eaten up by her domestic chores.[7] Troubled by her discontent, Charlie believes that there is only 'one right person to save us', namely her mother's younger brother Charles (Joseph Cotton), after whom she has been named and to whom she feels connected by a psychic affinity that exceeds their kinship relation. As she once observes, 'we're both alike . . . we're not just an uncle and a niece . . . we're sort of like twins'. In fact, she feels all the more confirmed in her expectation that her alter ego will restore the home to a site of happy belonging when she finds out that as if responding to a telepathic connection, he has already made plans to visit the family.

Hitchcock's film scenario not only picks up on Freud's metaphorical language in order to posit an analogy between the family home and the psychic apparatus of his heroine. His narrative also closely follows Freud's notion of the double as the harbinger of an uncanny knowledge. Initially, Charlie expects the arrival of her uncle to remedy her dissatisfaction with the monotonous everyday life of her family, but she gradually comes to realise that her home fantasy is troubled precisely by her desire for wholeness. As noted by Mladen Dolar, the film duplicates many of its scenes and details – but not the ring which Uncle Charlie gives to Charlie (1992a: 31–7). As an object that is not doubled, the ring both affirms their extraordinary bond and disrupts the imaginary relation on which it is based. The wrong initials set Charlie on her journey of detection in the course of which she discovers that the uncle, whom she believed to possess an imaginary surplus – 'something secret and wonderful' – is in fact wanted as a serial killer of wealthy widows in the East and that he attempts to kill her after she has found out.

While Uncle Charlie has come to see his relatives in order to hide out from the police, his criminal record simultaneously materialises a disturbing knowledge haunting the family. As if to offer a metaphor of the family secret he gives body to, but also to withhold the newspaper article about the 'Merry Widow Murderer' from the family, he builds a newspaper house for the children on the first night of his visit. Not only does the flimsy material of the house visualise the fragility of the home as a site of belonging, but as James McLaughlin puts it in his reading, 'the image also suggests a criminality concealed in the family's very construction' (1986: 145). As she traces the ripped-out article in the course of her investigations, Charlie comes to realise that her desire for happiness and wholeness implies a complicity with her criminal double. Aware that the disclosure of the uncle's crime would 'kill mother', she urges him to leave town. Yet she appears to do so knowing full well that she cannot get rid of the uncle, because her family is effectively held together by the imaginary surplus as well as the disturbing secret he embodies. As Uncle Charlie emphasises, he is indeed 'part of the family'. This becomes most evident at the party given in his honour. When he announces his plan to leave Santa Rosa in the presence of the guests, all of them social representatives of the town community, Charlie's mother publicly breaks out in tears, thus underlining the extent to which the mother and, in fact, the family and community are dependent on the uncle and his criminal secret.

Hitchcock further radicalises his double narrative by having Charlie increasingly resemble her criminal alter ego. Wishing to protect her family, she hesitates to turn him in and thus becomes complicit in the death of a wrongly suspected person. Moreover, she reciprocates her uncle's murderous impulse when she threatens to kill him if he does not leave. In the penultimate scene, she does, in fact, turn into his killer when acting in self-defence, she pushes him off the running train and to his death under another approaching train. This suggests that Charlie can liberate herself from her criminal double only by becoming to some degree like him. Replicating his criminal secrecy, she has to make a secret of his crime and the details of his death so as to protect both her family and herself. Hitchcock's narrative thus suggests a paradoxical twist. The figure who has been most persistent in her detection is ultimately forced to realise that her uncanny discovery must be suppressed so as not to endanger her family and community. In the final scene, Santa Rosa buries its new honorary citizen. By praising the deceased benefactor in public and accepting his seemingly generous but criminal bequest, the interest of which is going to support the local children's hospital, the town community literally encrypts the clandestine secret that underpins its stability.

Significantly enough, Hitchcock's final scene has Charlie stand outside the church so as to underline her ambiguous position. While she cannot forget the secret knowledge embodied by her uncle, she also cannot disclose his crime, nor can she endorse the normalising belief of her future fiancé, detective Jack Graham, who explains that 'the world's all right, it just goes crazy once in a while, like your Uncle Charlie'. As a representative of the symbolic law, Graham maintains a symbolic fiction which affirms the normality of the community but conceals its problematic foundation. Charlie, on the other hand, has woken up to a sobering knowledge. No longer idealising her double, to whom she felt connected precisely because he embodied a psychic part of herself, she appears to relinquish the dangerous home fantasy implicit in her wish for wholeness. Like the Hitchcock films already discussed earlier on, *Shadow of a Doubt* thus delineates a classic *rite de passage*. Its narrative draws on Freud's notion that a mature subject position entails not only a separation from the childhood home but also the knowledge that wholeness cannot be retrieved. Indeed, Hitchcock's heroine has come to realise that she cannot fully be at home, whether in her psychic apparatus, her family or town community. What Hitchcock is primarily concerned with in his repeated return to scenarios of home paranoia is a sense of psychic malaise. While subjects experience this alienation in their concrete homes, his aesthetics stages it in close exchange with Freud's allegorical language.

Like *Shadow of a Doubt*, the family narrative of Nabokov's *The Real Life of Sebastian Knight* also revolves around a configuration of doubles. Following the death of Sebastian Knight, the narrator V attempts to reconstruct the life of his half-brother, who established himself as an English writer after the family's exile from Russia. Nabokov's intricate narrative structure suggests various possible relations between the two half-brothers – V and Sebastian may or may not be two masks of one and the same person, and either one of them could be making up the entire memoir.[8] In either case, the (self-)doubling of the narrator through the figure he describes and the biography he writes about him is significant for a reading of the novel as an exilic text. The double structure can be seen in relation to the 'stereoscopic' situation of the exiled writer who hovers between two languages and cultures. At the same time, it provides an aesthetic principle which gestures towards a transcendence of loss also brought about by exile. As he composes his text about the dead other, Nabokov's narrator can both turn to the representational realm and recuperate an imaginary family home. Or put differently, it is the search for the half-brother and their shared childhood that allows him to produce his text and, in so doing, fashion himself as an author. *The Real Life of Sebastian Knight* thus proposes a trajectory that is very different from *Shadow of a Doubt*, where Charlie wakes up from her dream of imaginary wholeness. The novel posits a double loss – the exile from Russia and the death of the brother – as the precondition of textual production and an imaginary repossession of the past. In so doing, the text thematises a transformation of exile into an aesthetic trope that is characteristic of Nabokov's poetics. A reading of his novel alongside Hitchcock's film shows the extent to which his writing affirms an imaginary realm. It coincides not with narratives of home paranoia and Oedipal separation, but with a version of the Freudian family romance that hinges on an allegorical alignment of the homeland and the mother.

Both Sebastian and V are culturally displaced, but they respond to their exile and its doubling of cultures and languages by reinventing themselves in different ways.[9] Sebastian has been 'doubled' all along by the cultural legacy of his English mother, on the one hand, and his Russian stepmother, on the other. Following the family's flight from the Russian Revolution, he completely severs himself from the cultural context of his childhood in Russia and adopts the family name of his dead English mother, Virginia Knight. His self-invention as an English author appears to perform a return to his mother, 'an inveterate traveller' (SK: 9), who left the family when he was a child. Not only does he embrace her country and language, but he also falls in love with an

English girlfriend, Clare Bishop. All of a sudden, however, he leaves Clare and appears to lose his bearings. His premature death by angina pectoris returns him to his dual cultural affiliation. The rare variety of his fatal illness seems to have been transmitted from his English mother, while his Russian doctor used to be a friend of his Russian stepmother. Having rejected his cultural doubleness, Sebastian fails in his English assimilation, while his Russian past catches up with him shortly before he dies. By contrast, the narrator V oscillates between two cultures as he holds on to their Russian heritage in his Parisian exile. On the one hand, he decides to write in English, the language chosen by Sebastian, while on the other hand, his biographical text reclaims the past in a nostalgic fashion.

V's reconstruction of Sebastian's life is written against the earlier biography by Mr Goodman, Sebastian's English secretary. Goodman not only claims that the English writer was alienated by his Russian upbringing, but also relates his existential suffering to the disorientation and unrest following the First World War (SK: 13, 52–3). Arguing that Goodman has the wrong key, V insists on a reading which, no less metaphorical than Goodman's, reconstructs Sebastian's exile through a nostalgic lens. Each of the two biographers isolates a sentence in Sebastian's work which may describe his situation and supports their respective reading. While Goodman foregrounds the liberating effect of his exile – 'I shall never exchange the liberty of my exile for the vile parody of home' – V emphasises Sebastian's nostalgic longing for the homeland: 'I always think . . . that one of the purest emotions is that of the banished man pining after the land of his birth' (SK: 23). It is not just that V, who is never mentioned in Goodman's biography and was hardly noticed by his aloof half-brother in their childhood, tries to inscribe himself into the other's life. By claiming that Sebastian was like him and experienced the same nostalgic longing, he attempts to construct a shared past. 'His dark youthful broodings', V is convinced, 'the romantic – and let me add, somewhat artificial – passion for his mother's land, could not, I am sure, exclude real affection for the country where he had been born and bred' (SK: 23–4).

The letter which V unexpectedly receives shortly before Sebastian's death forms an important element in his quest and a turning point in the relationship of the two half-brothers, who have been living in separate cultural contexts. The fact that Sebastian should have written his last letter in Russian inspires V's reconstruction of how towards the end of his life, the English writer returned to the language of their childhood. In keeping with his nostalgic stance, V is certain that Sebastian's English was 'decidedly that of a foreigner' (SK: 40), and he later adds: 'I know

Sebastian's Russian was better and more natural to him than his English' (SK: 71). Privileging their shared Russian background over Sebastian's search for his English mother, he convinces himself that 'the missing link' in Sebastian's sudden transformation towards the end of his life – the reason why he leaves Clare and addresses him in the language of their childhood – is a Russian woman (SK: 99). When he attempts to find Nina Rechnoy, with whom Sebastian was unhappily but passionately in love, he simultaneously reconstructs his alleged return to the Russian homeland. 'What matters to V', Michael Wood writes, 'is that Sebastian loved a Russian woman, as if the very fact represented a return to Russia' (1994: 40). Nina not only reduplicates Sebastian's Russian stepmother and his first Russian beloved Natasha Rosanov, but V's search for her suggests an allegorical fusion of the lost woman with the lost land and language.[10]

By tracing Sebastian's return to his Russian roots, V's narration follows a classic family romance. Indeed, the text can be seen to resonate with psychoanalytic patterns as it restores the family through the elevated memory of a pre-exilic childhood – and puts its search under the auspices of the maternal. The lost woman, language and homeland form part of one and the same allegory harking back to the psychoanalytic notion that the mother represents the first object on which all further love choices come to be based. By treating the mother and her successor as figures of cultural belonging, V's search for Sebastian's Russian beloved Nina thus becomes an attempt to affirm a shared cultural legacy as well as to construct the memory of a supposedly intact family home. One might also say that V reconstructs Sebastian's biography so as to overcome separation and merge with the other – in contrast to Hitchcock's film, where Charlie's wish to surmount her domestic discontent comes to be disturbed by her double. Nabokov's novel invokes narrative patterns that are different from the ones used by Hitchcock. Indeed, his emphasis on a nostalgic family romance reverses the idea enacted by Hitchcock's scenarios of home paranoia, which argues that an abandonment of the home as a site of wholeness and integrity is inevitable. Using the family romance to restore a pre-exilic past, V's text transcodes geocultural displacement as a home narrative. However, it is precisely in order to transform exile into a family romance that his narrative makes use of tropes that are highly allegorical.

Nabokov's narrator V may well be deluded in his nostalgic quest. He rushes to the other's deathbed propelled by 'the belief in some momentous truth he would impart to me before dying' (SK: 170–1). His fusion with the dying half-brother is, however, based on a misunderstanding. Having registered under his Russian family name, Sebastian is already dead when V keeps vigil at the bed of another English patient. Yet, while death forestalls the reunion of the two half-brothers, V merges with Sebastian in his imagination. Although he learns about the mistake later, he is transformed by the few minutes during which he believed he was listening to Sebastian's breathing.

> Whatever his secret was, I have learnt one secret too . . . that any soul may be yours, if you find and follow its undulations . . . try as I may, I cannot get out of my part: Sebastian's mask clings to my face, the likeness will not be washed off. I am Sebastian, or Sebastian is I . . . (SK: 172–3)

On the one hand, the fusion of the two doubles suggests a precarious loss of identity, if not a lapse into madness. On the other hand, V's imaginary reunion with the dead half-brother, who may or may not be his invention, inspires his self-fashioning as a writer through the text he creates.

While *Shadow of a Doubt* underlines the extent to which Hitchcock aligns his home narratives with the language of Freud, *The Real Life of Sebastian Knight* performs a turn to representation and imagination that is characteristic of Nabokov's poetics of exile. Like Hitchcock's film, which doubles many of its elements, the novel also makes extensive use of textual reduplications. Yet, instead of invoking the double as a figure of the uncanny as Hitchcock does, Nabokov uses his doubles to thematise a transformation of cultural displacement into textual production. As argued above, the two mothers of Sebastian represent two cultural languages, while the two half-brothers suggest two different negotiations of exile. The death of the author Sebastian Knight inspires the writing of a text through which the narrator V doubles himself and which is itself doubled by quotations from Sebastian's books and Goodman's biography. Moreover, the textual technique of Nabokov's novel continually refers back to itself by revisiting recurrent patterns including multiple references to chess and the violet motif associated with Sebastian's English mother. In contrast to Hitchcock's film, which has Charlie discover and acknowledge an unresolvable psychic secret, Nabokov's novel suggests that its 'secret' is disseminated on the textual surface shaped by its reduplications. There is much in V's search to suggest that, like Sebastian's first novel, *The Real Life of Sebastian Knight* represents 'a rollicking parody of the setting of a detective tale' and, in so doing, runs counter to any interpretative trajectory or system (SK: 76).[11] As V transforms both Sebastian and himself into figures of the text he is writing, the two half-brothers become all the more elusive. The 'real life of Sebastian Knight' and also V as the narrator continually appear and disappear as the text turns towards the realm of representation. In fact, one might say that the novel's emphasis on textual reduplications and patterns undermines the very idea of hermeneutic interpretation and meaning.

In his rejection of psychoanalysis, Nabokov writes against the idea that his writing may be doubled by Freud's discourse and that Freud himself may constitute a 'double to his own authorial persona' (Green 1988: 78). He objects to 'symbols and allegories' because they refer to a collective dimension implicit in imagination (LO: 314). Yet he also seeks to distance psychoanalysis as a discourse which reads allegorically and, in so doing, posits latent layers beyond the textual surface. The fictional biography *The Real Life of Sebastian Knight* and the autobiographical text *Speak, Memory* are both remarkably attuned to allegorical tropes in general and the psychoanalytic notion of the family romance in particular. This suggests that it is virtually impossible to write about the home and imagination without touching on Freud's narrative patterns. At the same time, psychoanalysis threatens to impinge on a uniquely individual imagination not only by transcoding fantasies into a collective language. It also refers to the effects of 'another scene' and, in so doing, questions the conscious control of memory and imagination that are so important to Nabokov and his attempt to affirm an autonomous aesthetic realm in the face of loss and death. In *Speak, Memory*, Nabokov's turn to representation and imagination is simultaneously redoubled by troubling reminiscences. Perhaps his writing comes closest to the ineffable void that cannot be transformed into text and language when he notes the difficulty of writing about his dead brother Sergey: 'I find it inordinately hard to speak about my . . . brother. That twisted quest for Sebastian Knight . . . is really nothing in comparison to the task I balked in the first version of this memoir and am faced with now' (SM: 198). If Nabokov insists that his writing cannot be explained by psychoanalytic notions, this may well be because their allegorical hermeneutics comes too close to the disturbing impact of loss and death that underpins his writing as its 'absent cause'.

Hitchcock, too, foregrounds his aesthetic control as the *auteur* of his films. But in contrast to Nabokov's vehement rejection, his cinematic language prominently turns to psychoanalysis in 'creating nightmares' for his audiences. His work appropriates psychoanalytic tropes in order to translate them into narrative plots and visual images. Especially his psychothrillers use the psychic situation of his figures as an important motor of his film language. At the beginning of *Shadow of a Doubt*, Charlie talks about her daydreaming fantasies as if to signal that the subsequent events revolve around psychic material returning from Freud's 'other scene'. By using psychoanalytic structures, Hitchcock's films refer to psychic processes both as their actual theme and as part of their cinematic suspense. Or one might also say that they fascinate by invoking psychic ambivalence and uncertainty both in the diegesis and the spectator. Cinema has often been discussed in analogy to mental processes, for instance in reference to the ways in which dream thoughts are translated into images or the ways in which film represents a medium of collective fantasising and daydreaming.[12] Hitchcock's work in particular has frequently been treated as a model case by psychoanalytic film theory.[13] However, it is not just that his films invite psychoanalytic readings. The filmmaker also transforms Freud's tropes into a powerful source of aesthetic energy and, in so doing, highlights the 'doubleness' of his cinematic language.

Hitchcock's visual metaphors play on an ambiguity that is reminiscent of Freud's concept of overdetermination. In other words, they hark back to the notion that psychic representations condense several disparate thoughts and meanings.[14] In his appropriation of psychoanalysis, Hitchcock often makes tongue-in-cheek references to its master narratives. *North by Northwest*, for instance, invokes an Oedipal voyage but treats the resolution of its narrative blueprint in an ironic way. At the same time, it is precisely in its ambiguous overdetermination that Hitchcock's cinematic language can be seen to stage psychoanalytic tropes. In *Shadow of a Doubt*, this becomes particularly palpable in the *mise-en-scène* of the uncle's arrival. As the train carrying him pulls into Santa Rosa, the home town of the Newton family comes to be overshadowed by a huge cloud of black smoke. The visiting relative is helped in getting off the train so that it seems as if he were ill. For a brief moment, Charlie looks puzzled. But then the cloudy shadow disappears and the family welcomes Uncle Charlie. In condensing the family reunion with the image of the cloud, the scene plays on several conflicting associations. On the one hand, the uncle's arrival invokes the fantasy that the dark forces contaminating the idyllic world of Santa Rosa come from outside, which is reassuring as it implies that they may ultimately vanish like the smoke cloud. On the other hand, the same image also suggests that it is in fact the family that attracts this dark stain as an inherent part of itself. The ironical juxtaposition and convergence of the family reunion and its troubling resonance point to an ambiguous overdetermination. Or one might also say that in the way in which he chooses to edit and splice together his cinematic material, Hitchcock is interested in a psychic ambivalence in which the supposedly familiar comes to be enmeshed with uncanny desires and wishes.

A similar overdetermination also underpins the film's credit sequence and its repetition within the film itself. Accompanied by the soundtrack of Léhar's 'Merry Widow Waltz', we see several dancing couples, elegantly dressed in turn-of-the-century fashion with one of the women dressed in black, which suggests that she may be a widow in mourning. The nostalgically inflected scene obviously establishes a link to Uncle Charlie's secret, his criminal record as the 'Merry Widow Murderer'. Of particular interest is the way in which this cinematic element is structurally deployed as a 'foreign body'. Belonging to a different space and time period, the waltz scene returns and disrupts the narrative at various moments: first when Charlie receives the ring from her uncle, but also for example after she has pushed him off the train to his death. The return of the sequence in the course of the film suggests a psychic knowledge that cannot be attributed to any of the figures but instead circulates between them. After the presentation of the ring, the sequence is superimposed on Uncle Charlie's close-up, and afterwards Charlie 'can't get that tune out of my head'. Thinking that 'tunes jump from head to head', she asks the other family members to recall its title. The fact that the family appears to suffer from amnesia suggests that they need to repress the family secret which the tune would broadcast to them. In the course of the film, it becomes evident that 'attuned' to the melody, Charlie is willing to listen to its haunting message even as this implies the recognition that she indeed resembles her criminal double. As perhaps suggested by the Viennese operetta tune, Hitchcock's language, too, is attuned to the 'other scene' theorised by Freud in Vienna around 1900. It is the return of the desires, fears and anxieties from this inaccessible scene that nourishes the aesthetic scenarios of his films.

The readings I have proposed in this epilogue and the previous chapters are allegorical in several respects. Admittedly, allegorical interpretations run the risk of getting hooked on a single interpretative key. By relating Hitchcock's and Nabokov's texts to a psychoanalytic framework, I have kept returning to variations of the same figures of thought. To zero in on a particular aspect always means to disregard certain others. Because my interest is primarily a psychoanalytic one, I have, for instance, neglected the historio-cultural contexts of the overall cultural dynamics of exile in which Hitchcock and Nabokov participated. Thus I have neither embedded Nabokov's texts in the Russian émigré circles in Western Europe nor contextualised Hitchcock's films by discussing other European directors who emigrated to Hollywood. Instead I have followed a far more specific path by choosing to cross-map select texts from the two oeuvres and to read them through the lens of a circumscribed set of psychoanalytic patterns. The critical interest underpinning this type of reading is a thinking in analogies. At stake are not only the similarities and differences between the aesthetic texts, between the themes and narratives they bring into circulation. Equally important are the rhetorical gestures implicit in the way in which they depart from and intersect with Freud's discourse of dislocation. To read Hitchcock's and Nabokov's texts together with psychoanalytic tropes, and thus zoom in on their home and family narratives, thus my wager, allows us to trace concerns that would remain opaque in separate readings and opens the work of the two *auteurs* to issues of exile and migration. More specifically, a cross-mapping of Hitchcock and Nabokov highlights what tends to be overlooked in their relentless playfulness, namely the close connection between their imagination and real-life exile.

Psychoanalysis not only prefigures home and family narratives as a critical foil with and against which we can read Hitchcock's and Nabokov's aesthetic refigurations of exile. Its allegorical language also posits a doubleness which can be mapped onto processes of aesthetic refiguration. By focusing on the effects of an 'absent cause', Freud's theory is concerned with the division but also the transaction between representations and an inaccessible other scene. In a similar vein, aesthetic refigurations of exile raise questions concerning the specific ways in which they translate the 'absent cause' of real rupture and, in so doing, textualise what eludes representation. It is here that the most significant differences between Hitchcock and Nabokov emerge. Nabokov's exilic self-invention emphasises the double vision shaped by his oscillation between two cultural languages. By transforming geocultural displacement into an empowering trope of aesthetic creation, his writing is pitted against loss and death. Nevertheless his poetics comes to be uncannily redoubled by what resists full symbolisation. The textual surfeit created by his aesthetic patterns circle around a void that can be neither articulated nor undone. Although Nabokov seeks to rule out any doubleness beyond the reduplications of his textual surfaces, displacement and bereavement thus continue to inspire and haunt his texts as their ineluctable ground and vanishing point. By contrast, Hitchcock seeks to stage a 'contact with the unknown' precisely by turning to the psychoanalytic archive. The allegorical doubleness of the tropes he appropriates nourishes the psychic ambivalence evoked both by his scenarios of home paranoia and the overdetermination of his cinematic language.

The point of departure for my cross-mapping has been Hitchcock's and Nabokov's shared investment in aesthetic language. Rather than concentrating on the playful games of their textual proclivity, I have argued that their aesthetics can be read together with the notion that exile provokes a heightened turn to language as well as a valorisation of fantasy and imagination. Indeed, Nabokov's texts suggest a poetic re-creation of the world that is existential. His writing is pitted against history as that which according to Fredric Jameson 'hurts' by setting limits to the individual and his imagination. In contrast to Nabokov's texts, Hitchcock's films do not negotiate a traumatic loss as their 'absent cause'. Instead his scenarios of home paranoia enact the idea that it is precisely fantasy that registers the difficulty of being psychically at home. If Hitchcock emphasises the exilic effects of the subject's fantasy work, Nabokov asserts the protective function of his imagination in the face of history. Yet even while their oeuvres connect exile, language and imagination in different ways, they both refer us to a doubleness that remains unresolvable, namely the murky interface between the concrete experience of displacement and its allegorisation as a resilient trope of aesthetic production. Hitchcock and Nabokov follow divergent trajectories of geocultural displacement and create different figurations of exile. Yet they meet in the importance they attribute to an exilic imaginary.

Notes

1. In the foreword to *The Luzhin Defense*, Nabokov mentions that in his prefaces for the English editions of his Russian novels, 'I have made it a rule to address a few words of encouragement to the Viennese delegation' (LD: 10). In the preface to *King, Queen, Knave*, he points out: 'As usual, I wish to observe that . . . the Viennese delegation has not been invited. If, however, a resolute Freudian manages to slip in, he or she should be warned that a number of cruel traps have been set here and there in the novel' (KQK: viii).
2. In *Strong Opinions*, Nabokov confirms the assumption of one of his interviewers that his 'contempt' for Freudian analysis is 'based upon familiarity', albeit 'bookish familiarity only. The ordeal is much too silly and disgusting to be contemplated even as a joke' (SO: 23).
3. For discussions of Nabokov's relation to Freud and psychoanalysis, see also Jeffrey Berman (1985), Geoffrey Green (1988) and Barbara Straumann (1999).
4. 'One of the greatest pieces of charlatanic, and satanic, nonsense imposed on a gullible public', Nabokov argues in *Strong Opinions*, 'is the Freudian interpretation of dreams. I take gleeful pleasure every morning in refuting the Viennese quack by recalling and explaining the details of my dreams without using one single reference to sexual symbols or mythical complexes' (SO: 47).
5. My discussion of Hitchcock and psychoanalysis draws on Jonathan Freedman's text 'Alfred Hitchcock and Therapeutic Culture in America' (1999). While *Spellbound* and its treatment of psychoanalytic interpretation and crime detection nourished the popularisation of psychoanalysis in American postwar culture, Freedman argues that 'Hitchcock's cinema stages an extraordinarily complex return to Freud' (1999: 95). As his

reading of *Vertigo* demonstrates, Hitchcock criticises the optimism of American therapeutic culture by foregrounding notions such as the repetition compulsion or the death drive, which were largely ignored in this context. On death and the death drive in Hitchcock, see Laura Mulvey (2004). For a reading focusing on Hitchcock's ironic appropriation of psychoanalytic patterns, see Elisabeth Bronfen's chapter '"You Freud, Me Jane": Alfred Hitchcock's *Marnie*, the Case History Revisited', in *The Knotted Subject* (1998: 332–77). Virginia Richter (2000) explores not only how *Spellbound* and *Marnie* play out different attitudes towards the psychoanalytic cure. She also emphasises that although Hitchcock often criticises psychoanalytic tenets at the verbal and narrative level of his films, he does make use of psychoanalysis as a powerful source shaping the visual language of his 'pure' cinema.

6. In *Shadow of a Doubt*, which was to become one of his own favourite films, Hitchcock wished to create an atmosphere of contemporary small-town America. For the script, he turned to Thornton Wilder, whose play *Our Town*, equally set in small-town America, had won the Pulitzer Prize in 1938 (see Spoto 1983: 268). Teresa Wright, the actress who plays Charlie, began her career as an understudy in the Broadway production of Wilder's play (Spoto 1983: 269).

7. Also see the text on *Shadow of a Doubt* written by Elisabeth Bronfen and myself (2000).

8. Julian Connolly mentions several possible readings (1993: 39). Rather than by V, the text could, for example, be authored by Sebastian himself, who instead of having died, creates V as a narrator and has him encounter figures from his other fictional texts. Or else V could have invented both his quest for Sebastian and the quotations from his fictional texts.

9. In her reading of the novel, Elisabeth Bronfen also emphasises the different exilic figurations and cultural affiliations of the two figures (1993: 179–80).

10. Both Julia Kristeva (1991: 36) and Elisabeth Bronfen (1993: 179) make similar arguments in their readings of the novel.

11. 'I do not believe in *any* kind of "interpretation" . . .', Nabokov states in *Strong Opinions* (SO: 263). As suggested by John Lanchester, Nabokov's critical writings and lectures explain any one detail in reference to another, similar to the textual patterns he creates in his aesthetic texts. In so doing, he performs 'a movement which would be paradigmatically Derridean if it hadn't been paradigmatically Nabokovian first'. Lanchester goes on to argue that Nabokov's evasion of interpretation and an ultimate signified of meaning may be read together with his resistance against the Freudian discourse (1995: 180–2). In fact, Nabokov's relation to Freud can be seen to play through central issues also at stake in the debate between Derrida and Lacan (see the collection of texts edited by John Muller and William Richardson in 1988). For a reading along these lines, see my earlier text on Nabokov and psychoanalysis (Straumann 1999).

12. See, for instance, Christian Metz (1982), the essay collection *Psychoanalysis and Cinema* edited by E. Ann Kaplan (1990) and the overview provided by Vicky Lebeau (2001: 32–60). For a discussion of the 'parallel histories' of cinema and psychoanalysis, see the essay collection *Endless Night* edited by Janet Bergstrom (1999).

13. A prominent example is *Everything You Always Wanted to Know About Lacan and Were Afraid to Ask Hitchcock*, edited by Slavoj Žižek (1992).
14. In *The Interpretation of Dreams*, Freud writes: 'the elements of the dream are constructed out of the whole mass of dream-thoughts and each one of those elements is shown to have been determined many times over in relation to the dream-thoughts' (Freud 1958: 284).

Bibliography

Vladimir Nabokov

Ada or Ardor: A Family Chronicle (1971) [1969], London: Penguin.
Bend Sinister (1974) [1947], London: Penguin.
Dear Bunny, Dear Volodya: The Nabokov-Wilson Letters, 1940–1971 (2001), ed. Simon Karlinsky, revised and expanded edition, Berkeley, Los Angeles and London: University of California Press.
Despair (1981) [1965], London: Penguin; first published in Russian, 1934.
Invitation to a Beheading (1963) [1960], London: Penguin; first published in Russian, 1935.
King, Queen, Knave (1993) [1968], London: Penguin; first published in Russian, 1928.
Laughter in the Dark (1963) [1938], London: Penguin; first published in Russian, 1933.
Lectures on Literature (1980), ed. Fredson Bowers, San Diego, New York and London: Harcourt Brace.
Lectures on Russian Literature (1981), ed. Fredson Bowers, San Diego, New York and London: Harcourt Brace.
Lolita: A Screenplay (1997) [1961], New York: Vintage.
Look at the Harlequins! (1980) [1974], London: Penguin.
Mary (1973) [1970], Penguin: London; first published in Russian, 1926.
Pale Fire (1991) [1962], London: Penguin.
Pnin (1960) [1957], London: Penguin.
Selected Letters 1940–77 (1991), ed. Dmitri Nabokov and Matthew J. Bruccoli, London: Vintage.
Speak, Memory (1969) [1967], London: Penguin; first published as *Conclusive Evidence*, 1951.
Strong Opinions (1990) [1973], New York: Vintage.
The Annotated Lolita (1991) [1958], ed. Alfred Appel, Jr, London: Penguin; first published in Paris, 1955.
The Eye (1990) [1965], New York: Vintage; first published in Russian, 1930.
The Luzhin Defense (1994) [1964], London: Penguin; first published in Russian, 1930.
The Real Life of Sebastian Knight (1994) [1941], London: Penguin.
Transparent Things (1993) [1972], London: Penguin.

Alfred Hitchcock

Alfred Hitchcock Presents, USA: Revue Studios, 1955–62.
Aventure Malgache, UK: British Ministry of Information, 1944.
Bon Voyage, UK: British Ministry of Information, 1944.
Foreign Correspondent, USA: United Artists, 1940.
Frenzy, UK: Universal, 1972.
Lifeboat, USA: 20th Century-Fox, 1944.
Marnie, USA: Universal, 1964.
Mr and Mrs Smith, USA: RKO, 1941.
North by Northwest, USA: MGM, 1959.
Notorious, USA: RKO, 1946.
Psycho, USA: Paramount, 1960.
Rear Window, USA: Paramount, 1954.
Rebecca, USA: Selznick International Pictures, 1940.
Rope, USA: Warner, 1948.
Sabotage, UK: Shepherd, Gaumont British Pictures, 1936.
Saboteur, USA: Universal, 1942.
Secret Agent, UK: Gaumont British Pictures, 1936.
Shadow of a Doubt, USA: Universal, 1943.
Spellbound, USA: Selznick International Pictures, 1945.
Stage Fright, UK: Warner, 1950.
Strangers on a Train, USA: Warner, 1951.
Suspicion, USA: RKO, 1941.
The 39 Steps, UK: Gaumont British Pictures, 1935.
The Birds, USA: Universal, 1963.
The Lady Vanishes, UK: Gainsborough Pictures, 1938.
The Man Who Knew Too Much, UK: Gaumont British Pictures, 1934.
The Man Who Knew Too Much, USA: Paramount, 1956.
The Trouble with Harry, USA: Paramount, 1955.
The Wrong Man, USA: Warner, 1956.
To Catch a Thief, USA: Paramount, 1955.
Under Capricorn, UK: Transatlantic Pictures, Warner, 1949.
Vertigo, USA: Paramount, 1958.
Young and Innocent, UK: Gainsborough, Gaumont British Pictures, 1937.

References

Abraham, Nicolas and Maria Torok (1994), *The Shell and the Kernel*, vol. 1, Chicago: University of Chicago Press.
Abrams, M. H. (1985), *A Glossary of Literary Terms*, sixth edition, New York, Toronto and London: Harcourt Brace Jovanovich.
Aciman, André (ed.) (1999), *Letters of Transit: Reflections on Exile, Identity, Language and Loss*, New York: The New Press.
Alexandrov, Vladimir E. (1991), *Nabokov's Otherworld*, Princeton, NJ: Princeton University Press.
Alexandrov, Vladimir E. (ed.) (1995), *The Garland Companion to Nabokov*, New York and London: Garland.

Allan, Nina (1994), *Madness, Death and Disease in the Fiction of Vladimir Nabokov*, Birmingham Slavonic Monographs 23, Birmingham: Department of Russian Language and Literature, University of Birmingham.
Allen, Richard (2007), *Hitchcock's Romantic Irony*, New York: Columbia University Press.
Allen, Richard and S. Ishii Gonzalès (eds) (1999), *Alfred Hitchcock: Centenary Essays*, London: British Film Institute.
Allen, Richard and S. Ishii Gonzalès (eds) (2004), *Hitchcock: Past and Future*, London and New York: Routledge.
Alter, Robert (1975), *Partial Magic: The Novel as Self-Conscious Genre*, Berkeley, Los Angeles and London: University of California Press.
Alter, Robert (1991), 'Nabokov and Memory', *Partisan Review*, 58: 4, 620–9.
Améry, Jean (1966), 'Wieviel Heimat braucht der Mensch?', in Jean Améry, *Jenseits von Schuld und Sühne: Bewältigungsversuche eines Überwältigten*, Munich: Szcesny, pp. 71–100.
Appel, Alfred, Jr (1967), '*Lolita*: The Springboard of Parody', in *Nabokov: The Man and His Work*, ed. L. S. Dembo, Madison and London: University of Wisconsin Press, pp. 106–43.
Appel, Alfred, Jr (1974), *Nabokov's Dark Cinema*, New York: Oxford University Press.
Appel, Alfred, Jr (ed.) (1991), *The Annotated Lolita*, London: Penguin.
Assmann, Aleida (2002), 'Gedächtnis als Leitbegriff der Kulturwissenschaften', in *Kulturwissenschaft: Forschung, Praxis, Positionen*, ed. Lutz Musner and Gotthart Wunberg, Vienna: WUV, pp. 27–45.
Auiler, Dan (1999), *Hitchcock's Notebooks: An Authorized and Illustrated Look Inside the Creative Mind of Alfred Hitchcock*, New York: Avon Books.
Bakhtin, Mikhail (2002) [1975], 'Forms of Time and the Chronotope in the Novel', in Mikhail Bakhtin, *The Dialogic Imagination*, ed. Michael Holquist, Austin: University of Texas Press, pp. 84–258.
Barthes, Roland (1990) [1974], *S/Z*, trans. Richard Miller, Oxford: Blackwell.
Barthes, Roland (1993) [1981], *Camera Lucida: Reflections on Photography*, trans. Richard Howard, London: Vintage.
Barthes, Roland (2000) [1957], *Mythologies*, trans. Annette Lavers, London: Vintage.
Baumann, Sabine (1999), *Vladimir Nabokov: Haus der Erinnerung, Gnosis und Memoria in kommentierenden und autobiographischen Texten*, Basel and Frankfurt am Main: Stroemfeld.
Baxter, John (1976), *The Hollywood Exiles*, New York: Taplinger.
Beaujour, Elizabeth Klosty (1995), 'Bilingualism', in *The Garland Companion to Vladimir Nabokov*, ed. Vladimir E. Alexandrov, New York and London: Garland, pp. 37–43.
Beier, Lars-Olav and Georg Seeßlen (eds) (1999), *Alfred Hitchcock*, Berlin: Bertz.
Bell, Michael (1974), '*Lolita* and Pure Art', *Essays in Criticism*, 26: 2, 169–84.
Bellour, Raymond (2001), *The Analysis of Film*, ed. Constance Penley, Bloomington and Indianapolis: Indiana University Press.
Benjamin, Walter (1977) [1921], 'Zur Kritik der Gewalt', in Walter Benjamin, *Gesammelte Schriften*, ed. Rolf Tiedemann and Hermann Schweppenhäuser, vol. II.1, Frankfurt am Main: Suhrkamp, pp. 179–203.

Benton, Robert J. (1984), 'Film as Dream: Alfred Hitchcock's *Rear Window*', *Psychoanalytic Review*, 71: 3, 483–500.
Bergstrom, Janet (ed.) (1999), *Endless Night: Cinema, Psychoanalysis, Parallel Histories*, Berkeley, Los Angeles and London: University of California Press.
Berman, Jeffrey (1985), 'Nabokov and the Viennese Witch Doctor', in Jeffrey Berman, *The Talking Cure: Literary Representations of Psychoanalysis*, New York: New York University Press, pp. 211–38.
Bhabha, Homi K. (1994), *The Location of Culture*, London and New York: Routledge.
Bienstock, Beverley Gray (1982), 'Focus Pocus: Film Imagery in *Bend Sinister*', in *Nabokov's Fifth Arc: Nabokov and Others on His Life's Work*, ed. J. E. Rivers and Charles Nicol, Austin: University of Texas Press, pp. 125–38.
Bordo, Susan (2000), 'Humbert and Lolita', in Susan Bordo, *The Male Body: A New Look at Men in Public and in Private*, New York: Farrar, Straus and Giroux, pp. 299–322.
Botting, Fred (1991), 'Back to the Author: Romanticism, Postmodernism, de Man', *Textual Practice*, 5:1, 25–39.
Bowlby, Rachel (2003), '*Lolita* and the Art of Advertising', in *Vladimir Nabokov's Lolita: A Casebook*, ed. Ellen Pifer, Oxford: Oxford University Press, pp. 155–79.
Boyd, Brian (1993a), *Vladimir Nabokov: The Russian Years*, London: Vintage.
Boyd, Brian (1993b), *Vladimir Nabokov: The American Years*, London: Vintage.
Boyd, Brian and Robert Michael Pyle (eds) (2000), *Nabokov's Butterflies: Unpublished and Uncollected Writings*, London: Allen Lane and Penguin.
Brill, Lesley (1988), *The Hitchcock Romance: Love and Irony in Hitchcock's Films*, Princeton, NJ: Princeton University Press.
Bringing up Baby, film, directed by Howard Hawks, USA: RKO, 1938.
Brodsky, Joseph (1986), *Less Than One: Selected Essays*, New York: Farrar, Straus and Giroux.
Brodsky, Joseph (1994), 'The Condition We Call Exile: An Address', in *Altogether Elsewhere: Writers in Exile*, ed. Marc Robinson, San Diego, New York and London: Harcourt Brace, pp. 3–11.
Bronfen, Elisabeth (1988), 'Death's Liminality: With Reference to Nabokov's Prose', in *Proceedings of the XIIth Congress of the International Comparative Literature Association: Space and Boundaries*, vol. 2, Munich: Iudicum, pp. 591–7.
Bronfen, Elisabeth (1992), *Over Her Dead Body: Death, Femininity and the Aesthetic*, Manchester: Manchester University Press.
Bronfen, Elisabeth (1993), 'Exil in der Literatur: Zwischen Metapher und Realität', *Arcadia: Zeitschrift für Vergleichende Literaturwissenschaft*, 28: 2, 167–83.
Bronfen, Elisabeth (1998), *The Knotted Subject: Hysteria and Its Discontents*, Princeton, NJ: Princeton University Press.
Bronfen, Elisabeth (2001), 'Erschreckende Bilder vertrauter Art: Freuds Spiel mit einer Denkfigur', in *Die unheimliche Frau: Weiblichkeit im Surrealismus*, ed. Angela Lampe, Heidelberg: Edition Braus, pp. 113–26.
Bronfen, Elisabeth (2002), 'Cross-Mapping: Kulturwissenschaft als Kartographie von erzählender und visueller Sprache', in *Kulturwissenschaft:*

Forschung, Praxis, Positionen, ed. Lutz Musner and Gotthart Wunberg, Vienna: WUV, pp. 110–34.
Bronfen, Elisabeth (2004a), 'Uncanny Appropriations: *Rebecca*', in Elisabeth Bronfen, *Home in Hollywood: The Imaginary Geography of Cinema*, New York: Columbia University Press, pp. 31–63.
Bronfen, Elisabeth (2004b), *Liebestod und Femme Fatale: Der Austausch sozialer Energien zwischen Oper, Literatur und Film*, Frankfurt am Main: Suhrkamp.
Bronfen Elisabeth and Barbara Straumann (2000), 'Double Trouble in Hitchcock's *Shadow of a Doubt*', in *Das Unbewusste in Zürich: Literatur und Tiefenpscholgie um 1900*, ed. Thomas Sprecher, Zurich: NZZ Verlag, pp. 95–108.
Brooks, Peter and Alex Woloch (eds) (2000), *Whose Freud? The Place of Psychoanalysis in Contemporary Culture*, New Haven and London: Yale University Press.
Brougher, Kerry, Michael Tarantino and Astrid Bowron (eds) (1999), *Notorious: Alfred Hitchcock and Contemporary Art*, Oxford: Museum of Modern Art Oxford.
Burgin, Victor (1992), 'Fantasy', in *Feminism and Psychoanalysis: A Critical Dictionary*, ed. Elizabeth Wright, Oxford: Blackwell, pp. 84–8.
Caruth, Cathy (1996), *Unclaimed Experience: Trauma, Narrative, and History*, Baltimore and London: Johns Hopkins University Press.
Cavell, Stanley (1979), *The World Viewed: Reflections on the Ontology of Film*, Cambridge, MA and London: Harvard University Press.
Cavell, Stanley (1981), *The Pursuits of Happiness: The Hollywood Comedy of Remarriage*, Cambridge, MA and London: Harvard University Press.
Cavell, Stanley (1986), '*North by Northwest*', in *A Hitchcock Reader*, ed. Marshall Deutelbaum and Leland Poague, Ames: Iowa State University Press, pp. 249–64.
Cavell, Stanley (1987), *Disowning Knowledge in Six Plays of Shakespeare*, Cambridge: Cambridge University Press.
Certeau, Michel de (1986), 'Psychoanalysis and Its History', 'The Freudian Novel', in Michel de Certeau, *Heterologies: Discourses on the Other*, trans. Brian Massumi, Minneapolis and London: University of Minnesota Press, pp. 3–34.
Chabrol, Claude and Eric Rohmer (1975), *Hitchcock*, Paris: Editions Universitaires.
Chambers, Ian (1994), *Migrancy, Culture, Identity*, London and New York: Routledge.
Chandler, Charlotte (2005), *It's Only a Movie: Alfred Hitchcock, A Personal Biography*, London: Pocket Books.
Cohan, Steven (1995), 'The Spy in the Gray Flannel Suit: Gender Performance and the Representation of Masculinity', in *The Masculine Masquerade: Masculinity and Representation*, ed. Andrew Perchuk and Helaine Posner, Cambridge, MA and London: MIT Press, pp. 43–62.
Cohan, Steven (1997), 'The Spy in the Gray Flannel Suit', in Steven Cohan, *Masked Men: Masculinity and the Movies in the Fifities*, Bloomington and Indianapolis: Indiana University Press, pp. 1–33.
Cohen, Paula Marantz (1995), *Alfred Hitchcock: The Legacy of Victorianism*, Lexington: The University Press of Kentucky.

Cohen, Tom (1994), 'Hitchcock and the Death of (Mr) Memory (Technology of the Visible)', in Tom Cohen, *Anti-Mimesis from Plato to Hitchcock*, Cambridge: Cambridge University Press, pp. 227–59.
Cohen, Tom (2005a), *Hitchcock's Cryptonomies, Volume I: Secret Agents*, Minneapolis and London: University of Minnesota Press.
Cohen, Tom (2005b), *Hitchcock's Cryptonomies, Volume II: War Machines*, Minneapolis and London: University of Minnesota Press.
Colebrook, Claire (2004), *Irony*, London and New York: Routledge.
Connolly, Julian W. (1993), 'From Biography to Autobiography and Back: The Fictionalization of the Narrated Self in *The Real Life of Sebastian Knight*', *Cycnos*, 10: 1, 39–46.
Connolly, Julian W. (ed.) (1999), *Nabokov and His Fiction: New Perspectives*, Cambridge: Cambridge University Press.
Connolly, Julian W. (ed.) (2005), *The Cambridge Companion to Nabokov*, Cambridge: Cambridge University Press.
Conrad, Peter (2000), *The Hitchcock Murders*, London, New York: Faber.
Cook, Pam and Mieke Bernink (eds) (1999), *The Cinema Book*, second edition, London: British Film Institute.
Copjec, Joan (1994), *Read My Desire: Lacan Against the Historicists*, Cambridge, MA and London: MIT Press.
Corber, Robert J. (1993), *In the Name of National Security: Hitchcock, Homophobia, and the Political Construction of Gender in Postwar America*, Durham and London: Duke University Press.
Corliss, Richard (1994), *Lolita*, London: British Film Institute.
Cornwell, Neil (1999), *Vladimir Nabokov*, Northcote House: Plymouth.
Cornwell, Neil (2005), 'From Sirin to Nabokov: The Transition to English', in *The Cambridge Companion to Nabokov*, ed. Julian W. Connolly, Cambridge: Cambridge University Press, pp. 151–69.
Cowie, Elizabeth (1997), *Representing the Woman: Cinema and Psychoanalysis*, London: Macmillan.
Davidson, James A. (1997), 'Hitchcock/Nabokov: Some Thoughts on Hitchcock and Nabokov', *Images: A Journal of Film and Popular Culture*, 3, http://www.imagesjournal.com/issues03/features/hitchnab1.htm.
de Man, Paul (1983), *Blindness and Insight: Essays in the Rhetoric of Contemporary Criticism*, second edition, Minneapolis: University of Minnesota Press.
Derrida, Jacques (1988) [1966], 'Structure, Sign and Play in the Discourse of the Human Sciences', in *Modern Criticism and Theory: A Reader*, ed. David Lodge, London and New York: Longman, pp. 108–23.
Derrida, Jacques (2005) [2003], *Rogues: Two Essays on Reason*, Stanford: Stanford University Press.
Deutelbaum, Marshall and Leland Poague (eds) (1986), *A Hitchcock Reader*, Ames: Iowa State University Press.
Diment, Galya (1999), 'Vladimir and the Art of Autobiography', in *Nabokov and His Fiction: New Perspectives*, ed. Julian W. Connolly, Cambridge: Cambridge University Press, pp. 36–53.
Doane, Mary Ann (1987), *The Desire to Desire: The Woman's Film of the 1940s*, Bloomington and Indianapolis: Indiana University Press.
Dolar, Mladen (1991), '"I Shall Be with You on Your Wedding-Night": Lacan and the Uncanny', *October*, 58: 3, 5–23.

Dolar, Mladen (1992a), 'Hitchcock's Objects', in *Everything You Always Wanted to Know About Lacan and Were Afraid to Ask Hitchcock*, ed. Slavoj Žižek, London, New York: Verso, pp. 31–46.

Dolar, Mladen (1992b), 'A Father Who Is Not Quite Dead', in *Everything You Always Wanted to Know About Lacan and Were Afraid to Ask Hitchcock*, ed. Slavoj Žižek, London, New York: Verso, pp. 143–50.

Dolar, Mladen (1993), 'Beyond Interpellation', *Qui Parle*, 6: 2, 75–96.

Dolar, Mladen (1996), 'At First Sight', in *Gaze and Voice as Love Objects*, ed. Slavoj Žižek and Renata Salecl, Durham and London: Duke University Press, pp. 129–53.

Douchet, Jean (1986) [1960], 'Hitch and His Audience', in *Cahiers du Cinéma: The 1960s – New Wave, New Cinema, Reevaluating Hollywood*, ed. Jim Hillier, Cambridge, MA: Harvard University Press, pp. 150–7.

Douchet, Jean (1999) [1967], *Hitchcock*, Paris: Cahiers du cinéma.

Durgnat, Raymond (1978), *The Strange Case of Alfred Hitchcock or The Plain Man's Hitchcock*, Cambridge, MA: MIT Press.

Eagleton, Terry (1970), *Exiles and Emigrés: Studies in Modern Literature*, New York: Schocken.

Elsaesser, Thomas (1999), 'Ethnicity, Authenticity, and Exile: A Counterfeit Trade? German Filmmakers and Hollywood', in *Home, Exile, Homeland: Film, Media, and the Politics of Place*, ed. Hamid Naficy, New York and London: Routledge, pp. 97–124.

Evans, Dylan (1996), *An Introductory Dictionary of Lacanian Psychoanalysis*, London and New York: Routledge.

Fiedler, Leslie A. (1997) [1960], *Love and Death in the American Novel*, Normal, IL: Dalkey Archive Press.

Fink, Bruce (1995), *The Lacanian Subject: Between Language and Jouissance*, Princeton, NJ: Princeton University Press.

Fink, Bruce (1997), *A Clinical Introduction to Lacanian Psychoanalysis: Theory and Technique*, Cambridge, MA and London: Harvard University Press.

Finler, Joel W. (1992), *Alfred Hitchcock: The Hollywood Years*, London: Batsford.

Flaubert, Gustave (1980), *Correspondance: Juillet 1851–Décembre 1858*, ed. Jean Bruneau, vol. 2, Paris: Gallimard.

Flaubert, Gustave (1992) [1856–57], *Madame Bovary: Provincial Lives*, trans. Geoffrey Wall, London: Penguin.

Flaubert, Gustave (1997), *Selected Letters*, trans. Geoffrey Wall, London: Penguin.

Fletcher, John (1995), 'Primal Scenes and the Female Gothic: *Rebecca* and *Gaslight*', *Screen*, 36: 4, 341–70.

Flower, Dean (1993), 'Nabokov and Nastiness', *The Hudson Review*, 45: 4, 573–82.

Forrester, John (1997), *Dispatches from the Freud Wars: Psychoanalysis and Its Passions*, Cambridge, MA and London: Harvard University Press.

Foster, John Burt, Jr (1993), *Nabokov's Art of Memory and European Modernism*, Princeton, NJ: Princeton University Press.

Foucault, Michel (1977) [1963], 'Language to Infinity', in Michel Foucault, *Language, Counter-Memory, Practice: Selected Essays and Interviews*, ed.

Donald F. Bouchard, trans. Donald F. Bouchard and Sherry Simon, Ithaca, NY: Cornell University Press, pp. 53–67.
Fraysse, Suzanne (1995), 'Worlds Under Erasure: *Lolita* and Postmodernism', *Cycnos*, 12: 2, 93–100.
Freedman, Barbara (1991), *Staging the Gaze: Postmodernism, Psychoanalysis, and Shakespearean Comedy*, Ithaca and London: Cornell University Press.
Freedman, Jonathan (1999), 'Alfred Hitchcock and Therapeutic Culture in America', in *Hitchcock's America*, ed. Jonathan Freedman and Richard Millington, New York and Oxford: Oxford University Press, pp. 77–98.
Freedman, Jonathan and Richard Millington (eds) (1999), *Hitchcock's America*, New York and Oxford: Oxford University Press.
French, Philip (1985), 'Alfred Hitchcock: The Film-Maker as Englishman and Exile', *Sight & Sound*, 54: 1, 116–23.
Freud, Sigmund (1955a) [1919], 'The "Uncanny"', in Sigmund Freud, *The Standard Edition of the Complete Psychological Works of Sigmund Freud*, ed. James Strachey, vol. 17, London: The Hogarth Press, pp. 217–56.
Freud, Sigmund (1955b) [1920], 'Beyond the Pleasure Principle', in Sigmund Freud, *The Standard Edition of the Complete Psychological Works of Sigmund Freud*, ed. James Strachey, vol. 18, London: The Hogarth Press, pp. 1–64.
Freud, Sigmund (1958) [1900–1], *The Interpretation of Dreams*, in Sigmund Freud, *Standard Edition of the Complete Psychological Works of Sigmund Freud*, ed. James Strachey, vols 4–5, London: The Hogarth Press.
Freud, Sigmund (1959a) [1908], 'Creative Writers and Day-Dreaming', in Sigmund Freud, *The Standard Edition of the Complete Psychological Works of Sigmund Freud*, ed. James Strachey, vol. 9, London: The Hogarth Press, pp. 141–53.
Freud, Sigmund (1959b) [1909], 'Family Romances', in Sigmund Freud, *The Standard Edition of the Complete Psychological Works of Sigmund Freud*, ed. James Strachey, vol. 9, London: The Hogarth Press, pp. 235–41.
Freud, Sigmund (1963) [1916–17], *Introductory Lectures on Psycho-Analysis: Part III*, in Sigmund Freud, *The Standard Edition of the Complete Psychological Works of Sigmund Freud*, ed. James Strachey, vol. 16, London: The Hogarth Press.
Freud, Sigmund (1964) [1939], 'Moses and Monotheism', in Sigmund Freud, *The Standard Edition of the Complete Psychological Works of Sigmund Freud*, ed. James Strachey, vol. 23, London: The Hogarth Press, pp. 1–137.
Freud, Sigmund, and Wilhelm Fliess (1986) [1887–1904], *Briefe an Wilhelm Fliess 1887–1904*, ed. Jeffrey Moussaieff Masson, Frankfurt am Main: Fischer.
Fried, Debra (1999), 'Love, American Style: Hitchcock's Hollywood', in *Hitchcock's America*, ed. Jonathan Freedman and Richard Millington, New York and Oxford: Oxford University Press, pp. 15–28.
Frosch, Thomas R. (2003), 'Parody and Authenticity in *Lolita*', in *Vladimir Nabokov's Lolita: A Casebook*, ed. Ellen Pifer, Oxford and New York: Oxford University Press, pp. 39–56.
Gallafent, Ed (1988), 'Black Satin: Fantasy, Murder and the Couple in *Gaslight* and *Rebecca*', *Screen*, 29: 2, 84–103.
Gaslight, film, directed by George Cukor, USA: MGM, 1944.
Gay, Peter (1998), *Freud: A Life for Our Time*, New York, London: Norton.

Gottlieb, Sidney (ed.) (1997), *Hitchcock on Hitchcock*, London: Faber.
Gottlieb, Sidney (2002), 'Hitchcock and the Art of the Kiss: A Preliminary Survey', in *Framing Hitchcock: Selected Essays from the Hitchcock Annual*, ed. Sidney Gottlieb and Christopher Brookhouse, Detroit: Wayne University University Press, pp. 132–46.
Gottlieb, Sidney (ed.) (2003), *Alfred Hitchcock: Interviews*, Jackson: University Press of Mississippi.
Grabes, Herbert (1977), *Fictitious Biographies: Vladimir Nabokov's English Novels*, The Hague: Mouton.
Grayson, Jane (2001), *Vladimir Nabokov*, London: Penguin.
Grayson, Jane, Arnold McMillin and Priscilla Meyer (eds) (2002), *Nabokov's World, Volume 1: The Shape of Nabokov's World*, Basingstoke and New York: Palgrave.
Green, Geoffrey (1988), *Freud and Nabokov*, Lincoln, London: University of Nebraska Press.
Green, Geoffrey (1993), 'Visions of a "Perfect Past"': Nabokov, Autobiography, Biography, and Fiction', *Cycnos*, 10: 1, 55–62.
Greenblatt, Stephen (ed.) (1981), *Allegory and Representation*, Baltimore and London: Johns Hopkins University Press.
Greenblatt, Stephen (1988), *Shakespearean Negotiations: The Circulation of Social Energy in Renaissance England*, Oxford: Clarendon Press.
Hacking, Ian (1998), *Mad Travelers: Reflections on the Reality of a Transient Mental Illness*, Charlottesville and London: University Press of Virginia.
Haegert, John (2003), 'The Artist in Exile: The Americanization of Humbert Humbert', in *Vladimir Nabokov's Lolita: A Casebook*, ed. Ellen Pifer, Oxford and New York: Oxford University Press, pp. 137–53.
Hägglund, Martin (2003), 'Chronophobia: Vladimir Nabokov's Art of Memory', manuscript.
Halberstam, David (1993), *The Fifties*, New York: Fawcett Columbine.
Hamlet, film, directed by Laurence Olivier, UK: Two Cities Films, 1948.
Hartman, Geoffrey H. (1981), 'Plenty of Nothing: Hitchcock's *North by Northwest*', *Yale Review*, 71: 1, 13–27.
Haskell, Barbara (ed.) (1999), *The American Century: Art and Culture 1900–1950*, New York and London: Whitney Museum of American Art and Norton.
Hassan, Ihab (1993), 'Toward a Concept of Postmodernism', in *Postmodernism: A Reader*, ed. Thomas Docherty, New York, London and Toronto: Harvester Wheatsheaf, pp. 146–56.
Hayward, Susan (1996), *Key Concepts in Cinema Studies*, London and New York: Routledge.
Heath, Stephen (1992), *Gustave Flaubert: Madame Bovary*, Cambridge: Cambridge University Press.
Hesling, W. (1987), 'Classical Cinema and the Spectator', *Literature/Film Quarterly*, 15: 3, 181–9.
Hof, Renate (1980), 'Das Spiel des *Unreliable Narrator* in Nabokov's *Lolita*', *Amerikastudien/American Studies*, 25: 4, 777–94.
Hof, Renate (1984), *Das Spiel des unreliable narrator: Aspekte unglaubwürdigen Erzählens im Werk von Vladimir Nabokov*, American Studies: A Monograph Series 59, Munich: Fink.

Hollinger, Karen (1993), 'The Female Oedipal Drama of *Rebecca* from Novel to Film', *Quarterly Review of Film & Video*, 14: 4, 17–30.
Horkheimer, Max and Theodor W. Adorno (1988) [1944], *Dialektik der Aufklärung: Philosophische Fragmente*, Frankfurt am Main: Fischer.
Hüllen, Christopher (1990), *Der Tod im Werk Vladimir Nabokovs Terra Incognita*, Munich: Otto Sagner.
Hutcheon, Linda (1989), *The Politics of Postmodernism*, London, New York: Routledge.
Iles, Francis (1999) [1932], *Before the Fact*, London: Pan.
Israel, Nico (2000), *Outlandish: Writing Between Exile and Diaspora*, Stanford: Stanford University Press.
Jacobs, Karen (2001), 'From "Our Glass Lake" to "Hourglass Lake": Photo/graphic Memory in Nabokov's *Lolita*', in Karen Jacobs, *The Eye's Mind: Literary Modernism and Visual Culture*, Ithaca and London: Cornell University Press, pp. 264–80.
Jameson, Fredric (1981), *The Political Unconscious: Narrative as a Socially Symbolic Act*, Ithaca, NY: Cornell University Press.
Jameson, Fredric (1991), *Postmodernism, or, The Cultural Logic of Late Capitalism*, Durham: Duke University Press.
Jameson, Fredric (1992a) [1982], 'Allegorizing Hitchcock', in Fredric Jameson, *Signatures of the Visible*, New York and London: Routledge, pp. 99–127.
Jameson, Fredric (1992b), 'Spatial Systems in *North by Northwest*', in *Everything You Always Wanted to Know About Lacan and Were Afraid to Ask Hitchcock*, ed. Slavoj Žižek, London and New York: Verso, pp. 47–72.
Jaspers, Karl (1995) [1909], *Heimweh und Verbrechen*, Munich: Belleville.
Johnson, Barbara (1987), 'Apostrophe, Animation, and Abortion', in Barbara Johnson, *A World of Difference*, Baltimore and London: Johns Hopkins University Press, pp. 184–99.
Kaplan, E. Ann (ed.) (1990), *Psychoanalysis and Cinema*, London and New York: Routledge.
Kaplan, Louise J. (1991), *Female Perversions: The Temptations of Madame Bovary*, New York, London and Toronto: Doubleday.
Kapsis, Robert E. (1992), *Hitchcock: The Making of a Reputation*, Chicago: University of Chicago Press.
Karlinsky, Simon (ed.) (2001), *Dear Bunny, Dear Volodya: The Nabokov-Wilson Letters, 1940–1971*, revised and expanded edition, Berkeley, Los Angeles and London: University of California Press.
Kauffman, Linda (1993), 'Framing Lolita: Is There a Woman in the Text?', in *Lolita: Major Literary Characters*, ed. Harold Bloom, New York and Philadelphia: Chelsea House Publishers, pp. 149–68.
Keane, Marian (1980), 'The Designs of Authorship: An Essay on *North by Northwest*', *Wide Angle*, 4: 1, 44–52.
Kerouac, Jack (1972) [1957], *On the Road*, London: Penguin.
Kristeva, Julia (1991) [1988], *Strangers to Ourselves*, trans. Leon S. Roudiez, New York: Columbia University Press.
Krohn, Bill (2000), *Hitchcock at Work*, London: Phaidon.
Lacan, Jacques (1981), *The Seminar of Jacques Lacan, Book XI: The Four Fundamental Concepts of Psychoanalysis*, ed. Jacques-Alain Miller, trans. Alan Sheridan, New York and London: Norton.

Lacan, Jacques (1992), *The Seminar of Jacques Lacan, Book VII: The Ethics of Psychoanalysis 1959–1960*, ed. Jacques-Alain Miller, trans. Dennis Porter, London: Routledge.

Lacan, Jacques (1998), *The Seminar of Jacques Lacan, Book XX: Encore 1972–1973*, ed. Jacques-Alain Miller, trans. Bruce Fink, New York and London: Norton.

Lacan, Jacques (2002), *Écrits: A Selection*, ed. Bruce Fink, New York and London: Norton.

LaCapra, Dominick (2001), *Writing History, Writing Trauma*, Baltimore and London: Johns Hopkins University Press.

Lanchester, John (1995), 'Afterword', in Vladimir Nabokov, *The Real Life of Sebastian Knight*, London: Penguin, pp. 175–84.

Lange, Bernd-Peter (1999), 'Dislocations: Migrancy in Nabokov and Rushdie', *Anglia*, 117: 3, 395–411.

Laplanche, Jean (1999), *Essays on Otherness*, London and New York: Routledge.

Laplanche, Jean and Jean-Bertrand Pontalis (1986), 'Fantasy and the Origins of Sexuality', in *Formations of Fantasy*, ed. Victor Burgin, Donald James and Cora Kaplan, London: Routledge, pp. 5–34.

Laplanche, Jean and Jean-Bertrand Pontalis (1992), *Das Vokabular der Psychoanalyse*, Frankfurt am Main: Suhrkamp.

Larmour, David H. J. (ed.) (2002), *Discourse and Ideology in Nabokov's Prose*, London and New York: Routledge.

Lebeau, Vicky (2001), *Psychoanalysis and Cinema: The Play of Shadows*, London and New York: Wallflower.

Leff, Leonard J. (1987), *Hitchcock and Selznick: The Rich and Strange Collaboration of Alfred Hitchcock and David O. Selznick in Hollywood*, Berkeley, Los Angeles and London: University of California Press.

Lehman, Ernest (1999), *North by Northwest*, London: Faber.

Leitch, Thomas M. (1991), *Find the Director and Other Hitchcock Games*, Athens, GA: University of Georgia Press.

Levine, Robert T. (1979), '"My Ultraviolet Darling": The Loss of Lolita's Childhood', *Modern Fiction Studies*, 25: 1, 471–9.

Levy, Emanuel (1991), *Small-Town America in Film: The Decline and Fall of Community*, New York: Continuum.

Leys, Ruth (2000), *Trauma: A Genealogy*, Chicago: University of Chicago Press.

Lolita, film, directed by Stanley Kubrick, UK: A.A. Productions, 1962.

MacCannell, Dean (1993), 'Democracy's Turn: On Homeless *Noir*', in *Shades of Noir: A Reader*, ed. Joan Copjec, London and New York: Verso, pp. 279–98.

McCarthy, Mary (1994) [1972], 'A Guide to Exiles, Expatriates, and Internal Emigrés', in *Altogether Elsewhere: Writers on Exile*, ed. Marc Robinson, San Diego, New York and London: Harcourt Brace, pp. 49–58.

McGilligan, Patrick (2003), *Alfred Hitchcock: A Life in Darkness and Light*, Chichester: Wiley.

McLaughlin, James (1986), 'All in the Family: Hitchcock's *Shadow of a Doubt*', in *A Hitchcock Reader*, ed. Marshall Deutelbaum and Leland Poague, Ames: Iowa State University Press, pp. 141–52.

Maddox, Lucy B. (1993), 'Necrophilia in *Lolita*', in *Lolita: Major Literary Characters*, ed. Harold Bloom, New York and Philadelphia: Chelsea House Publishers, pp. 79–89.
Metz, Christian (1982), *The Imaginary Signifier: Psychoanalysis and the Cinema*, Bloomington and Indianapolis: Indiana University Press.
Michie, Elsie B. (1999), 'Unveiling Maternal Desires: Hitchcock and American Domesticity', in *Hitchcock's America*, ed. Jonathan Freedman and Richard Millington, New York and Oxford: Oxford University Press, pp. 29–54.
Miller, Jacques-Alain (1988), '*Extimité*', *Prose Studies*, 11: 3, 121–9.
Miller, Mark Crispin (1983), 'Hitchcock's Suspicions and *Suspicion*', *Modern Language Notes*, 98: 5, 1143–86.
Millington, Richard H. (1999), 'Hitchcock and American Character: The Comedy of Self-Construction in *North by Northwest*', in *Hitchcock's America*, ed. Jonathan Freedman and Richard Millington, New York and Oxford: Oxford University Press, pp. 135–54.
Modleski, Tania (1982a), '"Never to Be Thirty-Six Years Old": *Rebecca* as Female Oedipal Drama', *Wide Angle*, 5: 1, 34–41.
Modleski, Tania (1982b), 'The Female Uncanny: Gothic Novels for Women', in Tania Modleski, *Loving with a Vengeance: Mass-Produced Fantasies for Women*, Hamden, CT: Archon Books, pp. 59–84.
Modleski, Tania (1988), *The Women Who Knew Too Much: Hitchcock and Feminist Theory*, London and New York: Routledge.
Moore, Tony (2002), 'Seeing Through Humbert: Focussing on the Feminist Sympathy in *Lolita*', in *Discourse and Ideology in Nabokov's Prose*, ed. David H. J. Larmour, London and New York: Routledge: pp. 91–109.
Morrison, James (1998), *Passport to Hollywood: Hollywood Films, European Directors*, Albany: State University of New York Press.
Moses, Gavriel (1995), 'Memory Unreals', in Gavriel Moses, *The Nickel Was for the Movies: Film in the Novel from Pirandello to Puig*, Berkeley, Los Angeles and London: University of California Press, 39–61.
Muller, John P. and William J. Richardson (eds) (1988), *The Purloined Poe: Lacan, Derrida, and Psychoanalytic Reading*, Baltimore and London: Johns Hopkins University Press.
Mulvey, Laura (2004), 'Death Drives', in *Hitchcock: Past and Future*, ed. Richard Allen and S. Ishii Gonzalès, London and New York: Routledge, pp. 231–42.
My Favorite Wife, film, directed by Garson Kanin, USA: RKO, 1940.
Naficy, Hamid (ed.) (1999), *Home, Exile, Homeland: Film, Media and the Politics of Place*, New York and London: Routledge.
Naremore, James (1988), 'Cary Grant in *North by Northwest* (1959)', in James Naremore, *Acting in the Cinema*, Berkeley, Los Angeles and London: University of California Press, pp. 213–35.
Naremore, James (ed.) (1993), *North by Northwest*, New Brunswick, NJ: Rutgers University Press.
Naremore, James (1999), 'Hitchcock at the Margins of Noir', in *Alfred Hitchcock: Centenary Essays*, ed. Richard Allen and S. Ishii Gonzalès, London: British Film Institute, pp. 263–78.
Naremore, James (2004), 'Hitchcock and Humor', in *Hitchcock: Past and Future*, ed. Richard Allen and S. Ishii Gonzalès, London and New York: Routledge, pp. 22–36.

Olsen, Lance (1986), 'A Janus Text: Realism, Fantasy, and Nabokov's *Lolita*', *Modern Fiction Studies*, 32: 1, 115–26.

Packman, David (1982), *Vladimir Nabokov: The Structure of Literary Desire*, Columbia and London: University of Missouri Press.

Palmer, Barton R. (1986), 'The Metafictional Hitchcock: The Experience of Viewing and the Viewing of Experience in *Rear Window* and *Psycho*', *Cinema Journal*, 25: 2, 4–19.

Patnoe, Elizabeth (2002), 'Discourse, Ideology and Hegemony: The Double Dreams in and around *Lolita*', in *Discourse and Ideology in Nabokov's Prose*, ed. David H. S. Larmour, London and New York: Routledge, pp. 111–36.

Peters, John Durham (1999), 'Exile, Nomadism, and Diaspora: The Stakes of Mobility in the Western Canon', in *Home, Exile, Homeland: Film, Media and the Politics of Place*, ed. Hamid Naficy, New York and London: Routledge, pp. 17–41.

Píchová, Hana (2002), *The Art of Memory in Exile: Vladimir Nabokov and Milan Kundera*, Carbondale and Edwardsville: Southern Illinois University Press.

Pifer, Ellen (1980), *Nabokov and the Novel*, Cambridge, MA and London: Harvard University Press.

Pifer, Ellen (2003), 'Nabokov's Novel Offspring: Lolita and Her Kin', in *Vladimir Nabokov's Lolita: A Casebook*, ed. Ellen Pifer, Oxford and New York: Oxford University Press, pp. 83–109.

Poe, Edgar Allan (1977) [1850], 'Annabel Lee', in *The Portable Poe*, ed. Philip Van Doren Stern, London: Penguin, pp. 632–4.

Polan, Dana (1986), *Power and Paranoia: History, Narrative, and the American Cinema, 1940–1950*, New York: Columbia University Press.

Pomerance, Murray (2004), *An Eye for Hitchcock*, New Brunswick, NJ and London: Rutgers University Press.

Proffer, Carl R. (1968), *Keys to Lolita*, Bloomington: Indiana University Press.

Raskolnikov, Masha (1999), 'Pninian Performatives', in *Nabokov at the Limits: Redrawing Critical Boundaries*, ed. Lisa Zunshine, New York and London: Garland, pp. 127–59.

Richter, Virginia (2000), 'Strangers on a Couch: Hitchcock's Use of Psychoanalysis in *Spellbound* and *Marnie*', in *Psychoanalytic-ism: Uses of Psychoanalysis in Novels, Poems, Plays and Films*, ed. Ingrid Hotz-Davies and Anton Kirchhofer, Trier: WVT Wissenschaftlicher Verlag Trier, pp. 114–31.

Rimmon, Shlomith (1976), 'Problems of Voice in Vladimir Nabokov's *The Real Life of Sebastian Knight*', *PTL: A Journal for Descriptive Poetics and Theory of Literature*, 1, 489–512.

Rimmon-Kenan, Shlomith (1980), 'The Paradoxical Status of Repetition', *Poetics Today*, 1: 4, 151–9.

Rimmon-Kenan, Shlomith (1996), 'Vladimir Nabokov, *The Real Life of Sebastian Knight*: "The Painting of Different Ways of Painting"', in Shlomith Rimmon-Kenan, *A Glance Beyond Doubt: Narration, Representation, Subjectivity*, Columbus: Ohio State University Press, pp. 55–74.

Robbins, Bruce (1983), 'Homelessness and Worldliness', *Diacritics*, 13: 3, 69–77.

Robinson, Marc (ed.) (1994), *Altogether Elsewhere: Writers on Exile*, San Diego, New York and London: Harcourt Brace, 1994.

Rogin, Michael (1988), *Ronald Reagan, the Movie and Other Episodes in Political Demonology*, Berkeley, Los Angeles and London: University of California Press.

Rorty, Richard (1989), 'The Barber of Kasbeam: Nabokov on Cruelty', in Richard Rorty, *Contingency, Irony, and Solidarity*, Cambridge: Cambridge University Press.

Roth, Michael S. (ed.) (1998), *Freud: Conflict and Culture, Essays on His Life, Work, and Legacy*, New York: Alfred A. Knopf.

Roth, Phyllis A. (1982), 'Toward the Man Behind the Mystification', in *Nabokov's Fifth Arc: Nabokov and Others on His Life's Work*, ed. J. E. Rivers and Charles Nicol, Austin: University of Texas Press, pp. 43–59.

Rothman, William (1982), *Hitchcock: The Murderous Gaze*, Cambridge, MA and London: Harvard University Press.

Rothman, William (1988), '*North by Northwest*: Hitchcock's Monument to the Hitchcock Film', in William Rothman, *The 'I' of the Camera: Essays in Film Criticism, History, and Aesthetics*, Cambridge: Cambridge University Press, pp. 174–87.

Rushdie, Salman (1991), *Imaginary Homelands: Essays and Criticism 1981–1991*, London: Granta Books and Penguin.

Russ, Joanna (1972), 'Somebody's Trying to Kill Me and I Think It's My Husband: The Modern Gothic', *Journal of Popular Culture*, 6: 4, 666–91.

Ryall, Tom (1996), *Alfred Hitchcock and the British Cinema*, London and Atlantic Highlands, NJ: Athlone Press.

Said, Edward (1984), 'Reflections on Exile', *Granta*, 13: 3, 159–72.

Saito, Ayako (1999), 'Hitchcock's Trilogy: A Logic of Mise en Scène', in *Endless Night: Cinema and Psychoanalysis, Parallel Histories*, ed. Janet Bergstrom. Berkeley, Los Angeles and London: University of California Press, pp. 200–49.

Samuels, Robert (1998), *Hitchcock's Bi-Textuality: Lacan, Feminisms, and Queer Theory*, Albany: State University of New York Press.

Santner, Eric (1996), *My Own Private Germany: Daniel Paul Schreber's Secret History of Modernity*, Princeton, NJ: Princeton University Press.

Scheib, Ronnie (1976), 'Charlie's Uncle', *Film Comment*, 12: 2, 55–62.

Schiff, Stacy (2000), *Véra (Mrs Vladimir Nabokov)*, New York: The Modern Library.

Schmid, Hans (1988), *'Crimes of Passion': Die gestörte Idylle in den Filmen von Alfred Hitchcock*, Magisterarbeit, Ludwig-Maximilians-Universität Munich.

Schmid, Hans (1993), *Fenster zum Hof: Der Raum im Horrorfilm*, Munich: Belleville.

Schweighauser, Philipp (1999), 'Discursive Killings: Intertextuality, Aestheticization, Transcendence and Death in Nabokov's *Lolita*', *Amerikastudien/American Studies*, 44: 2, 255–67.

Sebald, W. G. (2003), 'Traumtexturen: Kleine Anmerkungen zu Nabokov', in W. G. Sebald, *Campo Santo*, ed. Sven Meyer, Munich and Vienna: Hanser, pp. 184–92.

Secret Beyond the Door, film, directed by Fritz Lang, USA: Diana Production Company, 1948.

Seidel, Michael (1985), 'Nabokov and the Aesthetics of American Exile', *The Yale Review*, 74: 2, 224–39.

Seidel, Michael (1986), *Exile and the Narrative Imagination*, New Haven and London: Yale University Press.

Shakespeare, William (1990), *Hamlet*, ed. Harold Jenkins, The Arden Shakespeare, London and New York: Routledge.

Shapiro, Gavriel (1999), 'Setting His Myriad Faces in His Texts: Nabokov's Authorial Presence Revisited', in *Nabokov and His Fiction: New Perspectives*, ed. Julian W. Connolly, Cambridge: Cambridge University Press, pp. 73–91.

Sharff, Stefan (1991), *Alfred Hitchcock's High Vernacular: Theory and Practice*, New York: Columbia University Press.

Shrayer, Maxim D. (1999), 'Jewish Questions in Nabokov's Art and Life', in *Nabokov and His Fiction: New Perspectives*, ed. Julian W. Connolly, Cambridge: Cambridge University Press, pp. 73–91.

Shute, Jenefer (1984), 'Nabokov and Freud: The Play of Power', *Modern Fiction Studies*, 30: 4, 637–50.

Shute, Jenefer (1995), 'Nabokov and Freud', in *The Garland Companion to Nabokov*, ed. Vladimir E. Alexandrov, New York and London: Garland, pp. 412–20.

Shute, Jenefer (2003), '"So Nakedly Dressed": The Text of the Female Body in Nabokov's Novels', in *Vladimir Nabokov's Lolita: A Casebook*, ed. Ellen Pifer, Oxford and New York: Oxford University Press, pp. 111–20.

Simpson, John (ed.) (1995), *The Oxford Book of Exile*, Oxford, New York: Oxford University Press.

Sloan, Jane E. (1995), *Alfred Hitchcock: A Filmography and Bibliography*, Berkeley, Los Angeles and London: University of California Press.

Smith, Susan (2000), *Hitchcock: Suspense, Humour and Tone*, London: British Film Institute.

Spoto, Donald (1983), *The Dark Side of Genius: The Life of Alfred Hitchcock*, New York: Ballantine Books.

Spoto, Donald (1992), *The Art of Alfred Hitchcock: Fifty Years of His Motion Pictures*, New York, London and Toronto: Anchor Books Doubleday.

Stam, Robert (1992), *Reflexivity in Film and Literature: From Don Quixote to Jean-Luc Godard*, New York: Columbia University Press.

Stam, Robert (2005a), 'Introduction: The Theory and Practice of Adaptation', in *Literature and Film: A Guide to the Theory and Practice of Film Adaptation*, ed. Robert Stam and Alessandra Raengo, Malden: Blackwell, pp. 1–52.

Stam, Robert (2005b), *Literature Through Film: Realism, Magic, and the Art of Adaptation*, Malden: Blackwell.

Sterrit, David (1993), *The Films of Alfred Hitchcock*, Cambridge: Cambridge University Press.

Sterritt, David (1998), *Mad to Be Saved: The Beats, the '50s', and Film*, Carbondale and Edwardsville: Southern Illinois University Press.

Straumann, Barbara (1999), '"Freudians keep out please"? Nabokovs Ablehnung von (Be)Deutung', *Rebus: Blätter zur Psychoanalyse*, 15, 19–51.

Straumann, Barbara (2002a), 'The Masculine Space of *North by Northwest*, or Mapping the Vicissitudes of Masculinity as Performance', in *Masculinities* –

Maskulinitäten: Mythos, Realität, Repräsentation, Rollendruck, ed. Therese Steffen, Stuttgart and Weimar: Metzler, pp. 56–76.

Straumann, Barbara (2002b), 'Rewriting American Foundational Myths in *North by Northwest*', in *American Foundational Myths*, ed. Martin Heusser and Gudrun Grabher, SPELL Swiss Papers in English Language and Literature 14, Tübingen: Gunter Narr, pp. 121–34.

Straumann, Barbara (2005), 'Revisiting Mnemosyne: (Un)canny Recollection in Nabokov's *Speak, Memory*', in *Inventing the Past: Memory Work in Culture and History*, ed. Otto Heim and Caroline Wiedmer, Basel: Schwabe, pp. 95–115.

Stuart, Dabney (1978), *Nabokov: The Dimensions of Parody*, Baton Rouge and London: Louisiana State University Press.

Suleiman, Susan Rubin (ed.) (1998), *Exile and Creativity: Signposts, Travelers, Outsiders, Backward Glances*, Durham and London: Duke University Press.

Sunset Boulevard, film, directed by Billy Wilder, USA: Paramount, 1950.

Sweeney, Susan Elizabeth (2005), '"By Some Sleight of Hand": How Nabokov Rewrote America', in *The Cambridge Companion to Nabokov*, ed. Julian W. Connolly, Cambridge: Cambridge University Press, pp. 65–84.

Tanner, Tony (1971), *City of Words: American Fiction 1950–1970*, London: Jonathan Cape.

Taylor, John Russell (1996), *Hitch: The Life and Times of Alfred Hitchcock*, New York: Da Capo Press.

The Manchurian Candidate, film, directed by John Frankenheimer, USA: United Artists, 1962.

The Philadelphia Story, film, directed by George Cukor, USA: MGM, 1940.

Timms, Edward and Naomi Segal (1988), *Freud in Exile: Psychoanalysis and Its Vicissitudes*, New Haven and London: Yale University Press.

The New Shorter Oxford English Dictionary, ed. Lesley Brown, fourth edition, Oxford: Clarendon Press, 1993.

Toker, Leona (1989), *Vladimir Nabokov: The Mystery of Literary Structure*, Ithaca and London: Cornell University Press.

Toker, Leona (1995), 'Nabokov and Bergson', in *The Garland Companion to Nabokov*, ed. Vladimir E. Alexandrov, New York and London Garland, pp. 367–73.

Toles, George (1984), '"If Thine Eyes Offend Thee . . .": *Psycho* and the Art of Infection', *New Literary History*, 15: 3, 631–51.

Trilling, Lionel (1958), 'The Last Lover: Vladimir Nabokov's *Lolita*', *Encounter*, 4, 9–19.

Truffaut, François (1985), *Hitchcock*, New York, London: Touchstone and Simon & Schuster.

Updike, John (1995) [1960], *Rabbit, Run*, London: Penguin.

Waldman, Diane (1983), '"At Last I Can Tell It to Someone!": Feminine Point of View and Subjectivity in the Gothic Romance Films of the 1940s', *Cinema Journal*, 23: 2, 29–40.

Williams, Linda (1984), 'When the Woman Looks', in *Re-Vision: Essays in Feminist Film Criticism*, ed. Mary Ann Doane, Linda Williams and Patricia Mellenkamp, American Film Institute Monograph Series 3, Frederick: University Publications of America, pp. 83–99.

Williams, Robert C. (1970), 'Memory's Defense: The Real Life of Vladimir Nabokov's Berlin', *The Yale Review*, 60: 2, 241–50.

Wollen, Peter (2004), 'Hitch: A Tale of Two Cities (London and Los Angeles)', in *Hitchcock: Past and Future*, ed. Richard Allen and S. Ishii Gonzalès, London and New York: Routledge, pp. 15–21.

Wood, Michael (1989), *America in the Movies*, New York: Columbia University Press.

Wood, Michael (1994), *The Magician's Doubts: Nabokov and the Risks of Fiction*, London: Pimlico.

Wood, Michael (1997), 'Afterword', in Vladimir Nabokov, *Pnin*, London: Penguin, pp. 161–70.

Wood, Robin (1989), *Hitchcock's Films Revisited*, New York: Columbia University Press.

Wright, Elizabeth (ed.) (1992), *Feminism and Psychoanalysis: A Critical Dictionary*, Oxford: Blackwell.

Wyllie, Barbara (2003), *Nabokov at the Movies*, Jefferson, NC and London: McFarland.

Wyllie, Barbara (2005), 'Nabokov and Cinema', in *The Cambridge Companion to Nabokov*, ed. Julian W. Connolly, Cambridge: Cambridge University Press, pp. 215–31.

Yates, Frances A. (1995) [1966], *The Art of Memory*, London: Pimlico.

Zimmer, Dieter E. (2001), *Nabokov's Berlin*, Berlin: Nicolai.

Žižek, Slavoj (1991), *Looking Awry: An Introduction to Jacques Lacan Through Popular Culture*, Cambridge, MA and London: MIT Press.

Žižek, Slavoj (ed.) (1992), *Everything You Always Wanted to Know About Lacan But Were Afraid to Ask Hitchcock*, London and New York: Verso.

Žižek, Slavoj (1993), *Grimassen des Realen: Jacques Lacan und die Monstrosität des Aktes*, ed. Michael Wetzel, Cologne: Kiepenheuer & Witsch.

Žižek, Slavoj (1997), *The Plague of Fantasies*, London and New York: Verso.

Žižek, Slavoj (2001) [1992], *Enjoy Your Symptom! Jacques Lacan in Hollywood and Out*, revised edition, New York and London: Routledge.

Index

Abraham, Nicolas, 56
Adorno, Theodor W., 9–10
advertising, 101, 117–18, 172, 177
aestheticism ('aesthetic bliss'), 7–8,
    34–5, 113, 115, 116, 119
  versus referentiality, 48, 88–91, 110,
    120, 169, 189–90, 193
Alexandrov, Vladimir, 42
allegory, 201–2
Améry, Jean, 18
anti-Semitism, 13, 36, 202–3
Appel, Alfred, 4

Barthes, Roland, 61, 111
  on myth, 103
  Camera Lucida, 39; *S/Z*, 46–7, 48
Baumann, Sabine, 39
Beat Generation, 10
Bellour, Raymond, 167–8, 176, 186
Bhabha, Homi K., 12
Boyd, Brian, 35, 60
Brodsky, Joseph, 17, 25, 195
Bronfen, Elisabeth, 2–3, 16, 20, 42, 66,
    88, 97, 107, 131, 167, 171
butterflies, 45–6, 50, 73, 102

Cahiers du Cinéma, 158
Caroll, Leo G., 171
Carroll, Madeleine, 149
Cavell, Stanley, 2, 99, 152–3, 165–6,
    168, 175, 182–5
chess, 49
chronophobia, 38–51
cinema
  in Berlin, 24

'will' of Hitchcock's camera, 23–4
  see also Cahiers du Cinéma;
    Hitchcock; Hollywood;
    photography; psychoanalysis
Colet, Louise, 154–6
common sense, 41–2
Copjec, Joan, 70, 151–2
Cotton, Joseph, 206
cross-mapping, 2–3
crypt, 56–8
Cukor, George, 2, 136

death, 66, 68–70, 139–40
  home movies and, 38–40
  in *Lolita*, 108–12
  see also murder
Doane, Mary Ann, 137, 150, 158
Dolar, Mladen, 148, 207
Donat, Robert, 149

espionage, 2, 75–6, 128, 173, 176, 190
ethics, 112–15
exile, 3, 201
  as 'absent cause', 201
  aesthetics of, 8–22, 160
  Freud on, 27, 201–4
  home and, 12, 15–21, 33–4
  language and, 17, 25, 28, 48–9
  poetics of, 74
  Said on, 14
'extimacy', 139

family, 21, 38, 51–2, 66, 202, 211
'family romance' *see under* Freud
fantasy, 18–19, 132, 139

female paranoia film, 136–7, 143, 150–1
Feydeau, Ernest, 155
film noir, 10, 151
Flaubert, Gustave, 154–8
Fontaine, Joan, 127–9
Foucault, Michel, 116–17
Frankenheimer, John, 191
Frankfurt School, 9–10
French, Philip, 10
Freud, Sigmund, 13–14, 16, 20, 130, 201–5, 207–8, 213–15
  on daydreams, 134, 140
  exile and, 13, 27, 201–4
  'family romance', 21, 38, 51–2, 66, 202, 211
  Nabokov versus, 204–5, 213
  'navel of the dream', 40–1, 79, 142, 160
  Beyond the Pleasure Principle, 16; *Moses and Monotheism*, 27, 202–3; 'The "Uncanny"', 17–18, 139
Frumkin, Yakov, 37
fugueur, 174–5, 181, 183

Gay, Peter, 203
Geddes, Barbara Bel, 182
general ideas, 205; *see also* common sense
Girardet, Christoph, 3
Gothic, 151, 157
Grant, Cary, 129, 132, 137, 148, 166
Greenblatt, Stephen, 3, 131

Hacking, Ian, 174
history, 66, 90, 100, 195, 217
  as 'absent cause', 11, 35, 70–1, 120–1, 202
Hitchcock, Alfred
  on actors, 6
  on audience, 143
  Hollywood and, 8, 10–11, 24, 127, 166, 188, 192–8
  'home paranoia' in, 130–1, 135, 202, 211
  meets Nabokov, 1
  movie appearances of, 4–5
  psychoanalysis and, 205–6, 212–14

psychothriller and, 131, 143–4
Alfred Hitchcock Presents, 5, 144; *The Birds*, 172; *Marnie*, 205; *North by Northwest*, 25–6, 132, 165–200, 214; *Psycho*, 172, 205; *Rear Window*, 149–50, 151; *Rebecca*, 38, 44, 74, 127–30, 135–7, 143–6, 149, 153, 157, 159, 167–8, 193; *Shadow of a Doubt*, 131, 137, 143–4, 153, 206–9, 212–15; *Spellbound*, 75, 205; *Suspicion*, 11, 25–6, 128–54, 157–60, 166, 168, 170, 179, 180, 184, 187; *The 39 Steps*, 149, 165, 186–7; *Vertigo*, 182, 187
Hitchcock (*née* Reville), Alma (wife), 8
Hitchcock, Patricia (daughter), 8
Hollywood, 192
  European exiles and, 9, 193
  Hitchcock and, 8, 10–11, 24, 127, 166, 188, 192–8
Holocaust, 8, 118
home, 12, 15–21, 33–4, 72–4, 96
  'home paranoia', 20–1, 130–1, 135, 173, 202
  'imaginary homeland', 17, 33, 72, 127, 159, 189
  see also exile; nostalgia
home movies, 38–40
homosexuality, 60
Horkheimer, Max, 9–10
House Committee on Un-American Activities *see* McCarthyism
hysteria, 171, 175

incest, 111
irony, 90–1, 114–16, 188, 196–7
Israel, Nico, 15

Jameson, Fredric
  on 'absent cause', 70, 120, 201–2, 203
  on history, 11–12, 35, 66–7, 90, 120–1, 195, 201–2, 217
  on the real, 119, 121, 201–2

Kaplan, Louise, 99, 155
Keane, Marian, 168
Kelly, Grace, 149

Kristeva, Julia, 138
Kubrick, Stanley, 1, 5, 103–4
Kuropatkin, General, 49–50

Lacan, Jacques, 21, 35, 139, 151
Lanchester, John, 48, 50
Lang, Fritz, 136
language, 17, 25, 28, 121
  Foucault on, 116–17
  Lolita and, 86–7, 105
  see also aestheticism; playfulness; self-reflexivity
Lehman, Ernest, 165
lepidopterology *see* butterflies
Lévi-Strauss, Claude, 70
Lyon, Sue, 104

McCarthyism, 10
'MacGuffin', 165, 190
McLaughlin, James, 207
'mad travellers', 173–4, 178, 183
Maddox, Lucy, 95
Manchurian Candidate, The, 191
Mason, James, 1–2, 104, 171
memory, 44, 66–8
Miller, Mark Crispin, 147
Milyukov, Pavel, 36, 64
Modleski, Tania, 131, 146, 158, 167
mourning, 35, 79
Müller, Matthias, 3
murder, 69, 139–44, 149–50
myth, 117–18

Nabokov, Dmitri (grandfather), 26
Nabokov, Dmitri (son), 8, 37, 43–5, 47, 50
Nabokov, Elena Ivanovna (mother), 38–9, 42, 47, 52–6, 69, 96, 128
Nabokov, Elena (sister), 61, 62
Nabokov, Kirill (brother), 59–60
Nabokov, Sergey (brother), 36, 58–62, 213
Nabokov (*née* Slonim), Véra (wife), 8, 36–7, 43–5, 73
Nabokov, Vladimir
  autobiography *see* Speak, Memory
  body size, 61–2
  childhood, 8, 35–6, 51
  English language and, 119–20
  'family romance' in, 38, 51–2, 66, 202, 211
  father *see* Nabokov, Vladimir Dmitrievich
  on Freud, 204–5, 213
  meets Hitchcock, 1: on Hitchcock, 7
  mother *see* Nabokov, Elena Ivanovna
  versus psychoanalysis, 204–5, 213
  on unconscious, 67
  Bend Sinister, 100; *Conclusive Evidence see Speak, Memory*; *Despair*, 24, 68–9, 76–7, 113; *The Eye*, 76, 77; *Invitation to a Beheading*, 76, 77–8, 100; *Lolita*, 26, 68, 86–124, 166–7, 169, 171, 177–8, 181–2, 188–90, 195–7, 204; *Pale Fire*, 76; *Pnin*, 100–3, 205; *The Real Life of Sebastian Knight*, 68, 206, 209–13; *Speak, Memory*, 9, 11, 26, 33–79, 99, 113, 117, 127–8, 130, 135, 145, 159, 189, 213; *Strong Opinions*, 5, 71–2
  see also aestheticism; home; irony; nostalgia; playfulness; self-reflexivity
Nabokov, Vladimir Dmitrievich (father), 36–7, 59–60, 62–6
Nazism, 8–9, 13, 100, 203
necrophilia, 108–9
nostalgia, 20–1, 35, 54–6, 66, 128
  in *Lolita*, 94
Novak, Kim, 182
nymphet, 97–9, 100, 181

Oedipus complex, 21–2, 146, 167, 186, 191
Olivier, Laurence, 128
Olympia Press, 86
otherworld, 42

perversion, 98–9
Phoenix Tapes, 3
photography, 39–40, 61, 73; *see also* cinema; home movies
playfulness, 4, 13, 47–8, 50, 89, 116, 143
protective fictions, 20
Poe, Edgar Allan, 93–4, 107

popular culture, 117–18; *see also* advertising
poshlost see general ideas
postcolonialism, 12; *see also* Bhabha; Rushdie; Said
postmodernism, 7, 12, 35; *see also* Rushdie; Žižek
poststructuralism, 7, 12, 17; *see also* Barthes; Foucault; Kristeva; Lacan
psychoanalysis, 13
  as critical method, 201–3, 215–16
  Nabokov versus, 204–5, 213
  see also Freud; Lacan

Rausch von Traubenberg, Yuri, 36
Reville, Alma *see* Hitchcock (*née* Reville)
rodina ('motherland'), 53, 54, 55, 71, 73
Royce, Jessie, 172
Rushdie, Salman, 16, 17, 34, 74
Russian Revolution, 8, 36, 56, 100

Said, Edward, 14–15, 195
Saint, Eva Maria, 168
Santner, Eric, 175
Schreber, Daniel Paul, 175–6
Seidel, Michael, 14
self-reflexivity, 3–6, 24, 47, 116–17, 121, 165
Selznick, David O., 131, 193–4, 205
sexual difference, 130, 149–52, 167, 173, 178–9, 184, 186–7
Shakespeare, William, 99, 153, 175
Shrayer, Maxim D., 42

Shute, Jenefer, 204
Slonim, Véra *see* Nabokov (*née* Slonim)
snow, 74–5
solipsism, 89, 100, 104, 107–8, 178
spies/spying *see* espionage
Stam, Robert, 103
stereoscopy, 74–6, 78, 127, 128
Sterritt, David, 10
Stewart, James, 149, 182
structuralism, 7
Sunset Boulevard, 24

thanatopoetics, 68–70, 108
Torok, Maria, 56
trains, 133, 170, 196
trauma, 40
travel bag, 57–8
Truffaut, Jean-François, 149, 165, 169, 188

unconscious, 3, 67; *see also* Freud; psychoanalysis

Waldman, Diane, 151
Warhol, Andy, 4–5
Wilder, Billy, 24
Winters, Shelley, 104
Wood, Michael, 48, 62, 65, 67, 73, 101, 119, 178, 195
Wright, Teresa, 206

Žižek, Slavoj, 70
  on Hitchcock, 4, 169, 172–3, 177, 183–4